For helpful information, see page 9.

Also by Sarah Bell

The British Columbia Lodge & Resort Guide
Also includes the Banff/Jasper area and the Yukon

The British Columbia & Alberta Adventure Travel Guide
Guided outdoor trips and more

Gordon Soules Book Publishers Ltd.
West Vancouver, Canada
Seattle, U.S.

Canadian Cataloguing in Publication Data

Bell, Sarah.
The British Columbia bed & breakfast guide, also includes the
Banff/Jasper area

Includes index.
ISBN 0-919574-50-5

1. Bed and breakfast accommodations—British Columbia—
Guidebooks. 2. Bed and breakfast accommodations—Alberta—
Banff Region—Guidebooks. 3. Bed and breakfast
accommodations—Alberta—Jasper Region—Guidebooks. I.
Title.
TX907.5.C22B73 1998   647.94711'03   C98-910596-2

Published in Canada by
Gordon Soules Book Publishers Ltd.
1354-B Marine Drive
West Vancouver, BC V7T 1B5
(604) 922-6588 or (604) 688-5466
Fax: (604) 688-5442
E-mail: books@gordonsoules.com
Web site: http://www.gordonsoules.com

Published in the United States by
Gordon Soules Book Publishers Ltd.
620—1916 Pike Place
Seattle, WA 98101
(604) 922-6588 or (604) 688-5466
Fax: (604) 688-5442
E-mail: books@gordonsoules.com
Web site: http://www.gordonsoules.com

Cover designed by Harry Bardal
Printed and bound in Canada by Printcrafters Inc.

Contents at a Glance
(for full contents, see pages 4 to 8)

4

Contents

5

8

Information for Users of This Book

1. Information in any guidebook is subject to change and error. It is advisable to confirm important information when making reservations.

2. While great care has been taken to ensure the accuracy of the information in this book, neither the author nor the publisher can accept responsibility for any outdated information, omissions, or errors.

3. Rates are in Canadian currency.

4. Distances are approximate.

5. For the B&Bs that accept credit cards for payment, the specific credit cards they accept are listed.

6. B&Bs are open year round unless otherwise indicated.

7. Ensuite bathroom describes a bathroom accessible directly from a guest room or from a bedroom in a suite or cottage, for the exclusive use of the guests in that room.

8. Private bathroom describes a bathroom for the exclusive use of the guests of one room or suite; the guests must exit their room or suite to get to it.

9. Bathroom in suite describes a bathroom in a suite, not accessible directly from a bedroom in the suite.

10. Bathroom in cottage describes a bathroom in a cottage, not accessible directly from a bedroom in the cottage.

11. Shared guest bathroom describes a bathroom shared by some or all guests; the hosts do not use this bathroom.

12. Shared bathroom describes a bathroom shared by guests and hosts.

13. Kitchen describes, at minimum, a sink, a stove, and a fridge.

14. Suite describes, at minimum, a bedroom with a large sitting area and a bathroom in the suite.

15. Honeymoon suite describes, at minimum, a bedroom with a bathroom in the suite.

16. Self-contained suite describes, at minimum, a bedroom with a large sitting area, a bathroom in the suite, and cooking facilities that include, at minimum, a sink, a hot plate, and a fridge.

17. Self-contained room describes, at minimum, a bedroom with an ensuite bathroom and cooking facilities that include, at minimum, a sink, a hot plate, and a fridge.

18. Examples of rates and bed types:

    Example 1: Four rooms. One person $50–60; two people $60–70. King-sized bed; queen-sized bed; twin beds. This means that the B&B has one or more rooms with a king-sized bed, one or more rooms with a queen-sized bed, and one or more rooms with twin beds.

    Example 2: Two rooms. One person $60; two people $65–75. Queen-sized bed. Ensuite bathroom. This means that each room has a queen-sized bed and an ensuite bathroom

    Example 3: Four rooms. One person $65–80; two people $80–90. Queen-sized bed, ensuite bathroom; double bed, shared guest bathroom; queen-sized bed and one twin bed, shared guest bathroom. This means that the B&B has one or more rooms with a queen-sized bed and an ensuite bathroom; one or more rooms with a double bed and a shared guest bathroom; and one or more rooms with a queen-sized bed, a twin bed, and a shared guest bathroom.

    Example 4: Three rooms. One person $50–55; two people $60–75. Queen-sized bed and one twin bed, ensuite bathroom; queen-sized bed and one twin day bed, private bathroom; double bed and one twin bed, private bathroom. This means that the B&B has one room with a queen-sized bed, a twin bed, and an ensuite bathroom; one room with a queen-sized bed, a twin day bed, and a private bathroom; and one room with a double bed, a twin bed, and a private bathroom.

    Example 5: Two rooms. One person $50; two people $60–70. Queen-sized bed; twin beds (or twin beds side by side with king-sized bedding). Ensuite bathrooms. This means that the B&B has one room with a queen-sized bed and an ensuite bathroom and one room with twin beds (or twin beds side by side with king-sized bedding) and an ensuite bathroom.

19. Maps of British Columbia are available from many sources, including bookstores, newsstands, gift shops, gas stations, automobile associations, tourist information offices, and the book's publisher, Gordon Soules Book Publishers Ltd. Information on how to obtain maps available from the book's publisher is included on the publisher's web site, http://www.gordonsoules.com. (Retailers, automobile associations, and tourist information offices can order maps of British Columbia from Gordon Soules Book Publishers Ltd. at wholesale prices; addresses are given on the copyright page of this book.)

BRITISH
COLUMBIA

Jasper National Park
Banff National Park

MAP 1:
North America

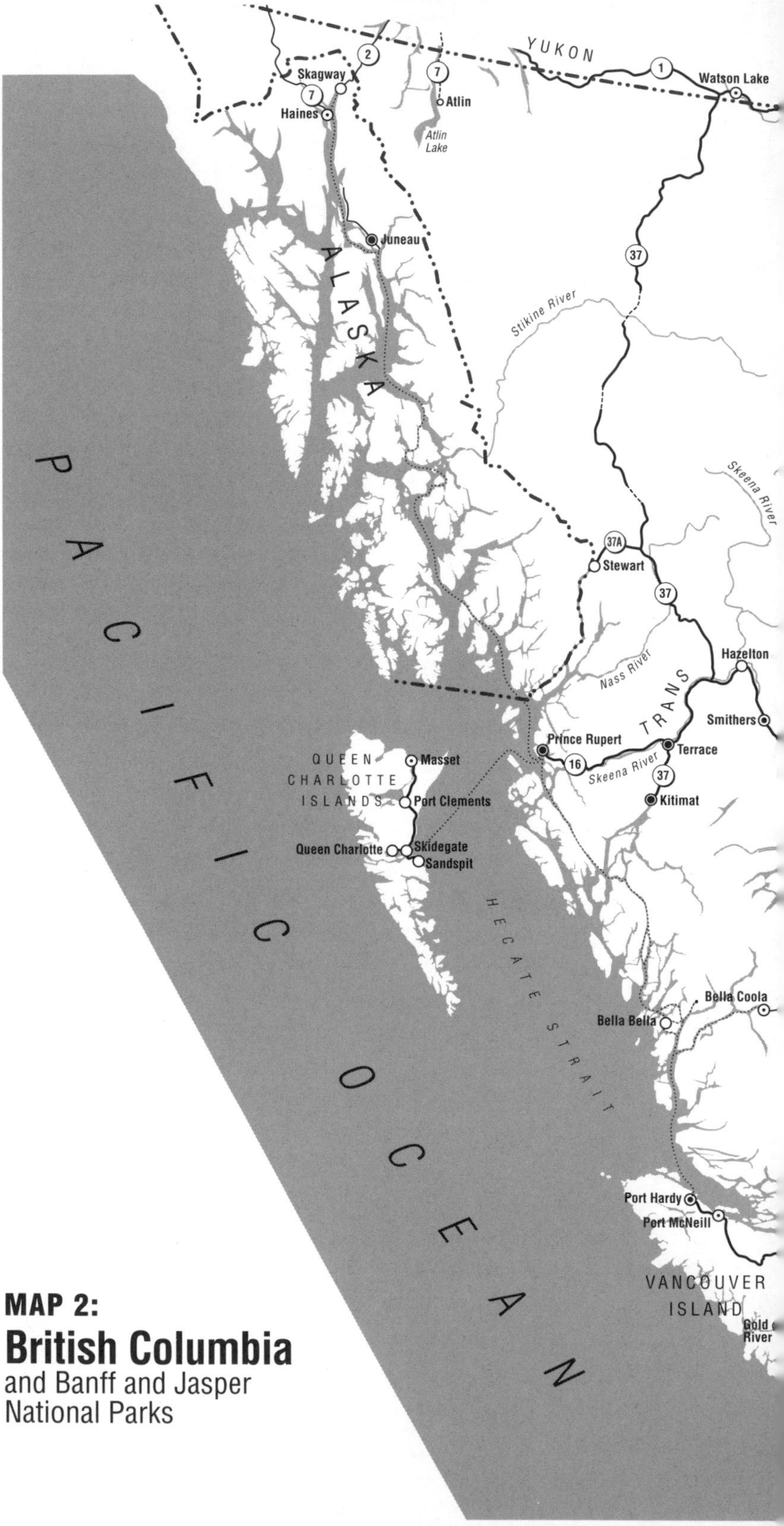

YUKON

Skagway
Haines
Atlin
Atlin Lake
Watson Lake

② ⑦ ①
⑦

ALASKA

Juneau

Stikine River

③⑦

Skeena River

③⑦A
Stewart
③⑦

Hazelton

Smithers

Nass River

TRANS

PACIFIC

QUEEN CHARLOTTE ISLANDS
Masset
Port Clements
Queen Charlotte
Skidegate
Sandspit

Prince Rupert
①⑥
Terrace
③⑦
Skeena River
Kitimat

HECATE STRAIT

Bella Coola
Bella Bella

OCEAN

Port Hardy
Port McNeill

VANCOUVER ISLAND
Gold River

MAP 2:
British Columbia
and Banff and Jasper
National Parks

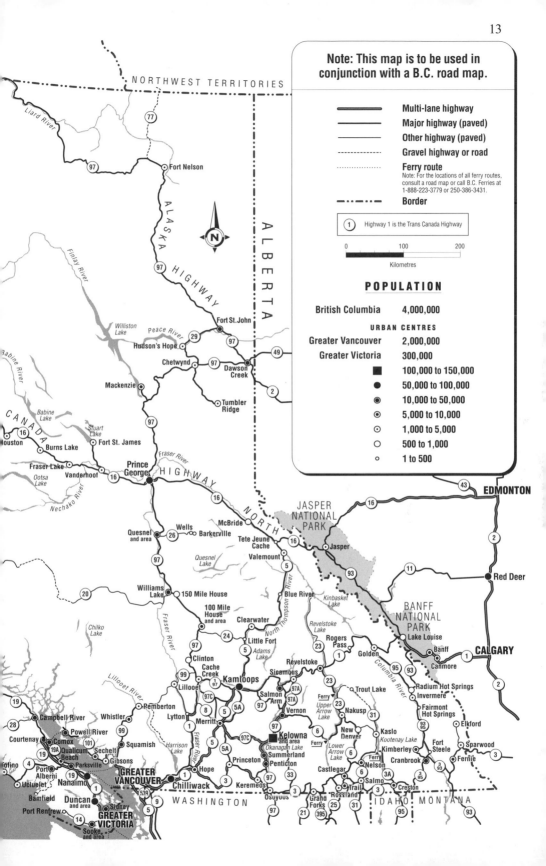

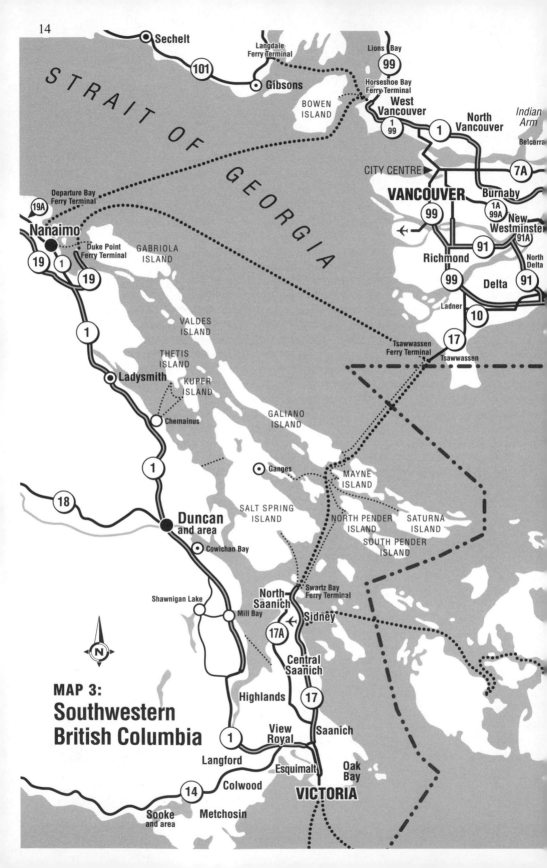

MAP 3:
Southwestern British Columbia

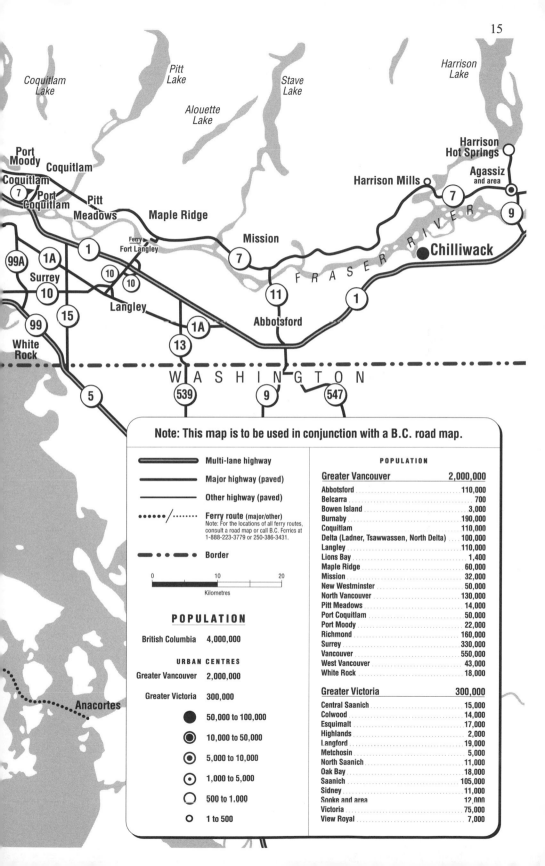

Coquitlam Lake
Pitt Lake
Stave Lake
Harrison Lake
Alouette Lake

Port Moody
Coquitlam
Coquitlam
Port Coquitlam
Pitt Meadows
Maple Ridge
Harrison Hot Springs
Harrison Mills
Agassiz and area

7
7
9

Ferry Fort Langley
Mission
Chilliwack
1
99A **1A** **1**
7
Surrey
10 **10**
10
11
1
Langley
15
1A
Abbotsford
99
White Rock
13

FRASER RIVER

WASHINGTON
5 **539** **9** **547**

Anacortes

Note: This map is to be used in conjunction with a B.C. road map.

Multi-lane highway
Major highway (paved)
Other highway (paved)
Ferry route (major/other)
Note: For the locations of all ferry routes, consult a road map or call B.C. Ferries at 1-888-223-3779 or 250-386-3431.
Border

0   10   20
Kilometres

POPULATION

British Columbia   4,000,000

URBAN CENTRES
Greater Vancouver   2,000,000
Greater Victoria   300,000

● 50,000 to 100,000
◉ 10,000 to 50,000
◉ 5,000 to 10,000
⊙ 1,000 to 5,000
○ 500 to 1,000
○ 1 to 500

POPULATION	
Greater Vancouver	**2,000,000**
Abbotsford	110,000
Belcarra	700
Bowen Island	3,000
Burnaby	190,000
Coquitlam	110,000
Delta (Ladner, Tsawwassen, North Delta)	100,000
Langley	110,000
Lions Bay	1,400
Maple Ridge	60,000
Mission	32,000
New Westminster	50,000
North Vancouver	130,000
Pitt Meadows	14,000
Port Coquitlam	50,000
Port Moody	22,000
Richmond	160,000
Surrey	330,000
Vancouver	550,000
West Vancouver	43,000
White Rock	18,000
Greater Victoria	**300,000**
Central Saanich	15,000
Colwood	14,000
Esquimalt	17,000
Highlands	2,000
Langford	19,000
Metchosin	5,000
North Saanich	11,000
Oak Bay	18,000
Saanich	105,000
Sidney	11,000
Sooke and area	12,000
Victoria	75,000
View Royal	7,000

AA-Accommodations West Reservation Agency

Doreen Wensley
660 Jones Terrace
Victoria, BC V8Z 2L7
(250) 479-1986 Fax: (250) 479-9999
E-mail: dwensley@vanisle.net
Web site: http://www.vanilse.net/gardencity

• One person $45–75; two people $55–125. King-sized beds, queen-sized beds, and double beds. Additional person from $15. Child from $5.

• A B&B reservation service covering Victoria and other Vancouver Island locations. Cottages and houses with ocean views, antiques, hot tubs, and swimming pools. All accommodations are inspected and are selected with attention to cleanliness, hospitality, and breakfasts. Many welcome families with children. Full descriptions given over the phone or detailed brochures mailed on request. No booking fees. Office is open Monday to Saturday from 8:00 a.m. to 9:00 p.m. and Sunday from 2:00 to 9:00 p.m. **In the agents' own words:** "We are pleased to offer country comfort and magnificent ocean views in a range of accommodations from rustic cottages to regal heritage houses. Our reservation service has been family owned since 1985. Your requirements are given caring, careful attention to ensure your satisfaction."

Canada-West Accommodations B&B Registry

Ellison Massey
Mail: Box 86607
North Vancouver, BC V7L 4L2
(604) 990-6730 Fax: (604) 990-5876
Toll-free from within North America, for
  reservations: 1-800-561-3223
E-mail: ellison@b-b.com
Web site: http://www.b-b.com

• One person $50–85; two people $75–125.

• A B&B reservation service covering British Columbia and Alberta, including Greater Vancouver, Victoria, Vancouver Island, the Okanagan, Whistler, Jasper, Banff, and Calgary. Accommodation for skiers at Whistler; Sun Peaks, near Kamloops; Big White, Silver Star, and Apex, in the Okanagan; and a number of locations in the Rockies. The B&Bs have one to three rooms and private bathrooms. Credit card payment required to hold reservation. Cancellation notice seven days; in Whistler during the ski season, thirty days. **In the agents' own words:** "We extend an invitation to call on us when planning to visit any location in British Columbia or Alberta."

Old English B&B Registry

Vicki Tyndall
1226 Silverwood Crescent
North Vancouver, BC V7P 1J3
(604) 986-5069 Fax: (604) 986-5069

• Rooms. Two people $85–175. Ensuite, private,
and shared guest bathrooms.
Self-contained suites. Two people $85–175.
Rate for one person is usually $10 less. Addi-
tional person $20.
Minimum stay two nights on holiday weekends.
• A B&B reservation service covering Vancouver, North Vancouver, and West Vancouver.
Most B&Bs are within twenty minutes of the city centre. Deposit required to hold reservation. Deposit less $20 administration fee is refunded if reservation is cancelled fourteen days
before arrival. Cash, traveller's cheques, credit cards. **In the agents' own words:** "All our
B&Bs have been personally inspected with attention given to cleanliness, hospitality, and
breakfasts. Our free professional reservation service offers European-style B&Bs with
warm, friendly West Coast ambience and with lots of breakfast table conversation about
places to explore and things to do. What is offered is definitely more than just a place to
stay."

Reservations Jasper Ltd.

Debbie Taylor
Mail: Box 1840
Jasper, AB T0E 1E0
(403) 852-5488 Fax: (403) 852-5489
E-mail: resjas@incentre.net
Web site: http://www.inshuttle.net/resjas/
   default.htm

• A reservation service covering Jasper, Banff,
Lake Louise, Canmore, Edmonton, Calgary, and
Mount Robson. B&Bs, in-house accommodation
without breakfast, hotels, motels, cabins, and bungalows. Booking fee of $20 for one desti-
nation; $5 for each additional destination. Additional $5 fee for overseas clients. Visa. Non-
commissionable. **In the agents' own words:** "We offer a fast, reliable, and informative service for our clients. You need only make one call for your Canadian Rockies vacation accommodations."

Town and Country B&B Reservation Service

Helen Burich
Mail: Box 74542
2803 West Fourth Avenue
Vancouver, BC V6K 1K2
(604) 731-5942 Fax: (604) 731-5942

• One person $55–95; two people $85–190.
Queen-sized beds, double beds, and twin beds.
Private and shared bathrooms.
• A B&B reservation service covering Vancouver,
Victoria, and Vancouver Island. Bookings for
other areas in BC and the Banff/Jasper area for guests who are making reservations for Vancouver, Victoria, and/or Vancouver Island. B&Bs range from modest to luxurious. Character houses to contemporary. Most B&Bs in residential areas are within twenty minutes of city centres and within walking distance of neighbourhood shops, restaurants, and parks. Some self-contained units and cottages. Personally selected and inspected. Deposit required. Cancellation notice seven days. **In the agents' own words:** "Our service has been established since 1980. We know our hosts and houses personally and do our best to meet your requirements according to facilities and availability."

The Denniston by the Sea B&B

Drew and Rosemary Denniston
430 Grafton Street
Victoria, BC V9A 6S3
(250) 385-5195 Fax: (250) 385-5100
Toll-free from within North America: 1-888-796-2699
E-mail: dennisto@datapark.com
Web sites: http://www.bbcanada.com
http://bcyellowpages.com/Advert/d/the_denniston.html
http://www.ivacation.com/p44.html

• From Victoria International Airport, the Anancortes ferry, or the Swartz Bay ferry terminal, take Highway 17 south. At exit 17, turn right onto McKenzie Avenue, which becomes Admirals Road. Turn right onto Esquimalt Road and left onto Grafton.
From the Inner Harbour, take Wharf Street to Johnson Street. Turn left onto Johnson and continue over the blue bridge. Johnson becomes Esquimalt Road after the bridge. Continue on Esquimalt and turn left onto Grafton.
• Four rooms. In summer, two people $85–115. In winter, two people $79–109. King-sized bed; queen-sized bed; double bed; twin beds. Each room has an additional twin bed, day bed, or hide-a-bed. Ensuite and private bathrooms. Additional person $20. Weekly rates during off-season.
• An early 1900s Tudor-style house on a hill with a view of the ocean and the Olympic Mountains. Seven minutes' drive from downtown and the Inner Harbour. Near transit to downtown, the Empress Hotel, ferries, the airport, and the University of Victoria. Beside a waterfront walkway from which birds, marine life, ferries, and ocean-going ships can be seen. Guest living room with fireplace has a view of Juan de Fuca Strait. Guest rooms have TVs, coffee, and tea. Daily housekeeping. One of the hosts is from Hawaii, and the other host is a third-generation Victoria resident. Full breakfast. Deposit required to hold reservation. Cancellation notice five days. Check-in 4:30 to 6:00 p.m. or by arrangement; check-out until 11:00 a.m. Credit cards for reservations only. No pets. Smoking in designated outdoor areas. **In the hosts' own words:** "We invite you to enjoy and rejuvenate in the peace and quiet of a serene, relaxing atmosphere—picturesque views in many directions will nurture your spirit."

Catherine House Harbour Walkway B&B

Joyce and Victor Holman
324 Catherine Street
Victoria, BC V9A 3S8
(250) 385-6945 Fax: (250) 385-6909

• From downtown Victoria, take Pandora Street southwest over the Johnson Street bridge and onto Esquimalt Road. Continue for 1 kilometre and turn left onto Catherine Street. The B&B is next to Spinnakers Pub.
• Rooms. Two people $95–125. Queen-sized bed. Ensuite and private bathrooms.
Monthly rates October to April.
• A B&B on the Inner Harbour walkway, near the ocean and fifteen minutes' walk from downtown, the Empress Hotel, the Royal British Columbia Museum, Chinatown, restaurants, pubs, and entertainment. Accommodates up to seven guests. Guest sitting room. Fridge. Facilities and supplies for coffee and tea. English breakfast. Deposit of one night's rate required to hold reservation. Reservations recommended. Cancellation notice seven days. Visa, MasterCard. No pets. No smoking. **In the hosts' own words:** "We welcome you to our large, modern, clean, and friendly house. Comfortable, quiet, and close to Victoria's beautiful Inner Harbour."

Norfolk House B&B

Val and Paul Ciceri
1225 Styles Street
Victoria, BC V9A 3Z6
(250) 384-8836

• From the Swartz Bay ferry terminal, take Highway 17 to downtown Victoria. Turn right onto Bay Street. Cross the Bay Street bridge and take Skinner to Banfield Park. Take the first right onto Styles Street. The B&B is the first house on the right.
• Four rooms. Two people $45–75. Queen-sized bed; double bed; twin beds. Shared guest bathrooms. Roll-away bed available for a fee. Off-season rates.
• A restored 1913 Tudor-style house with a view of the Gorge, Banfield Park, and the Selkirk trestle bridge. A few minutes from the start of the Galloping Goose Regional Park bicycle trail, which is sixty kilometres long. Ten minutes' walk from the Inner Harbour walkway, which leads to downtown and the Inner Harbour. Five minutes' drive or bus ride from the city centre; bus service every twenty minutes. Guest sitting room with TV. Tea and homemade baked goods. English breakfast. Reservations recommended. Cash, traveller's cheques. Children welcome. No pets. Smoking in the garden. **In the hosts' own words:** "At our B&B, a warm welcome awaits you."

The Gatsby Mansion

Rita A. Wilson
309 Belleville Street
Victoria, BC V8V 1X2
(250) 388-9191 Fax: (250) 920-5651
Toll-free from within North America, for reservations: 1-800-563-9656
E-mail: huntingdon@bctravel.com
Web site: http://www.bctravel.com/huntingdon/gatsby.html

• At Belleville and Oswego streets, one and a half blocks west of the Parliament Buildings.

• Eighteen suites. One person $125–285; two people $135–295. King-sized bed; queen-sized bed; double bed; twin beds. Ensuite bathrooms. Additional person $25. Off-season rates.

Romance, wedding, honeymoon, whale-watching, and golf packages.

• A restored Queen Anne–style mansion built in 1877 and a smaller house, both of which have views of the ocean, five minutes' walk from downtown, shopping, parks, and museums and one and a half blocks from the Parliament Buildings. Main house has antiques, frescoed ceilings, stained glass windows, mahogany panelling, and a large veranda with a view of the Inner Harbour. Rose and other flower gardens. Some of the guest suites have views of the harbour. Guest suites have TVs, movies, video games, and coffee makers. Some of the suites have sofa beds. Licenced lounge and fine dining restaurant that serves West Coast cuisine. Aromatherapy studio, gift shop, and currency exchange. Near golf courses. Across the street from the ferry terminals for the Clipper ferry, a passenger ferry that runs between Victoria and Seattle, and the Coho ferry, a passenger and vehicle ferry that runs between Victoria and Port Angeles. Full breakfast. Credit cards. No pets. Smoke-free environment. **In the hosts' own words:** "Our antiques, hand-painted ceilings, delicate stained glass windows, and mahogany panelling evoke a time of extravagance and prosperity; the fine dining restaurant and martini lounge complete the setting. Step back to a time when life was less complicated and pleasures were found at home."

Andersen House B&B

Janet and Max Andersen
301 Kingston Street
Victoria, BC V8V 1V5
(250) 388-4565 Fax: (250) 388-4563
E-mail: andersen@islandnet.com
Web site: http://www.islandnet.com/~andersen/

• At Kingston and Pendray streets, one and a half blocks west of the Parliament Buildings.

• Four suites in a house and one suite in a classic motor yacht. Two people $155–195. Queen-sized bed; king-sized bed and twin beds; queen-sized bed and a bed narrower than a twin bed; double bed. Ensuite bathrooms; on the yacht, a shower and two washrooms with toilets and washbasins. Discount of up to 50 percent November to January.

• A Victorian house built for a sea captain in 1891, with twelve-foot-high ceilings, stained glass windows, fireplaces, hardwood floors, and a garden with mature shrubs, fruit trees, and flowers. Three blocks from ferry and floatplane terminals. Antiques, original modern paintings, Peruvian rugs, and homemade Raku pottery throughout. Suites have private entrances, CD/cassette players, telephones, and books; some have views of mountains, gardens, the Parliament Buildings with passing horse-drawn carriages, or the downtown skyline. One of the suites has an ensuite bathroom with Jacuzzi tub. A second suite has a clawfoot soaker tub and a bar with sink, microwave, fridge, coffee maker, and electric kettle. A third suite has an antique four-post bed, a window seat/bed, and French doors that lead to a private deck. Fifty-foot 1927 classic motor yacht is docked at a marina five minutes' walk from the B&B and has a double bed, art deco teak cabinetry, a shower, two bathrooms, a skylight, and views of ships, kayaks, floatplanes, and seals. Full breakfast includes homemade jam. **In the hosts' own words:** "We are ideally located a short walk from Victoria's most popular attractions, and we can ensure that you enjoy the secret Victoria so many visitors miss."

Medana Grove B&B Inn

Noreen and Garry Hunt
162 Medana Street
Victoria, BC V8V 2H5
(250) 389-0437 Fax: (250) 389-0425
Toll-free from within North America: 1-800-269-1188
E-mail: medanagrove@pacificcoast.net
Web site: http://www.victoriabc.com/accom/medana.htm

• From Belleville Street at the Inner Harbour, go south on Menzies Street for three blocks. Turn left onto Simcoe and take the first right onto Medana.
• Rooms. One person $80; two people $85–110. Queen-sized bed; double bed and one twin bed. Ensuite and private bathrooms. Additional person $20. Child under 10 $10. Off-season rates.
• A 1908 house traditionally decorated and furnished with antiques, in a residential neighbourhood near downtown. Around the corner from shops, restaurants, and services. Guest living room on the main floor with TV and reading materials including local guidebooks and tourist publications. Full breakfast is served on an oak table in the dining room. Diets accommodated with advance notice. Visa, MasterCard. No pets. Smoke-free environment. **In the hosts' own words:** "Our B&B is reminiscent of a traditional English B&B and is within easy walking distance of the Inner Harbour ferry terminals, downtown Victoria, Beacon Hill Park, and the ocean. We are helpful but not intrusive. Experience our genuine Irish hospitality and guest rooms that are comfortable and tastefully decorated."

Heathergate House B&B and Cottage

Ann and Ned Easton
122 Simcoe Street
Victoria, BC V8V 1K4
(250) 383-0068 Fax: (250) 383-4320
Toll-free: 1-888-683-0068

• Ten minutes' walk from the Seattle and Port Angeles ferries.
• Three rooms. In summer (May 1 to October 15), one person or two people $99–125. In winter, one person or two people $79. Queen-sized bed; twin beds. Ensuite and private bathrooms.
Two-bedroom cottage (sleeps six). Two people $140. Queen-sized bed and twin beds. Private bathroom. Additional person $25. Hide-a-bed and roll-away cot available. In winter (October 1 to April 30), monthly rate of $1550.
• A B&B in the James Bay area of Victoria, fifteen minutes' walk from the Inner Harbour, the Parliament Buildings, the Royal British Columbia Museum, Fisherman's Wharf, and restaurants. Guest rooms have down comforters, robes, hair dryers, and ceiling fans. Coffee or tea is served on silver trays before breakfast in guests' rooms. Guest living room with fireplace, antique furniture, books, TV, and telephone with credit card service for long distance calls. Cottage has a kitchen, a washer and dryer, a dining room, a living room, a TV, a telephone, down comforters, ceiling fans, and a private garden. English breakfast or a daily entrée is served in the dining room in the main house. Continental breakfast is delivered to the cottage. Visa, MasterCard. Adult oriented. Children over nine welcome in the cottage. No pets. Smoking outdoors. **In the hosts' own words:** "Enjoy friendly West Coast hospitality combined with many of the comforts and traditions of a small English inn. We welcome world travellers, honeymooners, business travellers, and romantics."

At Craig House B&B

J. Hill
52 San Jose Avenue
Victoria, BC V8V 2C2
(250) 383-0339 Fax: (250) 383-0349
E-mail: craighouse@craighouse.bc.ca
Web site: http://www.craighouse.bc.ca

• From downtown Victoria, take Douglas, Menzies, or Government to Dallas Road. Turn right and continue to San Jose Avenue.

• Three rooms. One person $55–75; two people $60–80. Queen-sized bed; double bed. Shared bathroom.
Self-contained suite. One person $110; two people $120. Queen-sized bed and double sofa bed. Bathroom in suite. Additional person $15. Extended stay rates November 1 to May 31.

• A B&B in a quiet residential neighbourhood, twenty minutes' walk from Beacon Hill Park, the Empress Hotel, the Parliament Buildings, and the Inner Harbour. Half a block from the ocean. Guest rooms have TVs. Some guest rooms have fireplaces. Suite has a Jacuzzi tub, a fireplace, and a private garden entrance. Five minutes from downtown and ferries to Seattle. Full breakfast. Parking. Reservations recommended. Cancellation notice two days. Traveller's cheques, Visa, MasterCard. Children welcome by arrangement. No pets. Smoking on the deck. **In the hosts' own words:** "Comfort, relaxation, and hospitality await you at our quiet heritage B&B in James Bay. Our guest rooms are spacious and traditionally furnished. Awake refreshed."

Humboldt House B&B

Mila Werbik
867 Humboldt Street
Victoria, BC V8V 2Z6
(250) 383-0152 Fax: (250) 383-6402
Toll-free from within North America: 1-888-383-0327
E-mail: rooms@humboldthouse.com
Web site: http://www.humboldthouse.com

• In downtown Victoria, on Humboldt Street at Quadra.
• Five rooms. One person or two people $125–285. Queen-sized bed. Ensuite bathrooms.
Honeymoon and celebration packages available.
• An 1895 Victorian house on a quiet, tree-lined street, with guest rooms that have fireplaces and Jacuzzi tubs. One block from Beacon Hill Park. Three blocks from the Inner Harbour and the Royal British Columbia Museum. Guest rooms have down duvets, CD players, and flowers. Sitting room with fireplace, books, and telephone. Sherry is served in the sitting room in the afternoon. Full breakfast with champagne is delivered to guest rooms. Cash, Visa, MasterCard. Not suitable for children. No pets. Nonsmoking. **In the hosts' own words:** "Our B&B is a perfect choice for honeymoons, anniversaries, and retreats. Enjoy Victorian luxury, just steps from the heart of downtown."

The Beaconsfield Inn

Con and Judi Sollid
998 Humboldt Street
Victoria, BC V8V 2Z8
(250) 384-4044 Fax: (250) 384-4052
E-mail: beaconsfield@islandnet.com
Web site: http://www.islandnet.com/beaconsfield/

- At the corner of Vancouver and Humboldt streets.
- Six rooms and three suites. One person or two people $200–350. Queen-sized bed. Ensuite bathrooms. Additional person $65. Off-season rates.
- A 1905 English-style manor in a residential area, one block from Beacon Hill Park's 120 acres and four blocks from the Inner Harbour, downtown shops, galleries, and restaurants. Sixteen-foot beamed ceilings and mahogany floors. Guest rooms and suites have down comforters, canopied beds, antiques, and flowers. Most of the guest rooms and suites have fireplaces, Jacuzzi tubs, and stained glass windows. Sun room with a view of an English cottage–style front garden. Afternoon tea and sherry served by a fireplace in the library. Full breakfast is served in the dining room. Visa, MasterCard. Cancellation notice seven days. Full payment required to hold reservation. No children. No pets. No smoking. **In the hosts' own words:** "We offer fine service and luxury for discerning travellers. The style of our inn attracts many people celebrating special occasions."

Abigail's Hotel

Frauke and Daniel Behune
906 McClure Street
Victoria, BC V8V 3E7
(250) 388-5363 Fax: (250) 388-7787
Toll-free from within North America: 1-800-561-6565
E-mail: innkeeper@abigailshotel.com
Web site: http://www.abigailshotel.com

• At the corner of Quadra and McClure streets. From Vancouver Street, turn onto McClure Street.

• Twenty-two rooms. One person or two people $149–299. Ensuite bathrooms. Additional person $30.

Celebration and honeymoon packages. Winter rates.

• A European-style country inn with a garden, in a residential area, three blocks from downtown and the Inner Harbour. Guest rooms have antique furniture, down comforters, and flowers. Some guest rooms have fireplaces, sitting areas, and canopied beds. Some have Jacuzzis or soaker tubs. Snacks are available in the library, which has a stone fireplace. At 6:00 p.m., sherry and hors d'oeuvres are served by the fire. Full breakfast is served in the dining room. Cash, Visa, MasterCard, American Express. German spoken. No children under ten. No pets. No smoking. **In the hosts' own words:** "We greet you with smiling faces at our Tudor-style mansion, which has been lovingly restored. Charm, comfort, and sophistication make staying at our inn a quality experience."

Friends B&B

Jie and George Morrow
651 Trutch Street
Victoria, BC V8V 4C3
(250) 480-5504 Fax: (250) 480-5288
Toll-free: 1-888-480-5504
E-mail: friends@tthought.com
Web site: http://www.tthought.com/friends

• On the corner of Richardson and Trutch, one block east of Cook.
• Six rooms. One person $65–75; two people $80–105. Queen-sized bed;
queen-sized bed and one twin bed. Ensuite bathrooms. Additional person $20.
• A restored 1912 house on a quiet, tree-lined residential street, ten minutes' walk from the
Empress Hotel, antique row, the Dallas Road waterfront, Craigdarroch Castle, and downtown. Panelled hallway, hardwood floors, stained glass windows, and original fireplaces and
light fittings. Guest rooms have ensuite bathrooms, TVs, and down duvets. Afternoon tea is
served in a flower garden. Guest living room, dining room, and kitchen are separate from the
hosts' living quarters. Full breakfast includes fresh-squeezed orange juice and fresh fruit.
Parking. Cancellation notice two days. Visa, MasterCard. Children over five welcome. No
smoking. **In the hosts' own words:** "Let us introduce you to the many attractions of Victoria, including those often missed."

Prior House B&B Inn

Candis Cooperrider and Agnes Campbell
620 St. Charles Street
Victoria, BC V8S 3N7
(250) 592-8847 (250) 592-8223
E-mail: innkeeper@priorhouse.com
Web site: http://www.priorhouse.com

• Ten blocks from the Inner Harbour.

• Three rooms and three one-bedroom or two-bedroom suites. One person or two people $125–265. King-sized bed; two queen-sized beds; queen-sized bed. Ensuite and private bathrooms.
Additional person $35. Minimum stay two nights on weekends. Off-season rates October to June.

• A house built in 1912 as a private residence for the lieutenant governor of British Columbia, with oak-panelled walls and a Venetian glass chandelier. Within walking distance of historical sites, Victoria's antique row, and ocean beaches. Five minutes' drive from the Inner Harbour. High tea is served by a fireplace in a sitting room, in the library, or on a stone deck that has a view of landscaped grounds. Suites and rooms have down duvets, fireplaces, TVs, and antiques. Most of the guest rooms and suites have marble whirlpool tubs and views of English gardens or the ocean and the Olympic Mountains. Robes provided. Afternoon hostess, messages, fax, telephone, Internet, and laundry. Breakfast, including homemade scones, is served by a fireplace in the dining room or in guests' rooms. Parking on the grounds. Cancellation notice fourteen days. Check-in 4:00 to 6:00 p.m. or by arrangement; check-out until noon. Cheques, Visa, MasterCard for reservations; cash, traveller's cheques preferred for payment. Smoking in the garden and on decks. **In the hosts' own words:** "We welcome guests to our stately mansion and large landscaped grounds, where we recapture the graciousness and charm of the past in quiet luxury."

Dogwood Manor

Anne-Marie and Haji Dawood
1124 Fairfield Road
Victoria, BC V8V 3A7
(250) 361-4441 Fax: (250) 382-1618
E-mail: dogwoodmnr@coastnet.com
Web site: http://www.coastnet.com/home/dogwoodmnr/

• Between Cook and Trutch streets.
• Eight suites. One person $75–95; two people $90–145. Queen-sized bed and
sofa bed. Ensuite bathrooms. Breakfast ingredients supplied. Additional person
$20–25. Child under 13 $15. Off-season rates October to May. Extended stay
rates in winter.
• A 1910 house with a garden, six blocks from the Empress Hotel and the Inner Harbour and
two blocks from Beacon Hill Park. Suites have private entrances, kitchens, TVs, and telephones. Some of the suites have fireplaces. Coin laundry. Suites are supplied with ingredients for Continental breakfast. Reservations recommended. Deposit of one night's rate required to hold reservation. Cancellation notice three days. Check-in between 1:00 and 6:00
p.m. or by arrangement; check-out until 11:00 a.m. Visa, MasterCard. French, German, and
Spanish spoken. No pets. No smoking. **In the hosts' own words:** "We offer our house as
your home away from home."

The Sea Rose B&B

Pauline Boytim
1250 Dallas Road
Victoria, BC V8V 1C4
(250) 381-7932 Fax: (250) 480-1298
Toll-free from within North America:
** 1-888-335-7673**
E-mail: searose@compuserve.com
Web site: http://www.bctravel.com/
** searose.html**

• From downtown Victoria, take Douglas Street to Mile 0 of Highway 1. Turn left onto Dallas Road and continue to Howe.
• Four suites. Two people $115–170. Ensuite bathrooms.
Off-season and extended stay rates.
Furnished suites rented monthly November 1 to May 15.
• A B&B across the street from an ocean beach and a walkway along Dallas Road and five blocks from Beacon Hill Park. Sun room, beach, and walkway have views of the ocean, sunrises and sunsets over the ocean, the snowcapped Olympic Mountains, marine wildlife, ocean-going vessels, and hang-gliders. Birds and sea life can be seen in the waters off nearby Clover Point. Ten minutes' walk from Cook Street shops and restaurants. Twenty minutes' walk from the Empress Hotel. Suites have cooking facilities, fridges, and TVs. Full breakfast is served in the dining room at 8:30 a.m. Diets are accommodated. Cancellation notice seventy-two hours. Visa, MasterCard, American Express. Smoking outdoors. **In the hosts' own words:** "Our house is a beautiful characteristic 1920s house on a scenic marine drive. We offer friendly, hospitable service and accommodation. We will do our very best to ensure your comfort and enjoyment while visiting our beautiful city."

Piermont Place B&B

Trudy and Fred Jacobs
810 Piermont Place
Victoria, BC V8S 5J7
(250) 592-5703 Fax: (250) 592-5779
Toll-free from within Canada and the U.S.:
** 1-800-487-8397**

• From downtown, take Fort Street to Cook Street. Turn right onto Cook, left onto Rockland Avenue, and left onto Piermont.
• Three rooms and one suite. One person $65–100; two people $75–125. Queen-sized bed. Private bathrooms. Additional person $20. Extended stay and off-season rates. May 15 to September 15, minimum stay two nights.
• A Tudor-style house on a quiet residential street in the Rockland area of Victoria, a few minutes' walk from an art gallery, Craigdarroch Castle, and Government House, the Lieutenant Governor's official residence. Two kilometres from downtown and the ocean. Guest rooms and suite have down comforters. Some of the guest rooms have balconies and ocean views. Guest sitting room with TV and fireplace. Full breakfast is served on fine china in a formal dining room. Cancellation notice forty-eight hours. Check-in 4:00 to 7:00 p.m. or by arrangement. Visa, MasterCard. French and German spoken. No pets. No smoking. **In the hosts' own words:** "Enjoy our stately house with its spacious and elegant rooms, in one of Victoria's most beautiful neighbourhoods."

Claddagh House B&B

Ken Brown
1761 Lee Avenue
Victoria, BC V8R 4W7
(250) 370-2816 Fax: (250) 592-0228
E-mail: claddagh@pinc.com

• Four kilometres east of downtown Victoria. Take Fort Street east to Lee Avenue and turn right. There is no 1800 block; the B&B is the first house on the corner of the second block.

• Two rooms and one suite. Two people from $95. Ensuite bathrooms.

• A 1913 house in a quiet residential neighbourhood, eight minutes' drive from downtown and near the village of Oak Bay and ocean beaches. The main floor has guest rooms, a dining room, a living room with TV and videos, a sun room with fireplace, a front veranda, and a side deck. Guest rooms face south. Suite is on the upper level and has a bathroom with double Jacuzzi. Garden with patio, table, chairs, and hammock. Breakfast includes items from the garden, homemade bread, tea, coffee, and juice. Check-in 4:00 to 6:00 p.m.; check-out until 11:00 a.m. Visa, MasterCard, American Express. Smoking on the porch and in the garden. **In the hosts' own words:** "Our guests are number one."

Marion's B&B

Thomas and Marion Simms
1730 Taylor Street
Victoria, BC V8R 3E9
(250) 592-3070

• Five minutes from downtown Victoria. From Victoria International Airport or the Swartz Bay ferry terminal, take the Patricia Bay Highway, which becomes Blanshard Street. Turn left onto Hillside Avenue. Turn right onto Shelbourne Street and take the first left onto Myrtle, which becomes Taylor. The B&B is the fifth house on the left.

• Three rooms. One person $35–40; two people $50–60. Queen-sized bed; double bed. Shared guest bathroom and shared bathroom. Additional person $20. Child $10.

• A B&B on a quiet street, five minutes from downtown Victoria. Breakfast is served in a dining room that has a view of a field that was originally part of Victoria's first airport, with Mount Tolmie in the distance. Living room with a view of the Olympic Mountains. Beds with comforters, percale sheets, and homemade quilts. Jacuzzi. Full breakfast is served on bone china with silver cutlery. Reservations recommended. Cancellation notice two days. Cash, traveller's cheques. Smoking outdoors. **In the hosts' own words:** "We offer home accommodation with a friendly atmosphere."

Seabird House B&B

Ilima Szabo
1 Midwood Road
Victoria, BC V9B 1L4
(250) 479-2930
Web site: http://www.bbcanada.com.1854.html

• Ten minutes from downtown. Take Highway 1, turn left onto Helmcken, and turn left onto Midwood. Alternatively, take Highway 1A, turn right onto Helmcken, and turn right onto Midwood.

• Two rooms. In summer, one person $35–45, two people $55–70. In winter, one person $30–35, two people $40–55. Twin beds (or twin beds side by side with king-sized bedding). Shared guest bathroom. Additional person $10. Roll-away cot available. Weekly rates. December to February, monthly rates only.

• A quiet house on the edge of Portage Inlet, a tidal bird sanctuary connected to the ocean by the Gorge Waterway. Ten minutes from downtown. The second floor, which is one thousand square feet, is for guests. One of the guest rooms has a private deck and a view of the ocean. The other guest room has a partial ocean view. Living room, patio, and garden. Sitting area with TV, fridge, coffee, and tea. Kitchen and laundry facilities available, December to February. Full or Continental breakfast. Cancellation notice three days. Small pets. A non-smoking house. **In the hosts' own words:** "We offer you a home away from home on scenic Portage Inlet."

Swan Lake Chalet

Alan and Linda Donohue
948 McKenzie Avenue
Victoria, BC V8X 3G5
(250) 744-1233 Fax: (250) 744-2510
Toll-free: 1-888-345-1233
E-mail: swanlake@pacificcoast.net
Web site: http://www.swanlake@bctravel.com

• Five kilometres from downtown Victoria, near Saanich Road, between Highway 17 and Quadra Street.

• Three rooms. Two people $65–110. Queen-sized bed and double bed; queen-sized bed; double bed. Ensuite and private or shared guest bathrooms. Additional person $20.

• A modern chalet-style house across from Swan Lake nature sanctuary. Nature sanctuary has walking areas and views from Christmas Hill of the city, ocean, and mountains. One of the guest rooms has a double bed and a private bathroom with Jacuzzi tub. Another guest room has a sitting room and deck access through a gallery. The third guest room has a sitting room with TV and opens onto a deck. Full breakfast, including homemade muffins and homemade preserves, is served in the dining room, which has antique furnishings. Children welcome by arrangement. No pets. No smoking. **In the hosts' own words:** "Our guests return for the excellent food and hospitality."

Bender's B&B

Glenda Bender
4254 Thornhill Crescent
Victoria, BC V8N 3G7
(250) 472-8993 Fax: (250) 472-8995

• Eight kilometres from the city centre. From downtown Victoria, take Johnson Street east. As Johnson curves north, its name changes to Begbie and then to Shelbourne. Turn east onto Kenmore. At the first right, turn onto Thornhill Crescent.

• Six rooms. Two people $40–65. Two double beds, shared guest bathroom; queen-sized bed, shared guest bathroom; double bed, ensuite bathroom; double bed and one twin bed, shared guest bathroom; double bed and one twin bed, ensuite bathroom. Additional person $20.

• A B&B with six guest rooms, eight kilometres from the city centre. Two minutes' walk from a bus stop. Two of the guest rooms have TVs and ensuite bathrooms. Living room, deck, and guest family room. Full breakfast is served in a solarium before 10:00 a.m. Check-in by 10:00 p.m.; check-out until 10:00 a.m. Children welcome. No smoking. **In the hosts' own words:** "Our attractive house has a choice of pretty bedrooms."

Eagle's Nest B&B

Kathy McGuire
4769 Cordova Bay Road
Victoria, BC V8Y 2J7
(250) 658-2002 Fax: (250) 658-0135
E-mail: eagle@islandnet.com
Web site: http://www.victoriabc.com/accom/eagles.htm

• Fifteen minutes from downtown Victoria. From Victoria International Airport or the Swartz Bay ferry terminal, take Highway 17 (Patricia Bay Highway). Take the exit for Royal Oak Drive, turn left at the stop sign, and cross over an overpass. Continue on Royal Oak Drive to the intersection of Blenkinsop Road and Cordova Bay Road. Turn left onto Cordova Bay Road, continue for half a kilometre, and turn right into the B&B's driveway.

• Two rooms and one self-contained suite. Two people $75–125. King-sized bed, ensuite bathroom; queen-sized bed and sofa bed, private bathroom. Use of kitchen facilities in the suite $15.

Two-bedroom suite. Queen-sized beds. Ensuite bathroom. Breakfast not included. Minimum stay two nights.

Weekly and seasonal rates.

Honeymoon packages.

• A new house with a deck and ocean views, five minutes' walk from beachcombing by the ocean. Five minutes' drive from three golf courses, the Commonwealth Games pool, and a shopping centre. Near Mount Douglas Park and other areas for walking and hiking. Deer, raccoons, squirrels, eagles, and other wildlife can be seen. On bus route. Most beds have duvets. One of the guest rooms has a king-sized bed and an ensuite bathroom with Jacuzzi. Self-contained suite has kitchen facilities, a TV, a private deck with a view of the ocean, and a private entrance. Two-bedroom suite has kitchen facilities and a view of the ocean. Coffee available in the sun room. Varied, full breakfast. Most diets accommodated. Cancellation notice seven days. Visa, MasterCard, American Express. Children welcome. No pets. Smoking on the deck. **In the hosts' own words:** "We are well traveled and offer advice on sightseeing and restaurants. Our home is truly your home away from home."

Iris Garden Country Manor B&B

Dave and Sharon Layzell
5360 West Saanich Road
Victoria, BC V9E 1J8
(250) 744-2253 Fax: (250) 744-5690
E-mail: irisgarden@pacificcoast.net

• From downtown Victoria, take Highway 17 north for 12 kilometres, to the Royal Oak exit.

• Four rooms. One person $75–135; two people $85–145. Queen-sized bed, twin beds. Ensuite bathrooms. Additional person $20.

• A 1960 character house on three rolling acres, with irises in mixed gardens, large Douglas fir trees, and an indoor pool with a view of the gardens and forested hills. Guest rooms have vaulted ceiling, new fixtures, flowers, antiques, and contemporary furnishings. Two of the rooms have jetted tubs. One of the rooms has a double soaking tub. Guest living room with books and fireplace. A second guest living room, which has a high ceiling, beams, bricks, a TV, and a VCR, can be reserved for special occasions and meetings. Within walking distance of biking and hiking trails, tennis courts, and Prospect Lake beach. Ten minutes from the Butchart Gardens, the botanical gardens at the Horticultural Centre of the Pacific, the Victoria Butterfly Gardens, four public golf courses, restaurants, and shopping. Full breakfast, including homemade muffins and scones, fruit, German puffed pancakes, crêpes, French toast with warm berry sauce, and locally made sausage, is served in the living room that has a high ceiling. Visa, MasterCard. Children over twelve welcome. Nonsmoking house. **In the hosts' own words:** "We provide the charm and casual comfort of yesterday in combination with the amenities of today. Breakfast—decadent and delicious—is always an adventure."

Brentwood Bay B&B–Verdier House

Evelyn Hardy
7247 West Saanich Road
Box 403
Brentwood Bay, BC V8M 1R3
(250) 652-2012

• Twenty-five minutes east of Victoria, at the corner of Stelly's Cross Road and West Saanich Road.

• Three rooms. Two people $85-95. King-sized bed; queen-sized bed; twin beds. Ensuite and private bathrooms.

• A restored 1912 house with views of Brentwood Bay and Saltspring Mountain from a tea room and a balcony. Guest rooms have wood floors, lace curtains, braided rugs, and hand-made coverlets. One of the guest rooms has an ensuite bathroom with clawfoot tub. Two of the guest rooms have views of the bay; the other guest room has a view of the town of Brent-wood Bay. In the town and surrounding area are fine dining restaurants, boating, fishing, golf, Butterfly World, an observatory, scenic drives, a Native centre, and beaches. Veranda. Five minutes' drive from the Butchart Gardens. Breakfast includes vegetarian items; specialties are pear cobbler and homemade bread. Deposit of one night's rate required to hold reservation. Cancellation notice seven days. No pets. No smoking indoors. **In the hosts' own words:** "Enjoy our elegantly appointed rooms."

Island View Beach B&B

Sylvia Nicholson
7242 Highcrest Terrace
Saanichton, BC V8M 1W5
(250) 652-6842
Cel: (250) 744-7413

• Fifteen minutes from the Swartz Bay ferry terminal. From the ferry terminal, take Highway 17 (Patricia Bay Highway). Turn left onto Island View Road and continue for one block. Turn left onto Puckle. Turn right onto Lamont Road, which becomes Highcrest Terrace.

• Self-contained suite. Two people $69. Additional person $20.

• A B&B with a self-contained suite that has a view of Haro Strait and Mount Baker. Suite has a private entrance, a kitchen, a bathroom, a sun room, and a living room with TV and VCR. Fifteen minutes' drive from ferries and the Butchart Gardens. Twenty minutes' drive from Victoria. Coffee and tea supplies and homemade cakes and cookies are provided in the suite. Breakfast is served at guests' convenience in the sun room, which has a view of the ocean and a bird sanctuary. Breakfast includes blackberry muffins, fresh fruit with yogurt, and pancakes. Children welcome. Smoking outdoors. **In the hosts' own words:** "An ideal location for a quiet holiday, birdwatching, or just walking on our beach."

Guest Retreat B&B

Shirley and Ken Moncur
2280 Amity Drive
North Saanich, BC V8L 1B6
(250) 656-8073 Fax: (250) 656-8027

• Fifteen minutes from Victoria.
• Two suites. In summer, two people $115, four people $185. In winter, two people $85, four people $120. Queen-sized bed; queen-sized bed and hide-a-bed. Private bathrooms.
• A B&B on a half acre on the North Saanich peninsula, three hundred metres from a sandy beach. Front yard with fountain and flood-lights. Backyard with pond and bridge. One and a half kilometres from Victoria International Airport. Five kilometres from the Swartz Bay ferry terminal. Three kilometres from the Ana-cortes ferry in Sidney. Near the Butchart Gardens. One of the suites has a living room, arm-chairs, a TV, a VCR, an electric fireplace, and kitchen facilities. The other suite is wheelchair accessible and has a TV, a VCR, and a fridge. Suites have private entrances. Pickup from plane and ferry. Hosts provide information on the area. Full breakfast. Deposit of $50 re-quired to hold reservation. Cash, traveller's cheques. Adult oriented. **In the hosts' own words:** "Stroll over our pond bridge with a cool drink and enjoy the fresh air from the ocean. Over breakfast we will be happy to supply you with information on beautiful Vancouver Is-land and Victoria."

Pineneedle Place Waterfront B&B

Joan Buchanan
9314 Lochside Drive
Sidney, BC V8L 1N6
(250) 656-2095

• Ten minutes from the Swartz Bay ferry termi-nal on Highway 17. Turn left onto Beacon Avenue. Turn right onto Fifth Street, which becomes Lochside. Continue south for 1.6 kilo-metres.
• Suite. Two people $79. Queen-sized bed. Private bathroom. Additional person $20. Child $10. Double bed and twin bed available. Weekly and off-season rates.
• A cottage-style house with a garden on half an acre of beachfront property. Covered out-door area with barbecue. Suite is on the ground floor and has a private entrance and a liv-ing room with fireplace and TV. Less than two kilometres from Sidney. Less than a kilo-metre from ferries to Anacortes, Washington. Twenty-five minutes from Victoria. Ten min-utes from the Victoria International Airport. Twenty minutes from the Butchart Gardens. Tea and coffee in suite. Full breakfast is served at guests' convenience. Children welcome. No smoking indoors. **In the hosts' own words:** "Come to a peaceful place where you can stroll garden paths and beachcomb on the beach. Our suite is perfect for families and friends."

Lovat House Seaside B&B

Fran and Chris Atkinson
9625 Second Street
Sidney, BC V8L 3C3
(250) 656-3188

• Three rooms. One person $45; two people $55–75. Double bed and one twin
bed. Ensuite and private bathrooms. Additional person $20.
• A B&B in a quiet area of Sidney, within walking distance of shopping, restaurants, and
marinas and with a view of the ocean, islands, and mountains. A few minutes from B.C. and
U.S. ferries, Victoria International Airport, and the Butchart Gardens. Near beach access.
Boat charters, lessons, and whale watching can be arranged. Guest rooms have TVs. Two of
the guest rooms have sea views. Sitting area and patio. Full breakfast. Children over eleven
welcome. No pets. No smoking.

Orchard House

Gerry Martin
9646 Sixth Street
Sidney, BC V8L 2W2
(250) 656-9194

• From Highway 17, turn east onto Beacon Avenue. Turn south onto Fifth Street and continue for three blocks. Turn west onto Orchard Avenue and continue for one block to Sixth Street.

• Four rooms. One person $49–59; two people $59–69. Queen-sized bed; double bed. Additional person $20. Off-season rates October to April.

• A house built in 1914 by the founding family of Sidney, with beamed ceilings, built-in wooden cabinets with leaded glass windows, and English country-style gardens. Ten minutes' drive from the Butchart Gardens. Five minutes' walk from beaches and parks and from Sidney's shops and restaurants. Two blocks from ferries to Anacortes, Washington. A short drive from the airport and from ferries to Vancouver. Twenty minutes' drive from downtown Victoria. Full breakfast is served in a formal dining room. Children over twelve welcome. No pets. Smoking outdoors. **In the hosts' own words:** "Come stay with us in our beautiful heritage house and enjoy our large, healthy breakfasts and the small-town character of Sidney by the Sea. Sidney's main street comes alive with arts and crafts on the first weekend in July for Sidney Days."

Little Mermaid B&B

Leif and Kirsten Christensen
11064 Chalet Road
Sidney, BC V8L 5M2
(250) 656-4377 Fax: (250) 656-0949

• Directions are provided by mail or fax when reservations are made.

• Rooms. $85–95. King-sized bed; extra-long twin beds. Private bathrooms.

• A southwest-facing B&B on two and a half acres, on the ocean. Guest rooms have views of the ocean and sliding doors that lead to a patio with table and chairs. Ten minutes from ferries to Vancouver, Salt Spring Island, and Anacortes. Twenty minutes from the Butchart Gardens. Twenty-five minutes from downtown Victoria. Sitting room with TV and VCR and sliding doors that lead to the patio. Kitchen available for guests to prepare light meals. Tea and coffee. Breakfast includes homemade bread, muffins, jam, and jelly. Parking. Cash, traveller's cheques. Adult oriented. No pets. No smoking indoors. **In the hosts' own words:** "Enjoy beautiful sunsets from your rooms, or walk one hundred feet across our lawn to sit on the beach and watch the sun go down. We are lucky to have a little piece of paradise."

Cartref B&B

Josie and Malcolm Shrimpton
1345 Readings Drive
Sidney, BC V8L 5K7
(250) 656-1247 Fax: (250) 656-1247
E-mail: cartref@islandnet.com
Web site: http://www.victoriabc.com/
accom/cartref.html

• Thirty kilometres from Victoria. From the Swartz Bay ferry terminal, take the right lane. Turn right onto Wain Road and continue for 1 kilometre. Turn right onto Tatlow and continue for 2 kilometres. Turn right onto West Saanich Road and continue for 1 kilometre. Turn right onto Readings and continue for 1.3 kilometres. The B&B is on the right, opposite a walking trail sign.

• Two rooms. One person $60; two people $75–90. Queen-sized bed and one twin bed; double bed. Shared and private bathrooms. Additional person $15. Crib available. Rates for groups occupying both rooms. Extended stay and off-season rates.

• A new country-style house on one acre, on a south-facing hillside with a view of the village of Sidney, with guest room views of Sidney Channel, islands, and the Olympic Mountains. The grounds, in a natural rock setting, have been landscaped by one of the hosts, who is a retired botanist. Guest room drapes and duvets are made by the other host. Guest rooms are on the second floor and have dormer windows. Guest sitting room with TV and VCR. Hosts can recommend gardens to visit in the area. Full English breakfast or light breakfast of homeade bread and jam made from local fruit is served on a terrace by a rock pool and waterfall. Cash, traveller's cheques, Visa. Deposit of one night's rate required to hold reservation. Children welcome by arrangement. No pets. Nonsmoking house. **In the hosts' own words:** "*Cartref* is a Celtic word that means a warm, friendly home. We have traveled extensively and are knowledgeable about British Columbia. We welcome guests to our home, and we also love to talk about our garden."

Top o' Triangle Mountain

Henry and Pat Hansen
3442 Karger Terrace
Victoria, BC V9C 3K5
(250) 478-7853 Fax: (250) 478-2245
Toll-free: 1-800-870-2255
Web site: http://www.surfport.com/triangle

• From Highway 1, take Highway 14 west for 5.5 kilometres. Turn left onto Fulton Road. At the top of the hill, keep left on Fulton. Turn left onto Karger and continue to cul-de-sac.

• Two rooms and one suite. One person $55–75; two people $70–90. Queen-sized bed, ensuite bathroom; queen-sized bed and double hide-a-bed, bathroom in suite. Additional person $20. Child under 10 $5. Roll-away bed and crib available. Off-season rates.

• A cedar house surrounded by fir and arbutus trees, on a small mountain, with views of Victoria, Juan de Fuca Strait, Mount Baker, and the Olympic Mountains. Twenty minutes from downtown. Fifteen minutes from golf, fishing, swimming, hiking trails, and provincial and regional parks. Garden and wrap-around deck. Open-plan living area. Sitting area on the ground floor has a fridge, a kettle, and hot and cold drinks. Guest rooms and suite have TVs. Suite has a sitting room with a double hide-a-bed. One of the guest rooms and the suite face a back garden with trees. Another guest room has a view of the ocean and mountains and sliding glass doors that lead to the deck. Full hot breakfast is served in the solarium or in the dining room, both of which have a view of the ocean and mountains. Visa, MasterCard. No pets. Smoking on the deck. **In the hosts' own words:** "Up here we offer fresh air, a comfortable night's sleep, and a hearty breakfast each morning to get you started on your busy day of sightseeing or hiking."

Gracefield Manor

Shirley Wilde
3816 Duke Road RR 4
Victoria, BC V9C 4B2
(250) 478-2459 Fax: (250) 478-2447

• From Victoria, take Highway 1 west to the Colwood/Sooke exit (to Highway 14). Turn left onto Metchosin Road and continue for 7 kilometres. Turn left onto Duke Road. The B&B's address number is on an old tree at the end of a long driveway.

• Three rooms. One person or two people $85–100. Double bed; twin beds. Ensuite bathrooms.

• A colonial plantation–style manor with antique furnishings, restored in 1991, on eleven acres of pasture with apple trees, sheep in the fields, and views of the Olympic Mountains and Juan de Fuca Strait. Ten minutes' walk from a park, hiking trails, and a beach. Ten minutes' drive from golf courses and fishing. Twenty minutes' drive from downtown. Living room and front terrace. One of the guest rooms has a fireplace. Breakfast is served on fine china in a formal dining room. Reservations required. Cancellation notice seven days. Check-in 3:00 to 5:00 p.m. or by arrangement; check-out until 11:30 am. Cash, Visa. Adult oriented. No pets; dog in residence. Smoking outdoors. **In the hosts' own words:** "If you like quiet countryside, fabulous ocean and mountain views, fresh sea air, and clean beaches, then come to our manor."

Blue Castle B&B

Valerie and Gerry Walther
1009 Glen Forest Way
Victoria, BC V9C 3X7
(250) 478-2800 Fax: (250) 478-2800
E-mail: Bluecastle@bc.sympatico.com
Web site: http://www.surfport.com/Bluecastle

• From Highway 14, turn left onto Happy Valley Road. Turn left onto Glen Forest Way and continue for 1 kilometre. At the checkerboard, keep right.
• Two rooms. Two people $85. Queen-sized bed; twin beds. Private bathrooms. Two suites. Two people $120–130. King-sized bed; queen-sized bed. Ensuite bathrooms.
Extended stay rates.
• A Victorian house on a hill, with views of mountains and the ocean. Deer visit the property regularly. Wrap-around veranda with wicker furniture. Sitting room. Suite with king-sized bed has a seven-foot clawfoot bathtub, a solarium, and a balcony. Guest rooms have mountain views. Ten minutes from beach and parks. A few minutes from golf courses, riding stables, hiking and biking trails, fishing, and whale watching. Twenty-five minutes from Sooke and downtown Victoria. Full breakfast is served in the dining room. Visa, MasterCard. German spoken. Children over eleven welcome. No pets; cat in residence. **In the hosts' own words:** "We invite you to enjoy our comfortable house and its relaxed and casual atmosphere."

Wooded Acres B&B

Elva and Skip Kennedy
4907 Rocky Point Road
Victoria, BC V9C 4G2
(250) 478-8172
E-mail: swatt@netcom.ca
Web site: http://www.travelguides.com/lanier

• From Victoria, take Highway 1 north to Highway 1A. Take Highway 1A to
Highway 14. From Highway 14, turn left onto Metchosin Road, right onto
Happy Valley Road, and left onto Rocky Point Road.

• Two suites. Two people $110. Queen-sized bed. Bathrooms in suites.

• A log house on three treed acres in the country, thirty minutes from downtown, near beaches, wilderness parks, golf courses, fishing, birdwatching, and trails for walking, hiking, and mountain biking. Each suite has flowers, antiques, and down duvets. Hot tub with a view of the wilderness; robes provided. Full breakfast, including homemade baked goods, is served at guests' convenience. Cash, cheques. Adult oriented. No pets. Smoking restricted. **In the hosts' own words:** "Our secluded log house, built with the wood from our acreage, offers complete privacy for honeymooners, with friendly hospitality, comfort, relaxation, and good food. Candlelight and lace add a special touch."

A B&B at Swallow Hill Farm

Gini and Peter Walsh
4910 William Head Road
Victoria, BC V9C 3Y8
(250) 474-4042 Fax: (250) 474-4042
E-mail: swallowhill@pacificcoast.net
Web site: http://www.pacificcoast.net/~swallowhill

• Thirty minutes from Victoria. Take Highway 1 north to exit 10. Take Highway 1A west to Highway 14. Turn left onto Metchosin Road, which becomes William Head Road in the town of Metchosin. Continue for 2 kilometres past the town centre to the B&B.

• Two suites. In summer (May to October), one person $60–75, two people $70–95. In winter, one person $55–65, two people $65–75. Queen-sized bed, ensuite bathroom; queen-sized bed and twin beds, private bathroom.

• A B&B on an apple farm, with views of the ocean, mountains, and sunrises. Suites have private bathrooms, decks, feather beds, and down duvets. Whales, otters, seals, deer, and eagles and other birds can be seen. Five minutes from hiking, cycling, swimming, fishing, diving, and golf. Twenty minutes from whale watching. Antique Canadiana and handmade furniture made by one of the hosts. Sauna. Tea, coffee, and homemade cookies. Full breakfast includes farm-fresh eggs and juice made from the farm's apples. Cancellation notice five days. Advanced bookings preferred. Cash, credit cards. No pets; dog in residence. Nonsmokers. **In the host's own words:** "You'll enjoy the peaceful country setting of our little farm on Vancouver Island's beautiful southwest coast."

Lilac House Country B&B

Gail Harris
1848 Connie Road
Victoria, BC V9C 4C2
(250) 642-2809 or (250) 389-0252
E-mail: Lilac@pinc.com
Web site: http://vvv.com/~lilac/

• Twenty-six kilometres west of Victoria, on the road to Sooke.
• Two rooms. One person $45–75; two people $65–95. Queen-sized bed; double bed. Ensuite and shared bathrooms.
Discount of 10 percent on stays of three or more nights. Other discounts available.
• A custom-built house with views, vaulted ceilings, and skylights, on five acres of wooded trails and moss-covered hills. A creek runs through the property. Deck with hot tub. Living room with woodstove. Patio, garden, and walking trails. In the area are hiking, swimming, fishing, cycling, horseback riding, llama trekking, and bird and wildlife viewing. Five minutes' drive from the Galloping Goose Trail. Twenty-five minutes from Victoria. Ten minutes from Sooke. Ten minutes from lake, river, and ocean swimming. One kilometre from a pub. Deposit required to hold reservation. Cancellation notice seven days. Visa, MasterCard. Adult oriented. No pets; cat in residence. Nonsmoking. **In the hosts' own words:** "Our B&B is perched above the valley and surrounded by the beautiful Sooke hills. We offer all the comforts of a home away from home, in an atmosphere of warmth, elegance, and tranquillity. Come relax with us and enjoy a cool drink on the wraparound veranda or a soak in the hot tub under a canopy of stars."

Cape Cod B&B

Gwen Utitz and Peter Ginman
5782 Anderson Cove Road
Sooke, BC V0S 1N0
(250) 642-3253 Fax: (250) 642-3253
E-mail: pginman@aol.com

• Forty-five minutes southwest of Victoria. From Victoria, take Highway 14 towards Sooke. Turn left onto Gillespie Road (17 Mile Pub on the corner). At the end of Gillespie Road, turn right onto East Sooke Road. Turn right onto Anderson Cove Road, which is the first paved road on the right, and continue up the hill for 400 metres. The B&B is on the left.
• Self-contained suite. Two people $125. Queen-sized bed. Ensuite bathroom. Roll-away beds available at additional cost. Off-season rates.
• A Cape Cod–style house with a covered patio that has a view of Sooke Basin and sunsets. A base for day trips to Victoria, the Butchart Gardens, and the southern part of Vancouver Island. Suite has a private entrance, a modern kitchen, a dining area, a living room with TV, a bedroom with queen-sized bed, and an ensuite bathroom. Near hiking in East Sooke Regional Park and on the Galloping Goose Trail, kayaking, horseback riding, and windsurfing. Salmon fishing and crabbing year round. Hosts arrange fishing charters and whale-watching tours. Breakfast ingredients are provided, or, if guests prefer, breakfast is prepared by the hosts. Deposit of one night's rate required to hold reservation. Cash. French, German, and Dutch spoken. Nonsmoking. **In the hosts' own words:** "At our B&B total tranquillity is ensured."

Eliza Point B&B by the Sea

Cheryl and Doug Read
6514 Thornett Road
East Sooke, BC V0S 1N0
(250) 642-2705 Fax: (250) 642-2704
E-mail: eliza@tnet.net

• From Victoria, go west on Highway 1 to the Colwood-Sooke exit. Take Highway 14 (Sooke Road) west for 15 minutes. Just past a pub, turn left onto Gillespie Road and continue for 6 minutes. Turn right onto East Sooke Road and continue for 8 minutes. Turn right onto Eliza Point Road and look for the B&B's sign.

• Two rooms. Two people $75–95. Queen-sized bed and double sofa bed; double bed. Shared guest bathroom (or private bathroom by arrangement). Additional person $15.

• A B&B on Sooke Harbour, where deer, otters, great blue herons, kingfishers, and bald eagles can be seen. Guest rooms have views of the harbour, down duvets, and robes. One of the guest rooms has a sitting area, a queen-sized bed, a double sofa bed, a fireplace, a TV, antiques, and work by Native artist Victor Newman. Sitting room with ocean views and deck. Small deck with a view of the ocean is for guest use only. Forest and oceanfront yards. Ten minutes from hiking, tennis courts, and cycling and horseback riding trails. Hosts provide transportation to and from hiking in East Sooke. Whale watching, salmon fishing, and charters can be arranged from the B&B. Twenty-five minutes from Sooke. Forty minutes from downtown Victoria. Thirty-five minutes from a fine dining restaurant. Twelve minutes from a casual, pub-style restaurant. Near llama trekking, windsurfing, kayaking, crabbing, birdwatching, and beachcombing. Children welcome by arrangement. Smoking outdoors. **In the hosts' own words:** "Our casually elegant waterfront house has been designed with guests' pleasure in mind. It is ideally situated, whether you want to kick back and relax or go, go, go."

Hartmann House B&B

Ray and Ann Hartmann
5262 Sooke Road
Sooke, BC V0S 1N0
(250) 642-3761 Fax: (250) 642-7561

• Thirty minutes from Victoria, on the west coast of Vancouver Island, in the village of Sooke.
• Two rooms. $100–120. Double bed, private bathroom; king-sized bed, ensuite bathroom. Twin beds available.
Honeymoon suite. Two people $180. King-sized bed; ensuite bathroom.
• A handcrafted English cottage with ocean and sunset views, surrounded by gardens and lily ponds. Across the road from beaches and trails for hiking and walking. Five minutes' drive from restaurants, tea rooms, craft shops, and a golf course. Twenty minutes' drive from windsurfing. Fishing charters can be arranged by the hosts. Guest living area has books and a Count Rumford fireplace. Guest veranda with white wicker chairs. Guest rooms have canopied beds and eiderdown quilts. One of the guest rooms has a four-post double bed. Seven-hundred-square-foot honeymoon suite has a fireplace, a private courtyard, and a whirlpool bath for two. Bathrooms have robes, shampoo, lotion, and hair dryers. Champagne and fruit plate served when guests arrive. Breakfast includes strawberry waffles, homemade muffins, and omelettes. Entrées change daily. Off-street parking. Cancellation notice three days. Cash, traveller's cheques, Visa. German spoken. Adult oriented. No pets. Smoking on the veranda. **In the hosts' own words:** "Treat yourself to the charm of our country B&B— a unique romantic getaway."

Burnside House B&B

Renata Wuersch-Tilly
1890 Maple Avenue
Sooke, BC V0S 1N0
(250) 642-4403 Fax: (250) 642-4403
E-mail: wray_wuersch@bc.sympatico.ca
Web site: http://www.sookenet.com/burnside

• Less than 1 kilometre past Sooke; 37 kilometres west of Victoria.
• Four rooms. One person $65–85; two people $75–95. Queen-sized bed; double bed. Private bathroom. Additional person $20.
Off-season rates October 1 to May 1, excluding weekends and holidays.
• A restored Georgian-style country house on two acres of lawn and gardens. Built by John Muir in 1870, the B&B is the oldest inhabited house in Sooke. Two of the guest rooms have couches to accommodate an additional person. Some guest rooms have ocean and mountain views. Gazebo with Jacuzzi. Near golf, swimming, hiking, and trout and salmon fishing. Picnic lunches and bicycles available. Whales and seals can sometimes be seen from nearby beaches. Accessible by public transit. Full breakfast is served in the guest living room, which has a fireplace, a TV, and games. Vegetarian breakfast available. Deposit of one night's rate required to hold reservation. Cancellation notice three days. Visa, MasterCard. German spoken. Children over eleven welcome. Pets welcome. Nonsmokers preferred. **In the hosts' own words:** "An ideal base for exploring the Sooke area. We'd love to spoil you."

Salty Towers Guest Cottages

Linda and Glenn Thibault
1581 Dufour Road
Sooke, BC V0S 1N0
(250) 642-7034 Fax: (250) 642-7034
E-mail: salty@vicnet.net
Web site: http://www.sookenet.com/
**   saltytowers**

• Thirty-eight kilometres west of Victoria. One and one-half kilometres past Sooke, turn left onto Whiffen Spit Road. Turn left onto Dufour Road.
• Three self-contained cottages. Two people $115–140. Additional person $15. Weekly and off-season rates. Pet $10 per day.
Crabbing and fishing charters.
• Cottages on the ocean with a private wharf for moorage and a hot tub with views of Sooke Harbour, East Sooke, and Whiffin Spit Park. Cottages have private patios, skylights, wood stoves, down duvets, TVs, ensuite Jacuzzis, fridges, microwaves, toaster ovens, and hot plates. Five minutes' walk from fine dining at Sooke Harbour House restaurant. Complimentary breakfast at a nearby café or Continental breakfast in cottage. Deposit of one night's rate required to hold reservation. Cancellation notice three days. Visa, MasterCard. Pets welcome. No smoking indoors. **In the hosts' own words:** "Our B&B offers spectacular oceanfront scenery, fabulous décor, and seafood fresh from the ocean."

Richview House

Francois and Joan Gething
7031 Richview Drive
Sooke, BC V0S 1N0
(250) 642-5520 Fax: (250) 642-5520
E-mail: rvh@islandnet.com
Web site: http://www.islandnet.com/~RVH

• Thirty-two kilometres west of Victoria.
• Three suites. Two people $175–195. Queen-sized bed. Ensuite bathroom.
Additional person $25.
• A B&B on an eighty-foot cliff overlooking Juan de Fuca Strait, with a view of the Olympic
Mountains in Washington. Suites are in an addition to the original house and are separate
from the hosts' living quarters. Two of the suites are on the second floor, and one is on the
main floor. Furniture and woodwork, of red and yellow cedar, fir, and alder, was designed
and made by one of the hosts. Suites have hardwood floors, fireplaces, loveseats, and views
of Juan de Fuca Strait and the Olympic Mountians. The suites on the second floor have
vaulted ceilings with skylights and private Jacuzzi hot tubs on decks facing the ocean. The
third suite has a two-person steam room and a double shower; essential oils for the steam
room provided. Garden with benches. Eiderdown duvets, terry robes, and sherry. Shampoo
and hair dryers. Near salmon fishing charters, golf courses, ocean beaches, whale watching,
and mountain biking and hiking trails. Reflexology and massage therapy available. Guests
have access to a room for making tea or coffee throughout the day. Ice and ice buckets are
available. Breakfast includes fruit, homemade jam and jelly, bread, muffins, and an entrée;
menu changes daily. Breakfast is served in the dining area or in the suites. Cancellation notice three days. Cash, personal cheques, Visa, MasterCard. Adult oriented. No pets. Nonsmoking. **In the hosts' own words:** "Guests are welcome to stroll through our gardens—
benches are situated to enjoy the panoramic view of the water and mountains."

Gordon's Beach Farmstay B&B

Robyn Evans
4530 Otter Point Road
Sooke, BC V0S 1N0
(250) 642-5291 Fax: (250) 642-5291

• Ten kilometres west of Sooke's only traffic light on West Coast Road (Highway 14). Turn right onto Otter Point Road. The B&B is the second house on the left.

• Room. One person $55–75; two people $75–80. Double bed. Private bathroom.
Two suites. One person $55-75; two people $75-80. Queen-sized bed. Ensuite bathroom.

• A B&B across the road from an ocean beach, on ten acres with views of Juan de Fuca Strait and the Olympic Mountains. Suites and room have views of the ocean. Whales, sea lions, deer, and eagles can be seen from the B&B. Near hiking, biking, and nature trails. Suites have queen-sized beds, ensuite bathrooms, private entrances, patios, sitting areas, antiques, TVs, and coffee pots. One of the suites has a sink and a microwave. Outdoor gazebo hot tub, barbecue, and bicycles. Full breakfast is served in the dining room, on the patio, or in the suites. Check-in after 3:00 p.m; check-out until 11:00 a.m. Visa, MasterCard. **In the hosts' own words:** "We offer hospitality, privacy, and comfort."

Light House Retreat

Virginia Boyd
107 West Coast Road
Sooke, BC V0S 1N0
(250) 646-2345 Fax: (250) 646-2345
Toll-free for reservations: 1-888-805-4448
E-mail: light@islandnet.com
Web site: http://www.sookenet.com/lighthouse/

• Fourteen kilometres past Sooke's only traffic light. Cross two bridges and pass Muir Creek. The B&B's driveway is the first at the top of the hill, on the left.

• Suite and two-bedroom suite (sleeps up to six). One person $125–200; two people $150–225. Queen-sized bed; queen-sized bed and two double beds. Ensuite bathrooms. Additional person $25.
Self-contained one-bedroom cottage (sleeps up to five). Two people $150–225. Queen-sized bed and double futon. Ensuite bathroom.
Off-season rates.

• A B&B on the ocean with a private beach and suites that have a view of Juan de Fuca Strait and the Olympic Mountains. Eagles, whales, sunsets, and winter ocean storms can be seen from the B&B. Near hiking along the Juan de Fuca marine trail. Living room with fireplace and books. Two-bedroom suite has a fireplace, a private entrance, a deck, and a bathroom with Jacuzzi tub and family-sized shower. Suite has an ensuite bathroom with double Jacuzzi tub and double shower. Suites have French doors. Cottage is separate from the main house and has a loft, a fireplace, a kitchen, a barbecue, and an ensuite bathroom with clawfoot tub and shower. Host makes reservations in Sooke for fine dining restaurants, whale watching tours, fishing charters, kayaks, bicycles, surfboards, and guided hikes. Host can also arrange for massage. Continental breakfast includes fruit and homemade baked goods. Smoking outdoors. **In the hosts' own words:** "Our B&B is a wonderful place for small weddings, workshops, conferences, and corporate events or for gathering your family and friends together for a relaxing holiday in this seaside wilderness."

Ocean Wilderness Inn

Marion Rolston
109 West Coast Road
Sooke, BC V0S 1N0
(250) 646-2116 Fax: (250) 646-2317
Toll-free from within Canada and the U.S.: 1-800-323-2116
E-mail: ocean@sookenet.com
Web site: http://www.sookenet.com/ocean

• Forty-five kilometres west of Victoria. From Highway 1, turn onto Highway
14. Go through Sooke and continue for 14 kilometres.
• Nine rooms. Two people $115–175. Ensuite bathrooms. Additional person
$25 (hide-a-bed) or $15 (cot). Off-season rates.
Fishing and tour charters.
Weddings and group seminars.
• A house on the ocean with five acres of old-growth forest and views of Juan de Fuca Strait
and the Olympic Mountains. Orca whales, grey whales, seals, bald eagles, and deer grazing
under cedars can be seen. Guest rooms have sitting areas, antiques, and canopied beds. Some
of the guest rooms have tubs for two with ocean views. Full breakfast is served in a log dining room or in guest rooms. Reservations recommended. Cancellation notice seven days.
Credit cards. No smoking indoors. **In the hosts' own words:** "Relax, renew, and revitalize
yourself at our inn, in the peaceful setting of the ancient coastal rainforest. Enjoy natural
spring water, listen to waves breaking on our isolated beach, commune with seals and bald
eagles, watch for passing whales, and let our spa professionals massage away your stress and
release your enlightened spirit."

The Beach House

Ellie Thorburn
369 Isabella Point Road
Salt Spring Island, BC V8K 1V4
(250) 653-2040 Fax: (250) 653-9711
For reservations: 1-888-653-6334

• Fifteen kilometres from Ganges. Two kilometres from the Fulford Harbour ferry terminal and village. Follow the road up the hill to the left and around the end of the harbour. Go straight along the water's edge, past the Fulford Inn (on the right), for 1.3 kilometres. The B&B is on the left.

• Two rooms. One person $95–120; two people $110–150. King-sized bed; queen-sized bed. Ensuite bathrooms. Additional person $45, in an adjoining room with a double bed.

Self-contained one-bedroom suite. Two people $120–$140. Queen-sized bed, one twin bed, and queen-sized sofa bed. Breakfast is optional. Additional person $15–25. Weekly and off-season rates.

• A B&B with beach access, on the shore of Fulford Harbour, in a rural setting. Country décor and local artwork. Eleven steps lead down to a shell beach for beachcombing, crabbing, kayaking, swimming, and birdwatching. Each guest room has a private entrance, a sitting area with fireplace, a view of the shoreline, and French doors that lead to a patio. One of the guest rooms has a Jacuzzi tub and a king-sized bed. A room with a double bed is available for a third person accompanying the guests staying in either of the guest rooms. One-bedroom suite has a deck, a kitchen, a dining area, and a living room. Gas barbecue and outdoor fire pit. Bar, fridge, hot beverage bar, TV, and VCR. Guests are requested to refrain from wearing toxic products including perfume. Full breakfast. Diets are accommodated. Reservations recommended. Credit cards. Rooms are adult oriented and are not suitable for pets. Suite is suitable for families. Pets in the suite by arrangement. Smoking outdoors. **In the hosts' own words:** "Tasty, creative breakfasts served by the ocean provide memorable moments. Our location offers seclusion, tranquillity, and excellent ocean views. At low tide our beach invites hours of beachcombing, with numerous treaures to collect. A front-row seat to magnificent sunrises and glistening reflections of moonlight. A taste of paradise that is yours to enjoy."

Weston Lake Inn B&B

Susan Evans and Ted Harrison
813 Beaver Point Road
Salt Spring Island, BC V8K 1X9
(250) 653-4311 Fax: (250) 653-4340
Web site: http://www.bestinns.net

• Take the ferry from Vancouver (Tsawwassen), Victoria (Swartz Bay), or Crofton to Salt Spring Island. Located 3.6 kilometres from Fulford Harbour, on the road to Ruckle Provincial Park. Eleven kilometres from Ganges.

• Three rooms. One person $85–105; two people $95–120. Queen-sized bed; queen-sized bed and one twin bed. Ensuite bathrooms. Additional person $25. Charters on the hosts' 36-foot sailboat.

• A country house surrounded by gardens, on ten acres with a view of Weston Lake. A long driveway beside a split-rail fence winds past cows grazing in a pasture. Guest rooms have flowers, down duvets, and sitting areas. Antiques, art, and fine needlepoint throughout. Guest living room with stone fireplace, piano, CD player, and music collection. Second guest living room with woodstove, books, movies, TV, VCR, and collection of African musical instruments. Refreshment area with fridge and microwave. Hot tub. Decks, sitting areas, and paths through the gardens (rock, alpine, wildflower, rhododendron, herb, heather, cut flower, vegetable, and fruit). Pond, woodlands, pastures, birds, and wildlife on the property. Full breakfast includes home-grown organic produce; menu changes daily. Cancellation notice seven days. Check-out until 11:00 a.m. Visa, MasterCard. Children over thirteen welcome. No pets; sheep dog in residence. No smoking indoors. **In the hosts' own words:** "Our B&B offers serenity, privacy, outstanding food, and warm hospitality. We invite you to share our bit of heaven."

Daffodil Cove Cottage

John Gilman
146 Meyer Road
Salt Spring Island, BC V8K 1X4
(250) 653-4950
E-mail: sabine@unixg.ubc.ca

• Seven kilometres from the Fulford Harbour ferry terminal, on the south end of Salt Spring Island.

• Self-contained cottage (sleeps four or five). Two people $70–95. Queen-sized bed, twin beds in a loft, and double sofa bed. Private bathroom. Additional person $20. Nonperishable breakfast ingredients supplied. Weekly rates. Minimum stay two nights.

• A self-contained cedar and glass cottage on the ocean, adjacent to a nature reserve. Living room with glass-front wood stove, wrap-around deck, and view of the ocean and forest. Adjoining kitchen and sun room dining area. Electric heat. Cedar, ceramic tile, and floor-to-ceiling windows. Linen, stove, fridge, microwave, and coffee maker. Food staples, including tea, coffee, cereals, sugar, flour, and condiments, are provided for guests to prepare meals. Deposit required to hold reservation. Cancellation notice fourteen days. Children welcome. No pets. Nonsmoking establishment. **In the hosts' own words:** "The cottage has a spectacular setting and is completely private, with arbutus and Douglas fir forest, a garry oak meadow, and wildflowers. The nature and marine reserves provide an array of wildlife at the door and many hiking opportunities. Come and enjoy the beauty and quiet of this region from the comfort of our cottage."

Beddis House B&B

Terry and Bev Bolton
131 Miles Avenue
Salt Spring Island, BC V8K 2E1
(250) 537-1028 Fax: (250) 537-9888
E-mail: beddis@saltspring.com
Web site: http://www.saltspring.com/beddishouse

• Eight kilometres south of Ganges. Call for directions.

• Three suites in a coach house separate from the hosts' house. In winter, two people $125–155. In summer, two people $150–180. King-sized bed; queen-sized bed; twin beds. Ensuite bathrooms. One-person and weekly rates.

• A restored turn-of-the-century farmhouse on the ocean with a clam-shell beach. The house is between the ocean and an apple orchard and is surrounded by one and a quarter acres of flower gardens, lawns, and fruit trees. Deer, otters, seals, and eagles can be seen. Suites are in a coach house separate from the hosts' house. Each suite has a private deck that faces the ocean, a fireplace, a sitting area, and an ensuite bathroom with clawfoot tub and shower. Guest sitting room in the main house has a fireplace, a games table, and books. Afternoon tea is served in the sitting room or on the decks. Multi-course breakfast, including home-made baked goods, is served in the dining room in the main house; specialties include poached pear in blueberry sauce, apple pan puff, and barbecued salmon with scrambled eggs. Visa, MasterCard. Adult oriented. No pets. Nonsmoking. **In the hosts' own words:** "At our B&B, whether you choose rest, romance, or revitalization, you'll escape to quieter times in a spot that is truly magical all year round."

A Perfect Perch B&B

Libby and Michel Jutras
225 Armand Way
Salt Spring Island, BC V8K 2B6
(250) 653-2030 Fax: (250) 653-2045
E-mail: ljutras@saltspring.com
Web site: http://www.saltspring.com/
  perfect perch/

• Six kilometres south of Ganges. Three kilometres from the highway.
• Three rooms. $125–165. Queen-sized bed. Ensuite bathrooms.
• A West Coast–style contemporary house, with private entrances and decks, one thousand feet above sea level. Views of sunrises, the Sunshine Coast, and the San Juan Islands. At night, the lights of Vancouver, White Rock, and Bellingham can be seen fifty-five kilometres away across the Strait of Georgia. Guest rooms have ensuite bathrooms with double Jacuzzis, twin shower heads, or double soaker tubs. Beds have duvets and feather pillows. One of the hosts is a watercolour artist and instructor. Hosts arrange bookings and rentals for sailing, scuba diving, boating, fishing, horseback riding, kayaking, tennis, golf, mopeds, theatre, and artists' studio tours. Five-course breakfast includes farm-fresh eggs, homemade jam, and seafood or vegetarian alternatives. Check-in 4:00 to 6:00 p.m. Visa, MasterCard. Adult oriented. No pets. Smoke-free environment. **In the hosts' own words:** "For a romantic escape, we offer luxury accommodation in a dramatic setting."

Stonecutter's Rest B&B

Chris Gosset and Irene Heron
170 Simson Road
Salt Spring Island, BC V8K 1E2
(250) 537-4415 Fax: (250) 537-4462
E-mail: stonecuttersrest@saltspring.com

• Off Sunset Drive.
• Three rooms. One person $75; two people $85. Queen-sized bed; twin bed. Private bathrooms.
• A B&B on five acres with rooms that face the water, private decks, and views of Stonecutter's Bay and islands. A path winds down to three hundred feet of ocean shore. Swimming, fishing, and kayaking; kayaks available. Guest entrance and sitting room. Stair glide for those who have difficulty negotiating stairs. Near golf and walking and biking trails. Saturday market, an art centre, galleries, shops, cinema, and dining in nearby Ganges village. Full breakfast is served on the deck. Deposit or credit card number required to hold reservation. Cancellation notice seven days. Visa, MasterCard. Adults only. No pets; dog in residence. Smoke-free. **In the hosts' own words:** "At our B&B, enjoy fabulous sunsets and views of islands and ever-changing marine life."

Mallard's Mill B&B

Jack Vandort and Jan Macpherson
521 Beddis Road
Mail: Box 383
Ganges, Salt Spring Island, BC V8K 2E8
(250) 537-1011 Fax: (250) 537-1030
E-mail: mallardsmill@saltspring.com
Web site: http://www.saltspring.com/mallardsmill

• Four minutes south of Ganges.
• Three rooms and one cottage. Two people from $98–159. King-sized bed; queen-sized bed. Ensuite bathrooms. Additional person $30. Extended stay rates. Special occasion packages.
• A B&B built to replicate an 1880 mill, with a functioning eighteen-foot waterwheel, hand-made doors with hand-carved latches, and rough-sawn timbers. Guest rooms have fireplaces, old-fashioned quilts, antiques, and wicker. Guest living room/library with games and books. Outdoor hot tub; robes provided. Greenhouse with herbs, spices, and edible flowers. Cottage is across the pond from the mill and has a king-sized bed, a fireplace, a two-person Jacuzzi tub, a sitting area with books, and decks. Hot beverages and cookies. Island maps, local restaurant menus, and travel information material. Near kayaking, golf, horseback riding, boating, hiking, a farmers' market, galleries, studios, and fine dining restaurants. Guests can ride a miniature steam train that circles the property. Three-course breakfast, including homemade bread, fruit, and an entrée such as fruit crepes, Salt Spring–style lamb and eggs, or a seafood dish, is served in the mill or outside under a sun umbrella; for guests staying at the cottage, breakfast is delivered by steam train. Diets accommodated. Reservations recommended. Visa, MasterCard, Interac. Adult oriented. **In the hosts' own words:** "Let us take you on a magical first-class excursion. All aboard."

Water's Edge B&B

Helen Tara
327 Price Road
Salt Spring Island, BC V8K 2E9
(250) 537-5807 Fax: (250) 537-2862
Web site: http://www.islandnet.com/saltspring/

• Four kilometres south of Ganges. Take Fulford-Ganges Road. Turn southeast onto Beddis Road and continue for 2 kilometres. Turn left onto Price and continue for 1 kilometre to the waterfront.

• Room and one two-bedroom suite. One person $95–120; two people $115–135. Queen-sized bed and twin day bed; two queen-sized beds. Ensuite and private bathrooms. Additional person $35–45.

• A house with country gardens on Ganges Harbour, a few steps from a beach. Guest room and two-bedroom suite have views of the ocean. Guest sitting room with books, paintings, a fireplace, a fridge, a toaster oven, a microwave, kettles, and dishes for preparing light meals. Guest entrance. Rowboat. Covered brick patio with views of birds, sea life, and marine traffic. Breakfast, including fresh fruit, homemade cereals, yogurt, muffins, and scones, is served on the patio or in the guest sitting room, which has a view of the water. MasterCard. Smoking outdoors. **In the hosts' own words:** "We invite you to watch the sun rise over the water, stroll the beach, or row the boat along the shore."

White Fig Orchard B&B and Cottage

Cathie and John Wellingham
135 Goodrich Road
Salt Spring Island, BC V8K 1L2
(250) 537-5791

● From the Vesuvius Bay ferry terminal, take Vesuvius Bay Road for two blocks.
Turn right onto Bayview and continue for one block. Turn left onto Goodrich.
From the Fulford Harbour or the Long Harbour ferry terminal, take Vesuvius
Bay Road. Turn left onto Bayview and left onto Goodrich.
● Rooms. One person $70; two people $80. Queen-sized bed; twin beds. Private
and shared guest bathrooms.
Cottage (sleeps four). Two people $95. Private bathroom. Breakfast not included.
● A B&B with a view of the ocean, on two acres of landscaped grounds with an orchard. Two
to five minutes' walk from a public beach, a pub, a restaurant, and a store. Guest sitting room
in the main house has a stone fireplace, a TV, and a VCR. Cottage has kitchen facilities, a
bedroom, a living room with TV, a deck with barbecue, and a ground-level entrance.
Cancellation notice fourteen days. Visa, MasterCard. Smoking restricted.

Anne's Oceanfront Hideaway B&B

Rick and Ruth-Anne Broad
168 Simson Road
Salt Spring Island, BC V8K 1E7
(250) 537-0851 Fax: (250) 537-0861
Toll-free from within North America: 1-888-474-2663
E-mail: annes@saltspring.com
Web site: http://www.bbcanada.com/939.html

• Eight kilometres north of Vesuvius, off Sunset Drive; beside Stone Cutter's Bay on the northwest shore of Salt Spring Island.

• Four rooms and one honeymoon suite. In winter, $135–175. In summer, $175–210. Queen-sized bed; twin beds. Ensuite bathrooms.

• A seven-thousand-square-foot house with an elevator, a guest library with a fireplace, and a guest living room with a TV and a VCR. Covered veranda, exercise room, and outdoor hot tub are for guest use only. Guest entrance and east-facing deck. Guest rooms have ocean views, individual thermostats, recliners, down duvets, percale sheets, fruit trays, and terry robes. Ensuite bathrooms have hydromassage tubs. Honeymoon suite has a balcony overlooking the ocean, a fireplace, a canopied queen-sized bed, a hydromassage tub for two, and a separate shower for two. Canoe and bicycles. Refreshments served when guests arrive. Coffee is served to guests' rooms before breakfast. Full breakfast. Allergy aware; most diets are accommodated with advance notice. Reservations recommended. Cancellation notice seven days. Visa, MasterCard. Wheelchair accessible. Adult oriented. No pets. Smoke-free establishment. **In the hosts' own words:** "Enjoy the ever-changing ocean views, the sunsets, and our luxurious house. Come and share the experience of peace and tranquillity."

Moonshadows Guest House

Pat Goodwin and Dave Muir
771 Georgeson Bay Road
Mail: RR 1 Site 16 C–16
Galiano Island, BC V0N 1P0
(250) 539-5544 Fax: (250) 539-5544
Toll-free from within North America: 1-888-666-6742
E-mail: moonshadowsbb@bc.sympatico.ca
Web site: http://www.islandnet.com/~pixsell/bcccd/1/1000047.htm

• Three kilometres from Sturdies Bay. Go two kilometres on Sturdies Bay
Road and follow the curve to the left to Georgeson Bay Road.
• Two rooms. One person $90–95; two people $100–110. Queen-sized bed;
double sofa bed. Ensuite bathrooms. Additional person $20. Cot available.
Off-season rates mid-October to mid-May, excluding Christmas.
Honeymoon suite. Two people $135. Queen-sized bed. Ensuite bathroom.
Minimum stay two nights.
• A B&B on two acres with a view of a pond and a hundred-acre horse farm. Deck with hot
tub. Yard with picnic tables and chairs. Guest rooms are upstairs and have high ceilings,
books, and down duvets. Three-hundred-square-foot honeymoon suite is on the main floor
and has French doors that lead to a private covered patio with a view of a pond and pasture.
Suite has a private entrance, a TV, a VCR, a walk-in shower, a Jacuzzi, and an exercise bike.
Guest sitting room with books and games. Living room with TV, VCR, and videos.
Fireplaces in the living room and dining room and a wood stove in the entry hall. Hosts make
arrangements for biking, walking, kayaking, golf, fishing, picnics, and dinners. Morning
coffee or tea is served to the guest rooms and the suite. Full breakfast includes fruit, baked
goods, a hot dish, coffee, tea, and juice. Cancellation notice seven days. Check-in times are
flexible. Visa, MasterCard. Adult oriented. No pets; dogs in residence. Smoking outdoors.
In the hosts' own words: "We encourage our guests to be themselves, feel at home, and
enjoy our outstanding hospitality."

The Wheatleys' B&B

Clare McDuff-Oliver
2154 Sturdies Bay Road
Mail: S1 C–23 RR 1
Galiano Island, BC V0N 1P0
(250) 539-5980 Fax: (250) 539-5980
Toll-free: 1-888-539-5980
Toll-free fax: 1-888-539-5980
E-mail: mcduffwheatleys@gulfislands.com
Web site: http://www.victoriabc.com/accom/
   wheatleys.htm

• After the Burrill Road turnoff, turn into the second driveway on the left.
• In winter, two rooms. From $55. In summer, four rooms. From $65. Double bed; twin beds (or two twin beds side by side with king-sized bedding). Two shared bathrooms. In winter, breakfast is not included but is available for an additional fee.
Self-contained four-bedroom house. $185 per night, $1200 per week. Breakfast not provided.
Self-contained two-bedroom cottage. $100. Double bed and bunk beds. Private bathroom. Breakfast not provided.
• A B&B on landscaped property with trees, close to the Sturdies Bay ferry terminal, galleries, shops, beaches, and a market. Main house has a roof-top gazebo, a dining room, living areas, a south-facing deck, an old-fashioned porch, a barbecue, and a sauna in one of the two bathrooms. Self-contained cottage has a dishwasher, a washing machine, a vaulted ceiling, a sleeping loft with double bed, a sitting area with a view of the bay, a children's room with play area, and a fenced garden with barbecue, patio furniture, swing, sandbox, and toys. Private dock for kayakers and guests arriving by boat. Lawn volleyball and hiking trails on the property. Dishes, linen, TV, VCR, stereo, and woodstove in both house and cottage. Hosts arrange massages, bicycle and kayak rentals, and catamaran and fishing charters. Children and pets welcome. Nonsmoking. **In the hosts' own words:** "Come and absorb the island's peacefulness and enjoy its activities. Our B&B is a great place for family fun and relaxation and group retreats."

Sunrise/Sunset B&B

Donna Good
RR 1 Site 14 C–37
219 Sticks Allison Road
Galiano Island, BC V0N 1P0
(250) 539-5693
Web site: http://www.aebc.com/~sunrise

• Suites. Ensuite bathrooms. Continental breakfast ingredients supplied.
• An oceanside B&B with a hot tub in an oceanside gazebo and new suites that have private entrances, balconies, and views of the ocean. Near swimming. Videos and books. Barbecue. Continental breakfast ingredients supplied. **In the hosts' own words:** "You'll enjoy our homey hospitality and our deluxe sunny suites. Our B&B is close to all amenities. We'll make sure your visit to our island home is enjoyable and memorable."

Saturna Lodge

Bruce and Jennifer Griffin
130 Payne Road
Saturna Island, BC V0N 2Y0
(250) 539-2254 Fax: (250) 539-3091
Toll-free from within North America: 1-888-539-8800
E-mail: satlodge@gulfislands.com
Web site: http://www.gulfislands.com/saturna/satlodge

• Two rooms and five suites. One person $90–130; two people $100–140. Queen-sized bed and double sofa bed; queen-sized bed; twin beds. Ensuite and shared guest bathrooms.

• A newly refurbished country-style house overlooking Boot Cove, with guest suites that have ocean and garden views. Licensed restaurant and lounge with fireplace on the main floor, surrounded by a wrap-around deck. Living room with fireplace, books, and satellite TV. One of the suites is a honeymoon suite and has an ensuite bathroom with a soaker tub and a private balcony. Hot tub on the deck. Garden with croquet and bocci in summer. Mountain bicycles. Near a vineyard. West Coast–style Continental breakfast. Five minutes from the ferry terminal; bus service from and to the terminal. Visa, MasterCard. Smoking on the balconies. **In the hosts' own words:** "Tour our nearby vineyard."

Rose Arbor B&B

Richard and Jane Ferguson
3610 Trans-Canada Highway
Mail: Box 98
Malahat, BC V0R 2L0
(250) 478-0807 Fax: (250) 478-0837

• Twenty minutes north of downtown Victoria
on Highway 1.
• Suite. In summer (May to September), one
person $110, two people $120. In winter
(October to April), one person $89, two people
$99. Queen-sized bed and twin beds. Bathroom in suite. Additional person $20. Child 6
to 12 $15. Children under 6 free. Extended stay rates.

• A custom-designed Tudor-style house on three and a half wooded acres, with views of the
ocean and the mountains of Finlayson Arm. Suite has a deck, a hot tub, a stone fireplace, a
sleigh-style bed, a TV, a VCR, a small library, a microwave, and a fridge. Evening snacks
provided. Full breakfast. Reservations recommended. Cancellation notice seventy-two
hours. Check-in 4:00 to 7:00 p.m. or by arrangement; check-out until 11:00 a.m. Cash, traveller's cheques, Visa, MasterCard. Children welcome. No pets. Smoking outdoors. **In the
hosts' own words:** "Roses and breathtaking views await you at our mountain hideaway. Join
us for a stay you will never forget."

Norton's Green B&B

Clifford and Mary Norton
663 Frayne Road, RR 1
Mill Bay, BC V0R 2P0
(250) 743-8006

• Half an hour from Victoria. Forty-five minutes
from Nanaimo.
• Two rooms. One person $50; two people $55.
Queen-sized bed; double bed. Shared guest bathroom.
• A green house near the ocean, with a white balcony and flowers. Near Victoria's sightseeing and shopping and Chemainus's murals. TV.
Four o'clock tea is served. Full breakfast with fruit is served by a fireplace in the dining
room. Parking. No pets. No smoking. **In the hosts' own words:** "We give you a warm welcome. Experience comfort in a relaxed atmosphere. Stay with us—we love to spoil you."

Maple Tree Lane B&B

Dot and Jim Garbet
440 Goulet Road, RR 2
Mill Bay, BC V0R 2P0
(250) 743-3940 Fax: (250) 743-3959
E-mail: mapletre@cvnet.net
Web site: http://www.cvnet/cowb&b/maple

• From Highway 1, turn east onto Hutchinson Road, towards Arbutus Ridge.
Turn right onto Telegraph, left onto La Fortune Road, right onto Kilipi Road,
and left onto Goulet Road. Watch for signs on all corners.

• Two rooms. One person $50–60; two people $75–85. Twin beds (or twin beds
side by side with king-sized bedding); queen-sized bed. Bathrooms in suite.
Additional person $25. Child 6 to 14 $10. Double hide-a-bed. Crib and cot.
Family and weekly rates.

• A house on the ocean, thirty-five minutes from Victoria, with a beach and, in summer, a
swimming pool. Canoeing and kayaking from the B&B. Five to ten minutes from golf, fishing charters, hiking trails, Brentwood and Shawnigan College schools, shopping, and restaurants. Twenty minutes from Duncan. Thirty minutes from Chemainus. Fifty-five minutes
from Nanaimo. Garden-level guest room has a queen-sized bed and a private entrance.
Adjoining family room has a double hide-a-bed and a TV. Main-floor guest room has twin
beds and is wheelchair accessible. Full breakfast. Diets are accommodated. MasterCard.
Children welcome. Pets by arrangement; two cats in residence. Smoking outdoors. **In the
hosts' own words:** "Enjoy our country hospitality and scrumptious breakfasts, in a beautiful setting on Vancouver Island. Stroll the beach and collect shells and driftwood, canoe on
calm waters, and enjoy tea in the gazebo."

Arbutus Cove B&B

Carole and Bob Beevor-Potts
2812 Wiltshire Road
Mail: RR 2
Mill Bay, BC V0R 2P0
(250) 743-1435 Fax: (250) 743-1410
E-mail: arbutusc@cvnet.net
Web sites: http://www.bbcanada.com/1550.html
http://www.cvnet.net/cowb&b/arbutus

• From Highway 1, two traffic lights north of Mill Bay Centre, turn east onto Kilmalu Road. Continue for 1.5 kilometres. Turn left onto Whiskey Point Road. Turn right onto Wiltshire Road.

• Two rooms. One person $60; two people $85. Queen-sized bed. Ensuite bathrooms. Extended stay rates.

• A modern house on the ocean, with two wooded acres and a natural beach. Within walking distance of a nature park. Five minutes' drive from Brentwood College, a shopping centre, Mill Bay Marina, Arbutus Ridge golf course, and restaurants. Fifteen minutes from wineries, Duncan's totems, Shawnigan Lake, Cowichan Bay fishing village, and a forest museum. Thirty minutes from Victoria and from Chemainus's murals. Canoe and bikes. Guest rooms have views of the ocean. Guest entrance. Guest living room with TV, books, fireplace, and tea and coffee. Billiard room. Full breakfast is served in a modern kitchen with a view of the bay; guests' preferences are accommodated. Visa, MasterCard. Adult oriented. No pets. No smoking. **In the hosts' own words:** "Come and enjoy our quiet country atmosphere and yet be close to the attractions of the South Cowichan region and nearby Victoria."

Sea Lion B&B

Ruth and Ken Bushell
2643 Mill Bay Road
Mill Bay, BC V0R 2P0
(250) 743-1746 Fax: (250) 743-1749
E-mail: sealion@cvnet.net
Web site: http://www.cvnet/cowb&b/sealion/

• In Mill Bay (40 minutes north of Victoria; 55 minutes south of Nanaimo). From Highway 1, turn east onto Deloume Road and right onto Mill Bay Road.
• Two rooms and one self-contained suite. One person $50–65; two people $65–80. Twin beds; queen-sized bed and two pull-down double beds; queen-sized bed and one twin bed. Ensuite and private bathrooms. Additional person $20.
• A house on the ocean, with views of Mount Baker, Saanich Inlet, and marine life. Guest rooms and suite have views of the ocean. Access to beach for exploring. Five minutes' walk from a shopping centre and a marina where there are boat rentals. Ten minutes' drive from the Arbutus Ridge Golf and Country Club, a winery, and Shawnigan Lake, where there are beaches and boat rentals. Fifteen minutes' drive from the fishing village of Cowichan Bay. Twenty minutes' drive from totem poles in Duncan and a Native cultural village. Twenty-five minutes' ferry ride from the Butchart Gardens. Hot tub. Guest rooms are on the ground floor and share a sitting room with TV, VCR, and sliding glass doors that lead to a hot tub room and a garden. Self-contained suite is on the third floor and has a TV. Full breakfast is served in a country-style kitchen with a view of the ocean. Visa, MasterCard. Children welcome. No pets; cat in residence. No smoking. **In the hosts' own words:** "Treat yourself to the serenity of our oceanside setting. There is always something of interest to see—a graceful sailboat, a playful seal, or majestic, snow-covered Mount Baker."

Whistlestop Shawnigan Lakeside B&B

Ken and Shirley Charters
1838 Baden Powell Road
Mail: Box 39
Shawnigan Lake, BC V0R 2W0
(250) 743-4896 Fax: (250) 743-3301

• Forty minutes north of Victoria, on the east shore of Shawnigan Lake.
• Five rooms. Two people $125, $225 for two nights. Ensuite bathrooms. Honeymoon suite. Two people $199, $375 for two nights. King-sized bed. Ensuite bathroom.
Off-season rates.
• A B&B on the east shore of Shawnigan Lake, accessible by car and float plane. Docks for boats and float planes are a sixty-metre walk from the B&B. Close to E & N passenger train station. A few minutes' walk from the village of Shawnigan and a provincial park with walking/jogging trails and a beach. Guest rooms have down quilts, TVs, VCRs, and private decks with views of sunsets and the lake. Guest hot tub in a gazebo has a view of the lake, privacy glass windows, and a keyed entrance. Robes provided. Croquet sets and rowboats. Living room with stone fireplace, sun room, library, ice machine, and bar area. Suite has a private dining/bar area, a four-post king-sized bed, a two-person Jacuzzi, and a marble fireplace. Hosts help arrange small weddings, honeymoons, anniversaries, birthdays, and conferences. A karafe of fresh-ground coffee and assorted baked goods are served on a tray left at guests' doors before breakfast. Full breakfast; guests choose either an 8:30 or a 10:00 a.m. seating. Diets are accommodated by arrangement. Deposit of fifty dollars required to hold reservation. Cancellation notice seven days. Check-in 2:00 p.m. to midnight; check-out until noon. Visa, MasterCard, American Express. Smoking on decks and in the courtyard. **In the hosts' own words:** "We invite you to rediscover the country spirit of days gone by on southern Vancouver Island. Our house is set amongst magnificent ivy-covered maples on a secluded, sandy-beached acreage. We offer rooms decorated in a railroad theme, warm hospitality, and privacy. Curl up by the fireplace or relax on the balcony and enjoy the beautiful grounds, courtyard, and lakeside views. Our full breakfasts will satisfy even the heartiest appetites. The perfect romantic getaway."

Marifield Manor, an Edwardian B&B

Cathy Basskin
2039 Merrifield Lane
Mail: RR 1
Shawnigan Lake, BC V0R 2W0
(250) 743-9930 Fax: (250) 743-1667
E-mail: mariman@pccinternet.com
Web site: http://www.vancouverisland-bc.com/MarifieldManor/index.html.

• Forty minutes north of Victoria. Fifty minutes south of Nanaimo. From Highway 1, turn west onto Shawnigan-Mill Bay Road and continue to the four-way stop. Turn right onto Renfrew Road and continue past Mason's store and Shawnigan Lake School. Take the next right onto Linden, and then immediately turn right onto Merrifield.

• Rooms and two two-bedroom suites. One person or two people $75–150. Queen-sized bed; twin beds. Private and ensuite bathrooms. Group, off-season, and extended stay rates.

• A restored Edwardian house on a treed lot, with period furnishings, art, antique linen, and lake views. Close to Shawnigan Lake School, Brentwood College, and Maxwell International Baha'i School. Near sailing, rowing, hiking, lawn tennis, golf, cricket, farm markets, and Cowichan Valley wineries and cidery. Within walking distance of the village, the lake, and hiking and biking trails. Garden, hot tub, and benches with views of the lake. Suites have sitting rooms and views of Shawnigan Lake and Mount Baldy. Some of the guest rooms have lake views. Accessible by car, train, float plane, or bus. High tea is served. Breakfast is served in the dining room, on the wrap-around veranda, or in guests' rooms. Reservations recommended. Cash, traveller's cheques. Adult oriented. No pets. No smoking indoors. **In the hosts' own words:** "Discover the pleasures of conversation and elegant hospitality in our wonderful manor; we will strive to surprise you and surpass your expectations. Our B&B is a unique location for family get-togethers, corporate planning sessions, retreats, and group holidays."

Cobble House B&B

Ingrid and Simon Vermegen
3105 Cameron-Taggart Road, RR 1
Cobble Hill, BC V0R 1L0
(250) 743-2672 Fax: (250) 743-2672
E-mail: vermeges@brentwood.bc.ca
Web site: http://www.brentwood.bc.ca/vermeges/

• Forty-five minutes north of Victoria. One hour south of Nanaimo. Fifteen minutes south of Duncan.

• Three rooms. One person $55–65; two people $74–84. Queen-sized bed; queen-sized bed and double futon; twin beds. Ensuite bathrooms. Additional person $20.
Packages.

• A new one-level house with a cedar deck and a separate wing for guests, on forty forested acres with a creek. One of the guest rooms has an ensuite bathroom with Jacuzzi. Living room with Russian fireplace. In the area are wineries, private boarding schools, golf, kayaking, swimming, hiking, mountain biking, and fishing. Thirty minutes from Chemainus's murals. A base for exploring southern Vancouver Island. One of the hosts is a former executive chef. Full breakfast includes homemade baked goods. Deposit of 30 percent required to hold reservation. Cancellation notice four days. Dutch and German spoken. Two dogs in residence. No smoking. **In the hosts' own words:** "Our two friendly dogs would like to take you for a walk. We pride ourselves on offering a quiet, relaxing environment and on giving attention to every detail."

Heron Hill B&B

Vicki and Gordon Simpson
3760 Granfield Place, RR 2
Cobble Hill, BC V0R 1L0
(250) 743-3855 Fax: (250) 743-5821

• From Highway 1, north of Mill Bay and 10 minutes south of Duncan, turn east (towards Arbutus Ridge) onto Hutchinson Road. Turn left onto Telegraph, right onto Aros, and right onto Granfield.

• Three rooms. One person $50; two people $60–70. Queen-sized bed; twin beds; double bed and double hide-a-bed. Ensuite bathrooms.

• A house in a rural area, with views of the ocean, the Gulf Islands, and Mount Baker. An hour's drive from wineries, Chemainus's murals, the Butchart gardens, totems in Duncan, golf, tennis, sea kayaking, sailing, beachcombing, and birdwatching. Living room. Guest sitting room with fridge, microwave, and sink. One of the guest rooms has a private entrance. No pets; black Labrador in residence. No smoking. **In the hosts' own words:** "Our B&B is the place to stay that's really a home. While here, try the world-famous cobble cake."

Rainbow's End B&B

Sheila and Gray Thomson
1745 Ordano Street
Cowichan Bay, BC V0R 1N0
(250) 746-8320 Fax: (250) 746-8320
E-mail: rainbow@seaside.net
Web site: http://www.seaside.net/rainbow

• One hour north of Victoria. Forty-five minutes south of Nanaimo. From Highway 1, turn onto Cowichan Bay Road and continue to Glen Road. Take Glen Road to McGill Road. Turn left onto McGill Road and continue to the end. Turn right onto Ordano Street.

• Three rooms. One person $45; two people $60–70. Queen-sized bed or twin beds, shared guest bathroom; queen-sized bed, ensuite bathroom.
Weekly rates.
Fishing and sightseeing charters and evening cruises arranged.

• A country B&B with an outdoor pool and a barbecue, surrounded by tall trees. Wild birds in a nearby green belt are often seen and heard. Two minutes' drive from a maritime centre. Ten minutes from a Native heritage centre, Duncan's totems, and a forest museum. Twenty minutes from Chemainus's murals. Ten minutes from downtown Duncan and shopping for art, crafts, and antiques. Five minutes' drive from boat rentals, a boat ramp, fine dining restaurants, two par three golf courses, and three other golf courses. Hosts arrange evening cruises and fishing and sightseeing charters. No pets; cat in residence. Smoking outdoors.
In the hosts' own words: "In summer, bring your bathing suits and have your morning coffee by our outdoor pool."

Old Farm B&B

Barbara and George MacFarlane
2075 Cowichan Bay Road
Cowichan Bay, BC V0R 1N0
(250) 748-6410 Fax: (250) 748-6410
Toll-free from within Canada and the U.S.: 1-888-240-1482
E-mail: oldfarm@seaside.net
Web site: http://www.cvnet.net/cowb&b/oldfarm

• One hour north of Victoria. Five minutes south of Duncan. From Highway 1 turn onto Cowichan Bay Road, which is well marked from both directions. The B&B is 1 kilometre north of the village of Cowichan Bay, on the side of the road closer to the water.

• Three rooms. One person $65–110; two people $75–120. Queen-sized beds. Ensuite bathrooms. Additional person $20. Off-season rates.

• A restored century-old three-storey house, designed by architect Samuel Maclure for a retired English sea captain. Landscaped gardens, fruit trees, and a gazebo on two acres that slope down to tidal water. An estuary formed by the Cowichan and Koksilah rivers provides a sanctuary for resident and migrating birds. Guest sitting/reading room on the main floor, with fireplace, TV, VCR, and contemporary books. Guest rooms have high ceilings and are decorated in Laura Ashley style. One of the guest rooms has an ensuite bathroom with Jacuzzi. Coffee or tea is delivered to guest rooms before breakfast. Breakfast, including produce from the farm, is served with silver and linen, at guests' convenience. Diets are accommodated. Check-in and check-out times are flexible. Visa, MasterCard. Adult oriented. Dog and cat in residence. Smoking outdoors. **In the hosts' own words:** "We try to make sure that every guest will want to come back."

Fairburn Farm Country Manor

Anthea and Darrel Archer
3310 Jackson Road, RR 7
Duncan, BC V9L 4W4
(250) 746-4637 Fax: (250) 746-4637
E-mail: fairburn@gec.net

• Eleven kilometres southwest of Duncan. Fifty kilometres north of Victoria.
Fifty kilometres south of Nanaimo.
• Six rooms. Two people $95–140. Queen-sized bed; twin beds; queen-sized
bed and twin beds. Private and ensuite bathrooms. Additional person $15. Cots
available.
Self-contained cottage. One person to four people $750 for six days. Breakfast
not included. Additional person $10.
One-person and family rates. Open April to September.
• A nineteenth-century farmhouse and cottage surrounded by forested hills, on 130 acres of
rolling countryside, with walking trails beside a mountain stream and through woodlands
and meadows. Five thousand tree seedlings in a sustainable seventy-acre forest with birds,
wildlife, and old-growth trees. An hour north of Victoria. A base for touring the Cowichan
region. Some of the guest rooms have fireplaces. Some bathrooms have whirlpool tubs and
fireplaces. Robes provided. Guest room with a queen-sized bed and twin beds is suitable for
families, as are two rooms beside each other at the end of a corridor. Guest veranda and two
sitting rooms with fireplaces and books. Self-contained cottage, formerly the cottage of the
farm manager, is available by the week and has a washing machine. Hosts answer questions
about their country lifestyle, and guests may take part in farm chores. Breakfast includes
homemade granola, muffins and bread made from the farm's wheat, and butter, milk, preserves, bacon or sausage, and eggs, all of which are from the farm. Reservations required.
Deposit of one night's rate required to hold reservation. No pets; there are border collies for
herding and livestock guardian dogs who live with the sheep. No smoking. **In the hosts' own
words:** "We welcome you to step back in time, share our way of life, and experience the hospitality of a bygone era."

Grove Hall Estate B&B

Judy Oliver
6159 Lakes Road
Duncan, BC V9L 4J6
(250) 746-6152

• From Victoria, take Highway 1 north for 58 kilometres. In Duncan, turn right onto Trunk Road. Turn left onto Lakes Road and continue for 1.5 kilometres. The B&B is on the right; look for the brass number 6159 on pillars at the entrance to the driveway.

• Two rooms. One person $145–155; two people $175–185. Queen-sized bed; twin beds. Private bathroom and ensuite bathroom with shower. Additional person $30. Self-contained one-bedroom cottage. One person or two people $135. Minimum stay two nights. Weekly rate $750. Breakfast not included.

• A Tudor-style house on seventeen acres, on a lake. Guest rooms are decorated in an Asian theme. One of the guest rooms has an ornate antique Chinese wedding bed and a private bathroom with original clawfoot tub. The other guest room has batiks and art from Bali, a sitting room, a private balcony with a view of the lake, and an ensuite bathroom with shower. Antiques throughout, including an antique Brunswick billiard table. Tennis, walking by the lake. Tea or wine served on a veranda with a view of swans on the lake. Near golf courses, sailing and fishing in Cowichan Bay and Maple Bay, murals and antiques in Chemainus, and the arts community of Salt Spring Island. Full breakfast is served in a wood-panelled and wood-beamed dining room. Reservations required. Not suitable for children or for pets. No smoking indoors. **In the hosts' own words:** "Enjoy Edwardian elegance and the mysteries of the Orient in our mansion."

Saseenos Point B&B

Pat Neligan and Jan Leine
8241 Saseenos Point Road
Mail: Box 378
Youbou, BC V0R 3E0
(250) 745-3778 Fax: (250) 745-3778
Toll-free from within North America: 1-888-745-3778
E-mail: sasptbb@island.net

• From Duncan, take Highway 18 west for 42 kilometres. Follow signs to Youbou and the B&B.

• Two suites. Two people $85–100. Queen-sized bed, ensuite bathroom; queen-sized bed and double sofa bed, bathroom in suite. Additional person $15–20.
Weekly and off-season rates.
Charters on the hosts' 18-foot boat.

• A B&B on two acres on Cowichan Lake, with fifty metres of waterfront, a swimming beach, a private wharf, a boat launch, a beach fire pit, lawns, fern gardens, and large fir and cedar trees. Suites have views of the lake. Eighteen-foot bow rider boat available for water skiing and lake tour charters. Rowboat. Thirty minutes from three golf courses. Ninety minutes from Carmanah Walbran Provincial Park. Ten minutes from hiking, restaurants, shopping, and the Kaatza museum. Near walking trails and fishing. Suites have private entrances through a covered patio. One of the suites has a canopied queen-sized bed and a sitting area with wood stove, loveseat, stereo, coffee maker, fridge, and microwave. The other suite has a kitchen, a dining area, a sitting room with gas fireplace and TV, and a barbecue. Down duvets and robes. Choice of Continental or full breakfast is served in the suites or on the patio from 6:00 to 10:00 a.m. Visa, MasterCard. No pets. Smoking outdoors. **In the hosts' own words:** "Come to our B&B and experience a private, quiet getaway in comfortable surroundings with great food and hospitality."

Bird Song Cottage B&B

Larry and Virginia Blatchford
9909 Maple Street
Mail: Box 1432
Chemainus, BC V0R 1K0
(250) 246-9910 Fax: (250) 246-2909
Web site: http://www.vancouverisland-bc.com/BirdSongCottage

• In Chemainus (1 hour north of Victoria).

• Three rooms. One person $70–85; two people $85–110. Queen-sized bed;
queen-sized bed and one twin bed; double bed and one twin bed. Ensuite bathrooms. Additional person $20.

• A 1905 character house with antiques and oil paintings, half a block from the ocean, gift
and antique shops, restaurants, Chemainus's murals, and a dinner theatre. Guest living room
with fireplace, baby grand piano, pump organ, Celtic harp, and collection of fancy hats.
Guest rooms have duvets, flowers, and lace-trimmed cotton linen. Evening tea and cookies.
Breakfast is served on fine china in a sun room surrounded by a garden. Diets are accommodated. Visa, MasterCard, American Express, Interac. No pets; birds and cats in residence.
Smoking on the veranda. **In the hosts' own words:** "Warmth, gracious service, and unique
décor make our B&B what dreams are made of."

Clam Bay Cottage B&B

Donna Kaiser
121 Clam Bay Road
Thetis Island, BC V0R 2Y0
(250) 246-1016 Fax: (250) 246-1016
E-mail: dkaiser@islandnet.com

• From Chemainus (1 hour north of Victoria; half an hour south of Nanaimo), take the Thetis/Kuper Island ferry (30 to 45 minutes). From the ferry terminal, follow the B&B's signs for 3 kilometres to the B&B.
Direct float-plane service.

• Two rooms. One person $60; two people $65–80. In off-season, one person $55, two people $60–75. Queen-sized bed; twin beds. Ensuite and shared bath rooms.
Two-bedroom cottage (sleeps six). Four people $400 per three-day weekend, $850 per week. In off-season, four people $135 per night, $350 per three-day weekend, $600 per week. Queen-sized bed, bunk beds with double-width lower bunk, queen-sized futon sofa bed. Additional person $20 per night. In summer, breakfast is available for an additional cost.

• A cottage-style house and a cottage, both on the ocean, on a grassy point with arbutus trees. South-facing decks with views of the Gulf Islands and the B&B's three hundred feet of waterfront. Near birdwatching, snorkeling, paddling, hiking, and intertidal areas for exploring and photography. Guest room with twin beds has a view of Clam Bay. Sitting room with sofa, chairs, fireplace, books, and a view of the ocean. Cottage has a kitchen, a bathroom, antique furniture in the main bedroom, a stone fireplace, a private patio and garden, and a dining/living room that seats six. Full breakfast includes homemade bread and fresh local produce. Guests in the cottage have a choice of full breakfast, catered meals, or providing their own breakfast. Full-course dinner is available; specialty is Dungeness crab. Transportation from and to ferry terminal and marinas. Visa, MasterCard. Adult oriented; children welcome by arrangement. No pets; cat in residence. Smoking outdoors.

The Treasure House by the Sea

Vic and Dorothy Forster
11203 Chemainus Road, RR 4
Ladysmith, BC V0R 2E0
(250) 245-8092 Fax: (250) 245-4045
E-mail: treasure@island.net
Web site: http://www.vancouverisland-bc.com/TreasureHouse/

• In Saltair, on the old Chemainus Road, midway between Ladysmith and Chemainus. Seventy-five minutes from Victoria. Thirty minutes from Duncan and Nanaimo.

• Two rooms. One person $75; two people $85. Queen-sized bed; queen-sized bed and twin bed. Ensuite bathrooms. Additional person $15.

• A house on two acres, on a low bank above the ocean, a few steps from a pebbled beach. Guest rooms and guest living room are on a separate floor and have views of the ocean and mountains. Seals, herons, ducks, loons, and eagles can be seen from a guest patio. Seven minutes from golf, Chemainus's murals, antique shops, gift shops, and a theatre. Thirty minutes from a forest museum and a Native heritage centre in Duncan. Morning coffee or tea is delivered to guests' rooms before breakfast. Full breakfast, including juice, syrup, jam, and jelly made with fruit from the B&B's orchard, is served on a deck by the ocean or in a formal dining room. No children under twelve. No pets. Smoking on the deck and patio. **In the hosts' own words:** "Walk through our orchard or stroll down a few steps to the pebbled beach and watch the otters at play. We invite you to discover the treasures that await you."

Mañana Lodge

Jim and Ruth Bangay and Don and Gail Kanelakos
4760 Brenton Page Road
Mail: RR 1
Ladysmith, BC V0R 2E0
(250) 245-2312 Fax: (250) 245-2312
E-mail: manana@island.net
Web site: http://diane.island.net/~manana/

• Ten kilometres from downtown Ladysmith.
• Five rooms. Two people $59–99. Queen-sized bed; double bed; queen-sized bed and one twin bed. Ensuite bathrooms.
Two cabins. Two people $89. Queen-sized bed, double bed, and hide-a-bed.
Private bathrooms. Additional person $10.
• A lodge on the ocean built in the 1940s, with a licensed dining room and a marina. Ten kilometres from downtown Ladysmith. Guest rooms have views of the ocean. Three of the guest rooms have ensuite bathrooms with Jacuzzi tubs. Cabins have kitchens and TVs. Bicycles, canoe, and rowboat. Gift shop, marine store, laundry facilities, fuel, and overnight moorage and power. Hosts arrange car rentals. Near hiking, golf, fishing, biking, canoeing, scuba diving, mill tours, museums, waterfront parks, and Native heritage sites. Full breakfast is served in the dining room, which has a view of the ocean and mountains. Visa, MasterCard. **In the hosts' own words:** "We're a B&B inn with waterfront dining and spectacular views. A special place for special people."

Seaview Panorama B&B

Fred and Elizabeth Gardiner
5380 Kenwill Drive
Nanaimo, BC V9T 5Z9
(250) 756-3152

• Fifteen minutes from the Departure Bay ferry terminal; take Highway 19A. Thirty minutes from the Duke Point ferry terminal; take Highway 19 (the bypass highway) and the Mostar exit.

• Rooms. Two people $40–80. King-sized bed, ensuite bathroom; queen-sized bed, shared bathroom; double bed, shared bathroom; twin bed, shared bathroom.

Suite (sleeps five). One person $30; two people $55. Three twin beds (or two twin beds side by side with king-sized bedding and one twin bed) and queen-sized bed. Ensuite bathroom.

Children's rates depend on age.

• A five-year-old house in a quiet residential area, on a ridge with views of the Strait of Georgia and the mainland mountains. A base for day trips to a rainforest, beaches, waterfalls, lakes, caves, golf, fishing, and skiing. Five minutes from shopping malls and restaurants. Guest room with king-sized bed has a view and a Jacuzzi tub. Suite is on ground level and has a TV, a sitting area, an ensuite bathroom, coffee and tea, a patio, a garden, and a view of the ocean. Billiards and darts room. Electric heating. Sitting room. Gas fireplace. Deck. Choice of breakfasts; specialty is pecan waffles, maple syrup, and fruit. MasterCard. Children welcome in suite. Smoke-free. **In the hosts' own words:** "Watch spectacular sunsets, use the sitting room for snacking and chatting, and enjoy the deck in summer and the fireplace on cool evenings. Our aim is to make you as comfortable as possible. Honeymooners welcome. Come and enjoy the island."

The Koch's B&B

Vibeke Koch
435 Brechin Road
Nanaimo, BC V9S 2X1
(250) 754-6605

• From the Departure Bay ferry terminal, turn right at the first traffic light. The B&B has peach-coloured siding.

• Two rooms. One person $45; two people $55. Queen-sized bed; twin beds. Shared guest bathroom.

• A B&B with a view of the ocean, two minutes' walk from the Departure Bay ferry terminal. Living room with books. Private entrance. Within walking distance of downtown, along a harbour walkway. Near golf courses.

Beach Estates Inn

Neil and Fran Preston
800 Beach Drive
Nanaimo, BC V9S 2Y3
(250) 753-3597

• From the Departure Bay ferry terminal, take the first right onto Brechin Road and then the first right onto Beach Drive. The B&B is on the water side, just above the ferry terminal.

• Three rooms. One person or two people $38–53. Queen-sized bed, shared guest bathroom; double bed, shared guest bathroom; double hide-a-bed, shared bathroom. Self-contained suite. Two people $65; four people $85. Queen-sized bed and queen-sized hide-a-bed. Ensuite bathroom. Cots $10.

Extended stay rates.

Open March 15 to October 30.

• A quiet B&B on a nature park and ocean beach, two blocks from a seawall walkway, pubs, marinas, and restaurants. Thirty minutes' walk along the seawall from downtown, the Bastion, and shops in Pioneer Square. Forty-five minutes' drive from beaches, the Duncan Forest Museum, Whippletree Junction, Chemainus's murals, Cathedral Grove, Butterfly World, Bird Garden, and Coombs Market. Guest rooms and suite have TVs. Suite has a kitchen and a patio. Guest sitting area with a stone fireplace, a deck, and a view of the ocean. Large backyard with lawn chairs and picnic table. Wine and snacks served when guests arrive. Full breakfast is served in the dining room. Visa, MasterCard. Children over twelve welcome in the suite. No pets; two cats in residence. No smoking. **In the hosts' own words:** "Enjoy the views of cranes, eagles, mountains, ferries, and seaplanes from our waterfront B&B."

Westwood Tennis Club B&B

Allan Gale and Cheryl Miller
2367 Arbot Road
Nanaimo, BC V9R 6S9
(250) 753-2866 Fax: (250) 753-9683
E-mail: Westwood@bc.sympatico.ca

• On Westwood Lake, on Mount Benson.

• Rooms. Two people $75. Queen-sized bed. Ensuite bathrooms.

Tennis packages.

• A B&B at a private tennis club on Westwood Lake. Guests have use of indoor and outdoor tennis courts, a hot tub, and a log clubhouse that has a deck with a view of the lake. Café and licensed lounge. Guest rooms have separate entrances, sitting areas, TVs, radios, and coffee makers. Walking trail around the lake. Swimming and canoeing at the lake. Near hiking and golf courses. Pickup from the Nanaimo airport and the Departure Bay ferry terminal. Breakfast is served at guests' convenience. No pets. No smoking indoors.

B&B on the Green

Sharon Schwager
2471 Cosgrove Crescent
Nanaimo, BC V9S 3N9
(250) 758-4565
E-mail: bbgreen@island.net
Web sites: http://www.tourism.nanaimo.bc.ca/members/bbongreen/
   index.html
http://www.bbcanada.com/1849.html

• Five minutes from the Departure Bay ferry terminal.
• Room. One person $55; two people $60. Twin beds (or twin beds side by side with king-sized bedding). Private bathroom.
Suite. One person or two people $70. Queen-sized bed. Ensuite bathroom. Weekly rates.
• A B&B that borders on the seventeenth green of a golf course, in a quiet neighbourhood, with a view of Departure Bay. Five minutes' walk from the first tee. The main floor of the house is for guest use. Suite has a canopied queen-sized bed, a sitting area with TV, and a view of gardens and the golf course. Guest room has a view of the Strait of Georgia, mountains, and sunrises. Living room with piano and fireplace. Den with books, TV, VCR, and videos. Five minutes from the Departure Bay ferry terminal. An hour and a half from Victoria. Two hours from Tofino. A base for day trips to other golf courses. Afternoon and evening refreshments served. Morning coffee and juice on trays at guest room doors. Full breakfast, including fresh fruit, homemade baked goods, and coffee, is served in a formal dining room or on the patio. Breakfast can be served as early as 5:00 a.m. for golfers and business travellers. Kitchen available by arrangement for guests to prepare other meals. Off-street parking. Laundry facilities. Visa, MasterCard. Adult oriented. Smoke-free environment. **In the hosts' own words:** "My B&B is ideal for couples, small groups, and families. Experience the elegant comfort and charm of my home and garden—gracious hospitality, luxurious beds, down duvets, and fine linen and china. Independent serenity can be yours."

Jingle Pot B&B

Ivan
4321 Jingle Pot Road
Nanaimo, BC V9T 5P4
(250) 758-5149 Fax: (250) 751-0724
E-mail: jpotandb@nisa.net
Web sites: http://www.bbcanada.com/
1828html
http://www.islandnet.com/~pixsell/bcbbd/1/
1000055.htm

• From the Departure Bay ferry terminal, take
Highway 19A north for 10 minutes (7 traffic lights). Turn left onto Jingle Pot Road and
continue for one block. The B&B is on the right.
From the Duke Point ferry terminal, take Highway 19 north for 20 minutes. At exit 24,
turn right onto Mostar. Turn right onto Boban and left onto Jingle Pot.
• Self-contained suite. Two people $85. Queen-sized bed and queen-sized sofa bed. Ensuite
bathroom. Additional person $15. Business rates.
• A contemporary eight-hundred-square-foot self-contained suite in a house on a landscaped
half-acre with a fish pond and a waterfall. Private entrance, fireplace, steam bath, bidet, and
heated Italian marble floor. Air conditioning and air cleaner. Flowers throughout. Fruit, tea,
and coffee provided. Wheelchair accessible with aide. Visa, American Express, Diner's Club.
In the hosts' own words: "Let our B&B be your stepping stone to discovering Vancouver
Island's hidden beauty. Enjoy our deluxe private suite, designed with the discerning traveller
in mind."

Bonsai B&B

Pam and Ross White
5340 Kenwill Drive
Nanaimo, BC V9T 5Z8
(250) 758-8595 Fax: (250) 758-8595
E-mail: rwhite@island.net
Web site: http://www.island.net/~rwhite

• Ten minutes from the Departure Bay ferry ter-
minal. Take Highway 19A north. Turn right onto
Rutherford Road. Turn left onto Kenwill.
Twenty minutes from the Duke Point ferry termi-
nal. Take Highway 19. Turn right onto Mostar Road. Continue across Highway 19A to
Rutherford Road and turn left onto Kenwill.
• Two rooms. One person $45; two people $55–65. Queen-sized bed; extra-long twin beds.
Shared guest bathroom. Hide-a-bed and cot available.
• A modern house in a quiet neighbourhood, with views of the Winchelsea Islands, the Strait
of Georgia, and the coastal mountains. Near golf, ocean beaches, shopping, and the main island highway. Guest sitting room with fireplace and large-screen TV. Hot tub and deck. Guest
coffee bar with microwave, coffee maker, fridge, toaster oven, and kettle. Guest entrance.
Guest rooms have keyed doors. Fax machine, computer, and small meeting room. Small boutique with local crafts. Full or Continental breakfast includes homemade jam and baked
goods. Picnics arranged. Cash, cheques, Visa, MasterCard. No pets. No smoking. **In the
hosts' own words:** "We offer home comfort for vacationers and business guests, from the
welcoming entrance to the spectacular sunsets, ocean view, and hearty home-style breakfast."

Rocky Point Ocean View B&B

Mrs. Audrey Turgeon
4903 Fillinger Crescent
Nanaimo, BC V9V 1H9
(250) 751-1949
E-mail: aud@nisa.net
Web site: http://www.rockypoint.bc.ca

• From the Departure Bay ferry terminal, take Highway 19A north for 10 minutes. Turn right onto Rutherford Road. At the end of Rutherford, turn right onto Hammond Bay Road. Take the third left, onto Fillinger Crescent and into the Westworld subdivision.
From the Duke Point ferry terminal, take Highway 19 north for 20 minutes. At exit 28, turn right onto Aulds Road, which becomes Hammond Bay Road. Continue through four traffic lights. Turn left onto Fillinger Crescent and into the Westworld subdivision.
• Room. $65–85. Queen-sized bed. Private bathroom.
Self-contained two bedroom suite. $140–160. Two queen-sized beds. Private and ensuite bathrooms. Weekly rates.
• A B&B with views of the ocean, the mountains, eagles, deer, and whales. Self-contained twelve-hundred-square-foot two-bedroom suite with a private entrance, a convection microwave oven, a sink, a small fridge, and a bathroom with bidet and two-person Jacuzzi with stained-glass mural. Guest room has a Jacuzzi. Living room with fireplace. Both suites have TVs and VCRs. Flowers throughout. Coffee, tea, fruit, and chocolate provided. Near salmon fishing. Full breakfast is served in the dining room. **In the hosts' own words:** "Our guest rooms are decorated in monochromatic colours to blend into spectacular sunrises and sunsets. Enjoy a full breakfast in our large, opulent dining room."

Island View B&B

Darlene and Russ Dillon
5391 Entwhistle Drive
Nanaimo, BC V9V 1H2
(250) 758-5536 Fax: (250) 758-5536
E-mail: rdmts@islandnet.com
Web site: http://www.bbcanada.com/1017.html

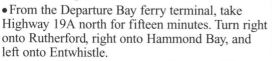

• From the Departure Bay ferry terminal, take Highway 19A north for fifteen minutes. Turn right onto Rutherford, right onto Hammond Bay, and left onto Entwhistle.
From the Duke Point ferry terminal, take Highway 19. Turn right onto Mostar, which becomes Rutherford. Turn right onto Hammond Bay and left onto Entwhistle. The B&B is halfway down the hill, on the left.
• Room. Two people $60. Twin beds. Private bathroom.
Self-contained suite. Two people $85. Queen-sized bed and queen-sized sofa bed. Bathroom in suite. Additional person $20. Call for one-person rates.
• A B&B on half an acre with a garden and views of the Strait of Georgia and the Sunshine Coast. Guest room has a TV and a view of the garden. Eight-hundred-square-foot one-bedroom suite has a view of the ocean, a private entrance, a kitchen, a living room with queen-sized sofa bed, a gas fireplace, a TV, a VCR, and a collection of videos. Sunsets can be seen from a deck. Half a block from a shoreline to walk on. Fresh fruit, snacks, and refreshments. Laundry facilities. Full breakfast is served in the dining room. Children welcome. Smoke-free environment. **In the hosts' own words:** "Enjoy quiet surroundings, tastefully served breakfasts, and magnificent sunsets in our garden paradise."

Courtyard B&B

Knut and Mara Hoglund
1569 Madrona Drive
Nanoose Bay, BC V9P 9C9
(250) 468-1720 Fax: (250) 468-1720

• From Nanaimo, take Highway 19 to the
Parksville north exit onto Highway 19A. At the
first set of lights after the tourist information office, turn right onto Franklin Gull Road, which
becomes North West Bay Road. Turn left onto
Beaver Creek Wharf Road. Turn right onto
Madrona Drive.

• Two rooms. One person $65; two people $75. Queen-sized bed. Ensuite bathrooms.

• A new house near ocean beaches, with a view of seals, sea lions, and other marine wildlife.
Near fishing and boating at Schooner Cove, a golf course, and scuba diving. Guest rooms
have sitting areas and TVs. Guest sitting room with fireplace. Guest rooms and sitting room
are on the ground floor. Air conditioning. Hosts share their knowledge of the area, restaurants, and shops. Breakfast, including homemade baked goods and fresh fruit, is served in
an eating area with an adjoining deck. Visa, MasterCard. Norwegian spoken. Adult oriented.
No pets; toy poodle in residence. Smoke-free environment. **In the hosts' own words:** "Our
tastefully decorated house is a good touring centre because of its central island location.
Come and enjoy Scandinavian comfort and charm. We offer rest and relaxation as part of
your Vancouver Island experience."

Creekside B&B

Kathy McMaster and Rolf Meier
1961 Harlequin Crescent
Nanoose Bay, BC V9P 9J2
(250) 468-9310 Fax: (250) 468-5990

• Twenty-four kilometres north of Nanaimo.
From Highway 19, turn right at the Petro Canada
gas station and follow signs to Fairwinds and
Schooner Cove. Two minutes after Schooner
Cove, turn left from Dolphin Drive onto Swal-
low Crescent. Turn right onto Harlequin.

• Three rooms. One person $65; two people $65–85. Queen-sized bed; twin beds. Private
and shared guest bathrooms.

• A modern house with a view of the ocean, on a wooded half acre, adjacent to a nature park
with a creek. Halfway between Victoria and ocean beaches. Two minutes' drive from sea
kayaking, sailing, and fishing at Schooner Cove. Three minutes' drive from a golf course.
Two minutes' walk from hiking, horseback riding, biking, and a beach for swimming. Guest
sitting room with leather couches, piano, guitar, books, and games. One of the guest rooms
has a TV and a separate entrance. Two guest rooms with washbasins share a guest bathroom.
One of the bathrooms has a Jacuzzi. Guests can visit the hosts' in-house stained glass studio. One of the hosts is a Swiss chef. Full breakfast is served in the dining room or on the
deck. German and Swiss spoken. Children over twelve welcome. No pets; dog in residence.
Smoking outdoors. **In the hosts' own words:** "We delight in sharing our house with those
who seek peace and quiet and a little West Coast adventure."

Marina View B&B

Dea and Art Kern
895 Glenhale Crescent
Parksville, BC V9P 1Z7
(250) 248-9308 Fax: (250) 248-9408
Web site: http://www.vancouverisland-bc.
**   com/MarinaViewBB/**

• Take Highway 19A north through Parksville. Past the French Creek Market, turn right onto Wright Road (at traffic lights) and take the first left onto Glenhale Crescent. Follow the B&B's signs.

• Three rooms. Two people $75–80. Queen-sized bed, ensuite bathroom; queen-sized bed, private bathroom; twin beds, ensuite bathroom. Additional person $20. Roll-away bed available.

• A B&B on the ocean with a view of the Strait of Georgia, the Gulf Islands, and mountains. Deck and solarium with views of Alaska cruise ships, sailboats, eagles, herons, seals, otters, and whales. Guest sitting room with books, TV, and games. Breakfast, including homemade baked goods, homemade preserves, and fresh fruit, is served in the dining room. Reservations recommended. Cancellation notice seven days. Check-in 3:00 to 6:00 p.m.; check-out until 10:30 a.m. Cash, traveller's cheques, Visa, MasterCard. French spoken. Adult oriented. No pets. No smoking. **In the hosts' own words:** "Our guest rooms are uniquely decorated, with emphasis on comfort and elegance. Come and share our delightful home, where the personal touches make the difference."

The Maclure House Inn

Penny and Michael McBride
1015 East Island Highway
Parksville, BC V9P 2E4
(250) 248-3470 Fax: (250) 248-6145
Web site: http://www.vancouverisland-bc.
**   com/MaclureHouse/**

• From the Nanaimo ferry terminal, take Highway 19 north for 24 kilometres. Take the Parksville exit and turn right at Beach Acres Resort.

• Four rooms. Two people $95–135. Queen-sized bed; twin beds. Ensuite and private bathrooms. Additional person $21. Child $12. Off-season rates.

• A Tudor-style B&B inn on the ocean on Rathtrevor Beach, a beach known for its sheltered warm waters. Views of islands and the snowcapped mountains of the Sechelt Peninsula. Steps from a sandy beach and walking trails. Light afternoon tea served when guests arrive. Coffee and juice outside the guest rooms in the morning. Restaurant, tennis, pool, hot tub, and sauna on the property. Five minutes from golf, kayaking, and horseback riding. Three-course breakfast is served on the patio, which has a view of the ocean, or by a fireplace in the dining room. Visa, MasterCard, American Express, Interac. **In the hosts' own words:** "Our heritage inn, visited by Rudyard Kipling in the 1920s, is full of charm and history. Our unobtrusive pampering brings guests back year after year."

Lily's Beach Retreat B&B

Jim Drake and Lily Mayall
Copley Road
Lasqueti Island, BC V0R 2J0
(250) 333-8849

• From French Creek (between Parksville and Qualicum Beach), take the foot-passenger ferry to Lasqueti Island, a 50-minute ride. Call for ferry schedule and parking information. Pickup on 40-foot sailboat can be arranged.
• Room. Two people $60. Queen-sized bed and twin bed. Outhouse and the use of the hosts' indoor bathroom and shower.
Self-contained suite. Two people $80. Queen-sized bed and two beds narrower than twin beds. Outhouse; shower in suite. Breakfast not provided.
Additional person $15.
Open May to September. Minimum stay two nights.
• An old homestead with electricity from alternative power sources—a waterwheel and solar panels—on one hundred and forty acres, with a private beach. Guest room is separate from the hosts' living quarters. Suite has hardwood floors, a kitchen, and a balcony with a view of the ocean. Horse and pony rides offered at neighbouring farm. Bicycles, canoes, and kayaks available for exploring Lasqueti and nearby islands. Children can feed the sheep. Massage and acupressure available. Breakfast is provided for guests staying in the room. **In the hosts' own words:** "We welcome you to step back in time to this beautiful, idyllic sanctuary beside the sea."

Hillcrest House B&B

Pauline and Terry Cross
350 Garrett Road
Qualicum Beach, BC V9K 1H4
(250) 752-7286 Fax: (250) 752-7586

• From Highway 19A, 2.5 kilometres north of the tourist information centre, turn left onto Garrett Road. The B&B is at the top of the hill, on the left.
• Two rooms. In summer, one person $45, two people $60. In winter, one person $35, two people $50. Queen-sized bed; double bed and one twin bed. Shared guest bathroom.
Additional person $15. Children under 5 free. Roll-away bed and cot available.
• A B&B with a view of the ocean, Texada and Hornby islands, and the mainland mountains, one minute's walk from a beach and five minutes' walk from restaurants and shops. A base for trips to Cathedral Grove, the Horne Lake Caves, and Little Qualicum River and Englishman River falls. Near golf, fishing, walking trails, kayaking, swimming in the ocean and in a municipal indoor pool, horseback riding, and shopping. Guest sitting room with gas fireplace, TV, VCR, tea and coffee, and a double hide-a-bed; the hide-a-bed is available for a large group occupying both rooms. Guest sitting room opens onto a patio and garden. Breakfast, which includes homemade bread and homemade preserves, is served at guests' convenience. Cash, traveller's cheques. Children welcome. No pets. Smoking on the patio and in the garden. **In the hosts' own words:** "Wake up to a view and enjoy breakfast with a view. Affordable comfort with old-fashioned hospitality. Beautiful Vancouver Island as you imagine it."

Hollyford Guest Cottage

Jim and Marjorie Ford
106 Hoylake Road East
Qualicum Beach, BC V9K 1L7
(250) 752-8101 Fax: (250) 752-8102
E-mail: fordj@island.net

• In downtown Qualicum Beach, between Highway 19 and Highway 19A. Turn onto Memorial
Drive and continue to Hoylake Road.
From Tofino or Port Alberni, take Highway 4,
which becomes Memorial Drive.
• Rooms. In summer, two people $90-125. In winter, two people $75-90. Ensuite bathrooms. Additional person $15. Discount of 10 percent on stays of seven days or longer.
• A 1924 English cottage-style house, surrounded by holly hedges and half an acre of fruit
trees, herbs, and flower gardens. A short walk from shops, a golf course, and a beach. A short
drive from the ferry terminals in Nanaimo. Near ski areas and year-round golf. Guest rooms
have ensuite bathrooms, private patios, traditional furniture, fine linen, duvets, robes, toiletries, and TVs. Atrium. Guest sitting room with information on local attractions and activities. Full or Continental breakfast is served on white linen with silverware in the dining
room or on the deck. Refreshments on sideboard. Business services. Off-street parking.
Transportation from and to plane, train, and ferry. One of the hosts is a former registered
nurse. Deposit of one night's rate required to hold reservation. Cash, Visa, MasterCard. Children over eleven welcome. Two cats in residence. Smoke-free. **In the hosts' own words:**
"We offer our guests friendly, professional hospitality and a truly memorable bed and breakfast experience."

Vista del Mar B&B

Anita and Roger Marion
343 Poplar Avenue
Qualicum Beach, BC V9K 1J7
(250) 752-1795 Fax: (250) 752-1795

• From Highway 19 south, take Memorial
Avenue. Turn left onto Crescent Road West, right
onto Bay Street, and left onto Poplar.
From Highway 19A, turn left onto Memorial,
right onto Crescent, right onto Bay, and left onto
Poplar.
• Two rooms. $85–95. Queen-sized bed, private bathroom; twin beds, ensuite bathroom.
Extended stay rates. Minimum stay two nights.
• A Mediterranean-style house in a quiet residential area, on a bluff overlooking the Strait of
Georgia, forty minutes north of Nanaimo. View from guest rooms and patio. Ten minutes'
walk from the village. Five minutes' walk from a beach and restaurants. Ten minutes' drive
from five golf courses. Guest rooms have sitting areas with TVs, VCRs, and books. One of
the guest rooms has a fireplace. Guest entrance. Guest patio and hot tub. Robes provided.
Full breakfast is served in the dining area or on the patio. Reservations recommended.
Cancellation notice three days. Check-in 3:00 to 6:00 p.m.; check-out until 11:00 a.m. Cash,
personal and traveller's cheques, MasterCard. French spoken. Adult oriented. No pets; dog
in residence. No smoking. **In the hosts' own words:** "We offer warm hospitality, breathtaking scenery, and luxurious guest rooms that make for a memorable experience."

Blue Willow B&B

Arlene and John England
524 Quatna Road
Qualicum Beach, BC V9K 1B4
(250) 752-9052 Fax: (250) 752-9039
E-mail: bwillow@qb.island.net

• From Highway 19, turn west onto Qualicum Road and then right onto Quatna Road.
• Rooms. One person $65–70; two people $80–85. Additional person $25.
Suite. Two people $95. Queen-sized bed and three twin beds. Additional person $25.
Off-season rates November to March.
• A Tudor-style house with beamed ceilings, leaded windows, and garden views, surrounded by evergreens. Five minutes' walk from an ocean beach. Fifteen minutes' walk from the village of Qualicum Beach. Suite has a separate entrance. Garden, patio, and guest sitting room with TV. Full breakfast. Visa, MasterCard. French and German spoken. Children welcome in the suite. Pets welcome by arrangement. Dachshund in residence. Nonsmoking house. **In the hosts' own words:** "We offer hospitality, comfort, quiet, and relaxation. Breakfast is a very special event."

Quatna Manor

Bill and Betty Ross
512 Quatna Road
Qualicum Beach, BC V9K 1B4
(250) 752-6685 Fax: (250) 752-8385
E-mail: neilgil@nanaimo.ark.com
Web site: http://www.islandnet.com/~pixsell/
  bcbbd.htm

• From Highway 19, take the Qualicum exit and continue to the beachfront. Turn right onto Highway 19A and continue for 1 kilometre. Turn right onto Hall Road. Take the first left, onto Quatna Road. Brochure with map is available at the Qualicum tourist information centre.

• Room. One person $65; two people $70–85. Queen-sized bed. Private or shared bathroom.

Two-bedroom suite. Two people $120–130. Queen-sized bed and twin beds. Bathroom in suite. Available May to November.

Self-contained suite. Two people $95. Queen-sized bed. Ensuite bathroom.

• A Tudor-style house with European and English antiques, down duvets, and crystal chandeliers. Guest room and suite are on the second floor. Guest entrance. Guest patio and TV room with fireplace. The self-contained suite is above the garage and has a private entrance, a fireplace, a TV, a VCR, and a kitchen with fridge, stove, microwave, and dishwasher. Laundry facilities available. Hosts arrange tee times at four local all-season golf courses, some of which provide reduced rates for guests of the B&B. Full or Continental breakfast is served in the dining room. Dachshund in residence. A smoke-free environment. **In the hosts' own words:** "Enjoy the peaceful luxury of our charming house. We offer exceptional privacy."

Falcon Crest B&B

Kurt and Lisa Zurbuchen
4265 Island Highway West
Qualicum Beach, BC V9K 2B1
(250) 752-1989 Fax: (250) 752-1989

• Forty-five minutes north of Nanaimo; 14 kilometres from Parksville; 55 kilometres from the Nanaimo ferry terminal; 168 kilometres from Victoria.

• Six rooms. Two people $75–90. King-sized bed; queen-sized bed; two double beds. Ensuite and private bathrooms. Additional person $20. Child $10–15. Off-season rates.

• A B&B on six and a half acres on a bluff, with a private trail to a beach. The trail leads through a forest with four-hundred-year-old trees. Sea lions, seals, eagles, deer, birds, and cruise ships can be seen. Swimming at the beach by the property or three kilometres away at Qualicum Beach. Near a shopping mall, golf, salmon-fishing charters, and boating. Three of the guest rooms have views of the ocean. Guest dining/recreation room has a fireplace, a TV, and games. Full breakfast, including homemade bread and local smoked salmon, is served in the guest dining/recreation room, which has an individual table for each guest room. Reservations recommended in summer, mid-June to mid-September. Cancellation notice seven days. Visa, MasterCard, traveller's cheques. Swiss, German, Chinese, and French spoken. Children welcome under parents' supervision. Nonsmoking house. **In the hosts' own words:** "Enjoy the ocean view, privacy, swimming, and relaxation."

Qualicum Bay B&B

Jillian and Len Ralph
6253 West Island Highway
Qualicum Bay, BC V9K 4E2
(250) 757-8802 Fax: (250) 757-8802
E-mail: qbbb@island.net
Web site: http://www.vancouverisland-bc.com/QualicumBayBB/

• Forty-five minutes north of Nanaimo, on Highway 19. Fifteen minutes north of Qualicum Beach.

• Three rooms. In summer (April to September), two people $75–$85. Queen-sized bed; double bed; twin beds (or twin beds side by side with king-sized bedding). Ensuite and private bathrooms. Additional person $20. Off-season rates October to March.

Self-contained cottage. Double bed and bunk beds. In summer (June to September), seven days $500; minimum stay seven days. Breakfast not included. Off-season rates October to May.

• A B&B on an ocean beach, near golf, fishing, hiking, and skiing. A base for day trips to Long Beach in Pacific Rim National Park. Secluded bay for swimming, beachcombing, clam digging, and bonfires. Guest rooms have coffee makers and private balconies with views of the ocean. One of the guest rooms has a queen-sized bed and a TV. The house's top floor is for guest use only and has games, a TV, a VCR, a billiard table, a piano, a chess set, books, and a small fridge. Self-contained waterfront cottage has a kitchen, a TV, and a stereo. Full breakfast for guests staying in the rooms is served in a sun room that has a view of the beach or on the patio. Cancellation notice for rooms in house and for winter rental of cottage, forty-eight hours; for summer rental of cottage, fourteen days. Visa, MasterCard. Children and pets welcome in the cottage; dog in the hosts' house. Smoking outdoors. **In the hosts' own words:** "Let us show you what true hospitality is all about."

Shoreline B&B

Dave and Audrie Sands
4969 Shoreline Drive
Deep Bay, BC
Mail: RR 1 Site 152 C–4
Bowser, BC V0R 1G0
(250) 757-9807 Fax: phone before faxing
E-mail: sands@nanaimo.ark.com

• In Deep Bay, off Highway 19A. From Highway 19 take the Cook Creek exit. Turn right at the E & N railway tracks. Turn left twice, the second time onto Shoreline Drive.

• Room. Two people $75. Queen-sized bed. Private bathroom.

• A house on a walk-on beach, with a guest room that has a view of a garden, Baynes Sound, the Chrome Island lighthouse, Denman and Hornby islands, and the Coast Mountain range. Guest room has antiques and a private entrance. Library/TV room with fireplace. Near ocean beaches, charter fishing, eco-tours, free or guided cave exploration at Horne Lake Caves, fish hatcheries, bird sanctuaries, and restaurants. A base for day trips to Long Beach, Mount Washington, and the northern half of Vancouver Island. Breakfast, including local eggs, bread, smoked salmon, homemade jam, and the hosts' berries and herbs, is served in the dining room or on the deck, both of which have a view of the ocean. Breakfast is customized to each guest's preferences and can be low fat, low salt, or vegetarian. Visa. Adult oriented. Pets welcome. No smoking indoors. **In the hosts' own words:** "Our B&B offers rural peace and quiet in the heart of lighthouse country. We try to treat our guests as we'd like to be treated when travelling; we want you to have an altogether enjoyable experience."

Seahaven B&B

Carol and Roy Richards
6660 South Island Highway
Mail: Site 3 C–12
Fanny Bay, BC V0R 1W0
(250) 335-1550
Toll-free from within North America:
  1-888-335-1550
E-mail: seahaven@island.net
Web site: http://www.victoriabc.com/accom/
  seahaven.html

• At Fanny Bay (20 minutes south of Courtenay; 3 hours north of Victoria), 1 kilometre from the Buckley Bay ferry terminal.
• Three rooms. One person $50; two people $60–65. Double bed; queen-sized bed; twin beds. Private bathrooms. Additional person $10.
• A two-level house on two hundred feet of waterfront, with a deck that has a view of sunrises, eagles, herons, seals, and otters. Guest sitting room has books, a selection of videos, and a view. In the area are Denman and Hornby islands, golf courses, hiking, swimming, kayak tours, and skiing at Mount Washington. Barbecue and picnic tables. Full breakfast includes fresh fruit, homemade bread, jam, and free-range eggs. Visa, MasterCard. Children over ten welcome. Smoking on the deck and in the garden. **In the hosts' own words:** "Take in our fantastic views. Our house is a very friendly and comfortable place to visit."

Good Morning B&B

Marian Sieg
7845 Central Road
Mail: Central 2–1
Hornby Island, BC V0R 1Z0
(250) 335-1094 Fax: (250) 335-1094
E-mail: hornbyi@mars.ark.com
Web site: http://mars.ark.com/~hornbyi

• On the corner of Central and Sandpiper.
• Three rooms. In summer, one person $60, two people $75. In winter, one person $55, two people $60. Queen-sized bed; double bed and one twin bed. Shared guest bathroom.
• A B&B on Hornby Island with a guest living room that has a fireplace, a TV, a VCR, and a radio. Guest entrance and deck. On Hornby are wildflowers, fossils (on Fossil Beach), three sandy swimming beaches, boating, hiking and biking trails, and nesting grounds of eagles, herons, and herring. Kayaks, bikes, and charter boats for fishing are available on the island. Breakfast, including homemade bread, muffins, jam, coffee, and a choice of pancakes or bacon and free-range eggs, is served in the dining room. Bike storage available. German spoken. No pets. Smoking on the patio. **In the hosts' own words:** "Enjoy our European hospitality and the spectacular views of Denman Island and the Comox Valley. Wir sprechen deutsch."

Orchard House B&B

Janet and Peter Hicken
1835 Shinglespit Road
Phipps Point
Hornby Island, BC V0R 1Z0
(250) 335-1111

• Two rooms. One person $75–95; two people $90–110. Queen-sized bed; twin beds (or twin beds side by side with king-sized bedding). Ensuite bathrooms. Roll-away cot and crib available. Self-contained cottage. Two to four people $500 per week. Breakfast not provided.

• A country-style house on two acres on the ocean, with a view of Lambert Channel. Guest rooms have ocean views, ensuite bathrooms, and coffee and tea facilities. Robes provided. Guest sitting room has an open fire, a TV, a VCR, books, and games. Garden with barbecue, picnic table, and garden chairs. Full breakfast, including local organic produce and fresh-squeezed juice, is served in the sitting room or on the porch, which has a view of the ocean; vegetarian breakfast is available. Cancellation notice seven days. Deposit of one night's rate required to hold reservation. Visa, MasterCard. Children welcome by arrangement. Dog and two outdoor cats in residence. Smoking on the porch. **In the hosts' own words:** "Our B&B offers a gracious, comfortable setting, delicious, healthy breakfasts, and a relaxing atmosphere. Watch eagles fly overhead, herons fish off the rocks, and spectacular sunsets."

Barb's B&B

Barb and Dave Roberts
4452 South Island Highway
Royston, BC V0R 2V0
Mail: RR 6 Site 664 C–2
Courtenay, BC V9N 8H9
(250) 338-7766

• Five kilometres south of Courtenay, on Highway 19A.

• Two rooms. One person $50; two people $75. Queen-sized bed. Shared guest bathroom.

• A new log-and-cedar house on the ocean, on an acreage in the Comox Valley recreation area, close to golf courses and marine activities, with guest rooms that have views of the ocean. A base for day trips to Campbell River and Denman and Hornby islands. Near hiking, beaches, and Mount Washington and Forbidden Plateau ski areas. A few minutes from Courtenay and Cumberland. Guest sitting room with rock fireplace and TV. Full breakfast is served on a glassed-in deck with a view of the ocean. **In the hosts' own words:** "You will enjoy our house with its spectacular views and easy access to the marine life of the beach. Our acreage gives you complete privacy and the sound of the ocean."

Wellington House B&B

Shelagh Davis and Doug Jackson
2593 Derwent Avenue
Mail: Box 689
Cumberland, BC V0R 1S0
(250) 336-8809 Fax: (250) 336-2455
E-mail: cma_chin@island.net
Web sites: http://www.vquest.com/stay/
  members.html
http://www.bbcanada.com/1341.html
http://www.islandnet.com/~pixsell/bcbbd/1/
  1000206.htm

• Take Highway 19 to Royston. Follow signs to Cumberland, 7 kilometres. Go through the village and turn left, towards Comox Lake. Take the first right onto Derwent.
• Two rooms. One person $50–55; two people $65–75. Queen-sized bed; double bed. Ensuite and private bathrooms.
Suite (sleeps four). $90. Additional person $20.
• A modern house in the foothills of the Beaufort Mountains, in the historical mining village of Cumberland. Garden-level guest entrance. Guest rooms have sitting rooms with TVs. Suite has a kitchen. Deck, covered patio, and garden. Five to forty-five minutes' drive from golf courses, skiing, sport fishing, fresh and saltwater activities, and nature parks for biking and hiking. Full breakfast with homemade preserves. Visa. No pets. Smoking on the patio.
In the hosts' own words: "This is one area where you can golf and ski on the same day. We look forward to sharing our peaceful surroundings and hospitality with you."

Forbidden Plateau B&B

Bruce and Mary Jaffary
4341 Forbidden Plateau Road
Mail: RR 4 Site 473 C–31
Courtenay, BC V9N 7J3
(250) 703-9622 Fax: (250) 703-9622
Toll-free from within North America:
  1-888-288-2144
E-mail: jaffary@island.net
Web site: http://www.island.net/~jaffary

• Twelve kilometres from Courtenay. Ninety minutes north of Nanaimo. Follow signs to the Forbidden Plateau ski area.
• Two rooms and one cottage. One person $50–60; two people $65–75. Twin beds (or twin beds side by side with king-sized bedding); queen-sized bed and double hide-a-bed; queen-sized bed. Ensuite bathrooms. Additional person $15–20.
• A recently remodeled house and a cottage among tall cedar trees on five acres of farmland. A thousand feet from the Puntledge River. Forest hiking trails from the B&B; some of the trails lead to swimming holes in the river. Twenty minutes from skiing and hiking at Forbidden Plateau and Mount Washington. Near golf, fishing, swimming, and birdwatching. Guest rooms and guest cottage have separate entrances. Sitting room with books, TV, VCR, and fireplace. Garden hot tub. Full breakfast includes chicken eggs or duck eggs, homemade baked goods, and jam. Guests are welcome to gather eggs for their breakfast. Visa, Master-Card. Pets in residence. Smoking outdoors. **In the hosts' own words:** "We welcome you. Our home is your home to enjoy. Experience a taste of the country at our B&B."

Mariposa Gardens B&B

Emerson (Red) and Mary DeGraw
4069 Haas Road
Mail: RR 6 Site 682 C–15
Courtenay, BC V9N 8H9
(250) 897-1807
E-mail: degraw@island.net
Web site: http://webfactory.base.org/
**   mariposa**

• From Courtenay, take Highway 19 south for 3 kilometres. Turn left onto Thomson Road. Turn right onto Haas Road.
• Two rooms. One person $45–55; two people $55–65. Queen-sized bed, shared bathroom; queen-sized bed, ensuite bathroom. Additional person $12. Seventh night free.
• A Cape Cod–style house with antiques and a view of Comox Bay and the Coast mountains, on an acre of gardens and woods. Near several golf courses and fresh and saltwater fishing. Three minutes from Courtenay. Ten minutes from beaches and ferries to Denman and Hornby islands. Thirty minutes from skiing at Mount Washington. Forty-five minutes from Campbell River. Guest rooms have down duvets. Family room for watching movies, reading, and playing cards. Living room with player piano, which guests are welcome to use, and stone fireplace. Full breakfast includes fresh fruit salad, homemade preserves, and homemade baked goods. Cancellation notice three days. Visa. No pets; two small shih tzu dogs in residence. Smoking on the deck. **In the hosts' own words:** "We treat our guests like old friends."

The Beach House B&B

Anke Burkhardt
3614 South Island Highway
Mail: RR 6 Site 688 C–28
Courtenay, BC V9N 8H9
(250) 338-8990 Fax: (250) 338-5651

• Two kilometres south of Courtenay on Highway 19.
• Three rooms. $35–65. Queen-sized bed; double bed; one twin bed. Private and shared guest bathrooms.
• A cedar house on the ocean, on a two-acre farm, with a private path along a beach, where trumpeter swans, seals, and ducks can be seen. Twenty minutes from downhill and cross-country skiing, four golf courses, hiking, and fishing. Deck, wood stove, pool table, darts area, and piano. Guest rooms have TVs. Two of the guest rooms are on the second floor and share a living room and a bathroom. The guest room on the main floor has a separate entrance, a deck, and an ocean view. Full breakfast includes eggs from the hosts' hens, homemade bread, and homemade yogurt. Kitchen facilities and barbecue available for guests to prepare other meals. Visa, MasterCard. German and French spoken. No pets. No smoking. **In the hosts' own words:** "Relax in our unique waterfront house."

Greystone Manor B&B

Mike and Maureen Shipton
4014 Haas Road
Mail: RR 6 Site 684 C–2
Courtenay, BC V9N 8H9
(250) 338-1422
Web site: http://www.bbcanada.com/1334.html

• From Courtenay, take Highway 19 south for 3 kilometres to Royston. Turn left onto Hilton and left onto Haas Road.
• Three rooms. One person $55; two people $75–80. Queen-sized bed; double bed; twin beds. Ensuite and private bathrooms.
• A 1918 house on the ocean, on one and a half acres with English flower gardens and old maples and firs. Perennial beds, rockeries, and herb and vegetable gardens. View across Comox Bay to mainland mountains. Seals, herons, sea birds, and eagles can be seen. Guest sitting room with fireplace, piano, books, and magazines. Twenty minutes from ferries to Denman and Hornby islands. Forty minutes from Mount Washington and Strathcona Provincial Park. Eight minutes from Courtenay. Ten minutes from golf courses. Halfway between Port Hardy and Victoria; a stopover point on the Sunshine Coast circle tour. The hosts, who came to Canada from Bath, England, share their knowledge about the local area and hiking and walking trails. Full breakfast. Visa, MasterCard. Children over twelve welcome. No pets. No smoking. **In the hosts' own words:** "A friendly welcome awaits you. Relax in our lovely heritage house and spectacular gardens."

Forest Glen B&B

Art and Lois Enns
5760 Sea Terrace Road
Mail: RR 2 Site 280 C–37
Courtenay, BC V9N 5M9
(250) 334-4374 Fax: (250) 334-4396
E-mail: forestgl@island.net
Web site: http://www.victoriabc.com/accom/forestgl.htm

• Fifteen minutes north of Courtenay. Ten minutes north of the Powell River ferry. From Courtenay, go north on Highway 19 for 6 kilometres. Turn right onto Hardy Road. Turn right onto Coleman. Turn right onto Loxley and continue to the end. Go down Avonlea and turn right onto Sea Terrace.
• Two rooms. One person $60–70; two people $70–80. Queen-sized bed. Ensuite and private bathrooms. Additional person $20. Roll-away cot available. Winter rates October 15 to April 30.
• A Cape Cod–style house in the Seal Bay Forest with walking trails from the B&B through Seal Bay Regional Park to Seal Bay. Deer, seals, eagles, and herons can be seen on the walking trails. Thirty minutes from skiing and hiking at Mount Washington in Strathcona Park. Five minutes' drive from fishing and kayaking at Bates Beach. Fifteen minutes' drive from ocean beaches. Living room with fireplace. Sun room has a TV and a view of flower gardens and leads to a deck with guest hot tub. Guest rooms have sitting areas. Full breakfast includes fresh fruit, juice, and homemade baked goods. Visa, MasterCard. Nonsmoking house. **In the hosts' own words:** "We've built our dream home, and now we invite you to come and enjoy it with us. Have a drink of wine or tea with us by the fireplace."

Foskett House B&B

Dove and Michael Hendren
484 Lazo Road
Comox, BC V9M 3V1
(250) 339-4272 Fax: (250) 339-4272
Toll-free: 1-800-797-9252
E-mail: foskett@island.net
Web sites: http://www.vquest.com/foskett/
http://www.bbcanada.com/1329.html

• At Point Holmes, 5 kilometres east of Comox.
• Two rooms. One person $65–75; two people
$80–90. Queen-sized bed and one twin hide-a-bed; queen-sized bed. Ensuite bathrooms.
Additional person $15. Seasonal rates.
• A 1920 South African–style ranch house with wrap-around verandas, on five acres of
wind-sculpted oaks and pines, across the road from the ocean. Views of the ocean, the Gulf
Islands, and winter storms. Interior is finished with cedar. Antiques. Beach-stone fireplace.
Guest rooms have private entrances. Ten minutes from ferries to Powell River. Hosts arrange
special rates for golf, kayaking, salmon fishing, and reflexology. Full breakfast includes
homemade baked goods, fresh fruit, and an entrée. Border collie in residence. Nonsmoking.
In the hosts' own words: "After the sound of the ocean has lulled you to sleep, awake from
a wonderful night's rest to our gourmet breakfast."

Levenvale B&B

Shirley and Alan Robb
2081 Murphy Avenue
Comox, BC V9M 1V4
(250) 339-3307 Fax: (250) 339-4036

• In Comox, near the hospital.
• Two rooms. One person $40; two people $55.
Queen-sized bed and hide-a-bed; twin beds (or
twin beds side by side with king-sized bedding).
Private bathrooms. Family rates.
• A B&B centrally located in a quiet residential
district, within walking distance of restaurants, a beach, a marina, and shopping. Near golf
courses. Deck, living room, and recreation room with TV. Guest room on the lower level has
a queen-sized bed, a hide-a-bed, a private entrance, and a sitting room with TV and books.
The other guest room is on the upper level and has twin beds, a deck, and a sitting room with
antiques. Pickup from bus, train, and plane. Full breakfast is served in a formal dining room
with antiques or on the deck, both of which have views of Comox Bay, a marina, and mountains. Cash, cheques. Children welcome. Smoking outdoors. **In the hosts' own words:** "We
look forward to meeting our guests and sharing our hospitality and travel experiences."

Fresh Tracks B&B

Kathy Penner and Bill Kossian
7250 Howard Road
Mail: Box 194
Merville, BC V0R 2M0
(250) 337-5956 Fax: (250) 337-5523

• From Courtenay, go north for 10 minutes. Turn left onto Merville Road (general store on the corner) and continue for 2 kilometres. Turn right onto Howard and continue for 1 kilometre.

• Two rooms. One person; $50–60; two people $70–80. Queen-sized bed. Ensuite and private bathrooms. Packages available.

• A modern country-style house on sixteen acres, with mountain, pasture, and garden views. One of the guest rooms, which is at ground level and leads to a garden patio, has a wood stove, a drying rack for wet gear, a fridge, local and world travel literature, games, a TV, and a VCR. On the main floor are a living room with a floor-to-ceiling stone fireplace, a dining room, a sun room, and a deck with an outdoor hot tub. Thirty minutes from Mount Washington. Ten minutes from Miracle Beach. Full breakfast includes homemade granola, organic coffee, preserves, and farm eggs. Afternoon refreshments served. Visa. Adult oriented. Two dogs in residence. No smoking indoors. **In the hosts' own words:** "Our home is a reflection of our passions—outdoor adventure, gardening, cooking, and two border collies who love to play frisbee. We offer an atmosphere conducive to both privacy and interaction. Our B&B is in an ideal location for skiers, hikers, cyclists, and birdwatchers."

Country Comfort B&B

Elaine and Ron Bohn
8214 Island Highway
Black Creek, BC V9J 1H6
(250) 337-5273
Web site: http://www.bbcanada.com/434.html

• From Courtenay, take Highway 19 north for 15 minutes; 2 kilometres north of the small Black Creek bridge, look for the B&B's sign.
From Campbell River, take Highway 19 south for 20 minutes; the B&B is one block south of the Black Creek country market.
• Three rooms. One person $40; two people $60. Queen-sized bed; double bed. Shared guest bathroom.
Family and extended stay rates.
• A split-level house on a fifty-acre hobby farm with lawns, orchards, and vegetable and flower gardens. Five minutes' drive from golf, hiking, trail riding, fishing, a provincial park, beaches, and fine dining restaurants. Hosts help guests arrange guided whale watching tours, guided helicopter tours, and visits to mines, a pulp mill, and timber operations. Twenty minutes' drive from Mount Washington ski resort; near a daily ski bus stop. Mount Washington's hiking trails, chairlift, and restaurant are also open in the summer months. A stopover point on the way to Strathcona Park and to the ferries from Port Hardy to Prince Rupert. Solarium and family room with TV, VCR, and books. Small gift shop. Full breakfast, including fresh fruit, homemade baked goods, and farm-fresh eggs, is served at guests' convenience; special diets accommodated. **In the hosts' own words:** "After a long day's travel, take this opportunity to stop and smell the flowers. Please let us pamper you on your holiday."

Tudor Acres B&B

Betty and Peter Cartwright
2065 Endall Road
Black Creek, BC V9J 1G8
(250) 337-5764 Fax: (250) 337-5764

• From Courtenay, go north for 15 minutes. Pass Black Creek Building Supply, which is on the right, continue for 2 kilometres, and turn left onto Endall Road.
• Two rooms. One person $45; two people $60. Queen-sized bed; two double beds. Shared guest bathroom.
Suite. Two people $70. Queen-sized bed and twin day beds. Private bathroom. Additional person $15. Family rates.
• A Tudor-style house on twelve acres, where the hosts raise Romney sheep. Five minutes from Miracle Beach, an ocean beach. Fifteen minutes from Courtenay and ferries to Powell River. Thirty minutes from Campbell River, Mount Washington, and Strathcona Provincial Park. Guest living room with open brick fireplace, Hammond organ, TV, and VCR. Deck with hot tub, lawn furniture, and a barbecue overlooks a garden. Suite has a living room with a day bed that converts into twin beds and a kitchen with stove, fridge, and microwave. Washer and dryer available. Breakfast includes an entrée, fruit from the garden, and home-made bread and preserves. Visa. No pets. Smoking outdoors. **In the hosts' own words:** "Welcome to our home. We will do our very best to make your stay with us as comfortable and enjoyable as possible."

The Grey Mouse B&B

Hanayo and John Oughtred
2012 Eyre Road, Saratoga Beach
Black Creek, BC V9J 1B2
(250) 337-5795 Fax: (250) 337-2036
Web site: http://www.bbcanada.com/
**   1332.html**

• Twenty-two kilometres north of Courtenay. Twenty kilometres south of Campbell River. From Highway 19, follow the signs to Saratoga Beach resort area.
• Three rooms. One person $40–50; two people $60–70. Queen-sized bed; double bed; twin beds. Shared guest bathroom. Additional person $20.
• A house on the ocean with guest rooms that have views of the Strait of Georgia and the Coast Mountains. Sandy beach and bonfire pit. Court for tennis, basketball, volleyball, and shuffleboard. Ten minutes' walk from a marina, fishing, hiking, and golf. Forty minutes' drive from Mount Washington ski resort and Strathcona Provincial Park. Five minutes' drive from restaurants and pubs. Guest rooms, guest living room with TV, and shared guest bathroom are on one floor of the house. Guest entrance. Full breakfast is served in the guest dining room, which has a view of the ocean. Japanese spoken. Pets by arrangement. No smoking indoors.

Arbour's Guest House

Sharon and Ted Arbour
375 South Murphy Street
Campbell River, BC V9W 1Y8
(250) 287-9873 Fax: c/o (250) 287-2353
E-mail: crfish@oberon.ark.com

• Five minutes from downtown.
• Two rooms. One person $60–80; two people
$70–95. Queen-sized bed; twin beds. Ensuite
and private bathrooms. Additional person $20.
Open seasonally. Weekly rates.
• A B&B with antique décor, on treed property, with a view of the mountains, ocean, and
fishing grounds. Glass of wine served when guests arrive. Near golf courses. Bicycle rentals
available. Boat rentals arranged. Experienced fishing guides available for saltwater salmon
fishing. One of the guest rooms has a kitchen and a TV and accommodates up to four people; the other guest room has a living room with TV. Reservations recommended. Visa,
MasterCard. Adult oriented. No pets. No smoking. **In the hosts' own words:** "Hospitality
is our business. We are in the sport fishing capital of the world."

Blue Heron B&B

Gunnar and Emilia Hansen
Potlatch Road
Mail: Box 23
Manson's Landing
Cortes Island, BC V0P 1K0
(250) 935-6584

• Twenty kilometres from the Whaletown ferry
landing; 1 kilometre from Smelt Bay Provincial
Park.
• Two rooms. One person $40–65; two people
$45–70. King-sized bed; twin beds. Ensuite and shared bathrooms. Additional person $15.
• A country-style house on the ocean with a garden and a view of Sutil Channel and
Vancouver Island, a few steps from a sand and rock beach. Guests can walk along the beach,
explore tidal pools, and watch sunsets. Living room and deck with views of ocean and
mountains. Wood-fired sauna available for a fee. Guest entrance. Full breakfast includes
fresh fruit, homemade baked goods, free-range eggs, and homemade preserves. Cancellation
notice seven days. Danish spoken. No pets; dog and cat in residence. No smoking in the
guest rooms. **In the hosts' own words:** "We invite guests to relax and read in our pleasant
living room and enjoy the view deck."

Fairhaven Farm and B&B

David and Margaret Hansen
Mail: Box 141, Manson's Landing
Cortes Island, BC V0P 1K0
(250) 935-6501

• Two and a half kilometres from the centre of
Manson's Landing.
• Three rooms. One person $60; two people $70.
Queen-sized bed; twin beds. Ensuite and private
bathrooms. Additional person $15. Crib available.
• A modernized turn-of-the-century log house on a
seventeen-acre farm, with views of an orchard and
a pasture with grazing sheep. Twenty minutes' walk from a gravel ocean beach. Five minutes'
drive from two sandy beaches, one on the ocean and the other on Hague Lake. Near kayak
rentals. Library. Hot tub. Terry robes and down duvets in guest rooms. Full breakfast, including farm-fresh eggs from the B&B's hens, is served between 8:00 and 10:00 a.m. Afternoon
tea is served indoors or under a grape arbour. Children welcome. No pets; cat in residence. No
smoking indoors. **In the hosts' own words:** "After a day of exploring scenic Cortes, come and
enjoy the quiet pleasures of life down on our farm."

Roseberry Manor B&B

Diane and Robert Hitchcox
810 Nimpkish Heights Drive
Port McNeill, BC V0N 2R0
(250) 956-4788 Fax: (250) 956-4788
Toll-free from within North America:
  1-888-956-7673
Web sites: http://www.bbcanada.com/
  1989.html
http://www.islandnet.com/pixsell/bcbbd/
  1/1000050.htm

• From Highway 19, 7 kilometres south of Port McNeill, turn onto Nimpkish Heights
Drive. The B&B is on the left side of the road, a short distance from the highway turnoff.
• Three rooms. One person $60; two people $65–75. Queen-sized bed; double bed; twin
beds (or twin beds side by side with king-sized bedding). Private and shared guest bathrooms.
• A house on two acres in a quiet rural setting, decorated in Victorian country style with family heirlooms, dolls, and teddy bears. Guest living room with fireplace. Guest entrance. Dining
room, sun rooms, and porch. Books, magazines, and tourist information. Guest rooms have
feather pillows, flowers, chocolates, toiletries, hair dryers, curling irons, robes, and slippers.
Guest room with twin beds has a TV and a VCR. Thirty minutes from whale watching tours
and forestry tours, Native culture, caving, scuba diving, kayaking, windsurfing, golf, and ferries to Prince Rupert and Bella Coola. Thirty minutes from lake, stream, and ocean fishing.
Afternoon tea and evening cappuccino and hot chocolate are served in the guest living room.
Breakfast, including fresh-ground coffee, regular and herbal teas, fruit, baked goods, homemade preserves, and a choice of a hot entrée including eggs Benedict, blueberry pancakes, or
omelettes, is served on china, silver, and crystal, by candlelight and with music and flowers,
in a Victorian-style dining room, from 7:30 to 10:00 a.m. Laundry facilities. Reservations recommended. Check-in after 3:00 p.m.; check-out until 11:00 a.m. or by arrangement. Cash,
traveller's cheques. Adult oriented. No pets; small dog in residence. Smoking in a designated
area. **In the hosts' own words:** "Please allow us the pleasure of your company."

Tranquil Space B&B

Wayne and Joyce McKamey
2702 Brockington Place
Mail: Box 991
Port McNeill, BC V0N 2R0
(250) 956-2002

• From Campbell River, go north for 2 hours to
Port McNeill. Turn right onto Mine Road (gas
station on the corner), left onto Kingcome, and
right onto Brockington.
• Three rooms. One person $45; two people
$55–60. Queen-sized bed; twin beds. Shared guest bathroom.
Winter rates. Group rates. Children's rates.
• A B&B near fishing and whale watching, two hours north of Campbell River. A base for
day trips to Malcolm Island and Cormorant Island. Rooms are in the basement and have
TVs. Entrance, breakfast area, and recreation room with a fireplace are also in the basement
and are separate from the hosts' living quarters. Near totem poles in Alert Bay on Cormorant
Island. Two kilometres from the world's largest burl (a knot of wood formed on a tree trunk).
Near ferry to Sointula on Malcolm Island and Alert Bay on Cormorant Island. Cruise ships
can be seen in summer. Cooking facilities available. Continental breakfast. Cash, traveller's
cheques. Children and pets considered. Smoking outdoors. **In the hosts' own words:** "We
simply offer a good night's rest in pleasant, clean surroundings at an affordable price."

Barbara Bruner's B&B

Larry and Barbara Bruner
8835 Seaview Drive
Mail: Box 193
Port Hardy, BC V0N 2P0
(250) 949-2306

• Two rooms. One person $40–$60. Twin beds;
one twin bed. Shared guest bathroom.
• A quiet house four blocks from a bus depot,
restaurants, stores, recreation facilities, and Port
Hardy's seawall walkway. Guest sitting room with
fireplace, piano, TV, pool table, books, magazines, and telephone. Garden with patio and
picnic table. Tea, coffee, and hot chocolate available in the sitting room. Shuttle bus service
between the ferry terminal and the B&B. Full breakfast includes fresh fruit, fresh eggs, juice,
homemade baked goods, and preserves. Cash, traveller's cheques. Smoking on the garden
patio. **In the hosts' own words:** "We invite you to spend a night or a few days enjoying the
North Island attractions and our hospitality."

Oceanview B&B

Bob and Chantal Charlie
7735 Cedar Place
Mail: Box 1837
Port Hardy, BC V0N 2P0
(250) 949-8302
E-mail: oceanvue@trinet.bc.ca
Web site: http://www.trinet.bc.ca/~oceanvue

• In Port Hardy ($2^{1}/_{2}$ hours north of Campbell River).
• Two rooms. One person $75; two people $85. Queen-sized bed. Shared guest bathroom.
Suite. Two people $100; three people $115; four people $125. Two queen-sized beds. Ensuite bathroom.
Off-season rates.
• A house with a perennial garden, a pond, and views of the ocean, cruise ships, and snow-capped mountains. Eagles are often seen. Ten minutes' walk from a beach, restaurants, and the town centre. Guest rooms have down comforters, small tables, chairs, and armoires with TVs and VCRs. Suite has down comforters, a small reading corner, a sofa, a love seat, a coffee table, and a TV. Guest rooms and suite have flowers, chocolates on the pillows, homemade chocolate chip cookies, and folders containing information on local attractions and activities. Guest sitting room with fireplace, piano, books, and magazines. Hosts arrange transportation from and to ferries to Prince Rupert and Bella Coola. Guests making round trips on ferries can leave their vehicles at the B&B. Breakfast, including homemade bread, muffins, cereal, fruit, cold cuts, cheese, jam, jelly, juice, and choice of tea, coffee, or hot chocolate, is served in the kitchen, which has a view of the ocean. Cash, traveller's cheques. No children under twelve. No pets. Smoking outdoors. **In the hosts' own words:** "Our house is your home. Wander through our wonderful garden or sit by the pond and watch the gold fish swim. If there is anything we can do to make your stay more memorable, please ask. Enjoy West Coast hospitality at its best."

C-View B&B

Cathy and Jim Witton
6170 Hardy Bay Road
Mail: Box 526
Port Hardy, BC V0N 2P0
(250) 949-7560 Fax: (250) 949-7560
Toll-free: 1-800-515-5511
E-mail: catala@capescott.net
Web site: http://www.capescott.net/labrador/

• Immediately after crossing the Quatze River
Bridge, turn right onto Hardy Bay Road. Con-
tinue for 1.5 kilometres. The B&B is on the left.
• Three rooms. One person $45–55; two people $60–70. Queen-sized bed and one twin
bed; queen-sized bed and double hide-a-bed; bunk beds and one twin bed. Shared bathroom and shared guest bathroom. Additional person $15. Cots available.
Charters.
• A house in a quiet residential area, on a bay where eagles, seals, and other birds and marine
life can be seen. Hosts offer boat charters for scuba diving, whale watching, and fishing in
Quatsino Sound and Queen Charlotte Strait, which are known for halibut, rockfish, lingcod,
and chinook, coho, and pink salmon. One of the guest rooms has a sitting area with TV and
movies. Patio with lawn chairs and a coffee table. Three minutes' drive from the city centre.
Ten minutes' drive from the Bear Cove ferry terminal. Continental breakfast is served in the
sun room, which has a view of the bay. Parking. Children and pets welcome. Smoking outdoors. **In the hosts' own words:** "We offer a clean, comfortable, quiet home for your stay."

Rocklands B&B

Rosaline Glynn
5096 Peel Street
Mail: Box 1145
Port Hardy, BC V0N 2P0
(250) 949-7074 Fax: (250) 949-7072
Toll-free for reservations: 1-888-766-7625
E-mail: dfaber@direct.ca
Web site: http://www.bbcanada.com/1964.html

• From Highway 19, turn onto Fort Rupert
Road (airport sign). Turn right onto Byng Road,
left onto Beaver Harbour Road, and left onto Peel.
From the Bear Cove ferry terminal, take Bear Cove Road. Turn left onto Highway 19,
left onto Byng, left onto Beaver Harbour, and left onto Peel.
• Three rooms. One person $50–60; two people $65–70. Queen-sized bed; twin beds.
Shared guest bathroom. Additional person $15–20.
• A B&B with hardwood floors, antiques, family heirlooms, local art, and a view of the ocean.
Guest entrance. Afternoon tea is served in a guest sitting room. Guest rooms have flowers,
robes, chocolates on pillows, bottled water, hair dryers, curling irons, and toiletries. Ten minutes' drive from downtown Port Hardy and ferries to Prince Rupert. Twenty minutes from a
golf course. In the area are orca whale tours and forestry tours, caving, scuba diving, kayaking, windsurfing, and lake, stream, and ocean fishing. Host arranges shuttle service from and
to the Queen of the North and Discovery Coast ferries. Breakfast is served on fine china in
the dining room. Off-street parking. Guests travelling on overnight ferries may leave vehicles
at the B&B. **In the hosts' own words:** "You'll enjoy your stay with us, because we treat our
guests like royalty."

Imperial Eagle Lodge

Jim and Karen Levis
Mail: Box 59
Bamfield, BC V0R 1B0
(250) 728-3430 Fax: (250) 728-3430
E-mail: impeagl@cedar.alberni.net
Web site: http://travel.bc.ca/i/imp-eagle/

• From Port Alberni, $1\frac{1}{2}$ hours on logging roads. From Duncan, $2\frac{1}{2}$ hours on logging roads.

• Two rooms in a lodge and two rooms in a duplex cottage. One person $55–75; two people $85–115. Four twin beds; queen-sized bed or twin beds; queen-sized bed and one twin bed; double bed and one twin bed. Private bathrooms and ensuite bathrooms with showers. Additional person $30.

Self-contained two-bedroom cottage (sleeps four). $125–155. Twin beds in each bedroom.

Sport fishing charters. Kayak rentals.

Meal plans available.

• A country-style lodge and cottage with a garden and a view of the harbour, on the west side of Bamfield Inlet, which is in Barkley Sound. Hosts arrange sport fishing packages, guided charters, guided marine tours, and kayaking and hiking excursions. Guest dining and living area in the lodge has a fireplace, books, cards, a cribbage board, and a view of the harbour. Deck with hot tub. Cottage has a kitchen, a dining and sitting area, and a harbour view. Guest rooms have private entrances. Two of the guest rooms are in a duplex cottage adjacent to the lodge and share a veranda. Three of the guest rooms look out onto a garden. One of the guest rooms has a sink in the room and an ensuite bathroom. Full breakfast. Free parking in a lot on the east side of the harbour; hosts arrange ferry transportation across the harbour to the B&B. Reservations recommended. Cancellation notice thirty days; in August, sixty days. Visa, MasterCard. Adult oriented; children over eleven welcome in the cottage. No pets. Smoking outdoors. **In the hosts' own words:** "Whether you are looking for an outdoor adventure or a quiet retreat, we are pleased to accommodate your West Coast vacation getaway. Come and experience our special brand of hospitality."

The Tide's Inn on Duffin Cove B&B

Val and James Sloman
160 Arnet Road
Mail: Box 325
Tofino, BC V0R 2Z0
(250) 725-3765 Fax: (250) 725-3325
E-mail: tidesinn@island.net
Web site: http://www.vancouverisland-bc.com/TidesInnBB/

• In Tofino, turn left onto First Street. Turn right onto Arnet Road. The B&B is a brown house, the first house after the Y in the road.

• Rooms. In summer (June 15 to October 15) and on long weekends, one person $80, two people $85–90. In off-season, one person $65, two people $75–85. Queen-sized bed. Ensuite bathrooms.

Two-bedroom suite. In summer (June 15 to October 15) and on long weekends, two people $90. In winter, two people $70. In spring and fall, two people $80. Queen-sized bed, twin beds, and pull-out couch. Additional person $20.

In summer and on long weekends, minimum stay two nights.

• A house on Duffin Cove, with views of the cove, Duffin Passage, and the mountains and islands of Clayoquot Sound. Shoreline with tidal pools. Ten minutes' walk from Tonquin Beach, a sandy beach protected from the open ocean by Wickaninnish Island. Five to fifteen minutes' drive from other beaches in Tofino and Pacific Rim National Park and Long Beach. Ten minutes' walk from the village centre's galleries, restaurants, and charters and tours including whale watching, kayaking, hot springs, Clayoquot Sound harbour, and Meares Island hiking. Guest rooms face the ocean and have private entrances, fridges, and facilities for making coffee and tea. One of the guest rooms has a Jacuzzi. Another guest room has a private balcony. Two-bedroom suite has a sitting room with fireplace, pool table, TV, coffee bar, and fridge. Decks and guest hot tub. Full breakfast includes baked goods, a hot entrée, fruit, juice, and fresh-ground coffee. Cancellation notice three days. Children over ten welcome. No pets; cat in residence. Smoking on decks. **In the hosts' own words:** "We welcome you to Tofino and our home. We'll help in every way we can to make sure your visit to Clayoquot Sound is a comfortable and memorable one."

Midori's Place B&B

Midori Matley
370 Gibson Street
Mail: Box 582
Tofino, BC V0R 2Z0
(250) 725-2203 Fax: (250) 725-2204

• Three rooms. In summer, two people $65, three people $75. In winter, two people $45, three people $65. Queen-sized bed; twin beds. Ensuite and private bathrooms.
• A quiet B&B, two blocks from the centre of Tofino. Ten minutes' walk from Tonquin Park's hiking trails and Tonquin Beach. Full breakfast. Japanese spoken. No pets. Nonsmokers.

Wilp Gybuu (Wolf House) B&B

Wendy and Ralph Burgess
311 Leighton Way
Mail: Box 396
Tofino, BC V0R 2Z0
(250) 725-2330 Fax: (250) 725-1205
E-mail: wilpgybu@island.net
Web site: http://www.vancouverisland-bc.
com/WilpGybuuBB/

• In Tofino, turn left onto First Street. Turn right onto Arnet Road. Turn left onto Leighton Way. The B&B is the first driveway on the right.
• Three rooms. One person $70–80; two people $80–90. Queen-sized bed; twin beds. Ensuite bathrooms. Minimum stay of two nights may apply. Off-season rates.
• A West Coast–style contemporary cedar house with a view of Duffin Passage and islands in Clayoquot Sound. Within walking distance of restaurants, galleries, kayaking, whale watching, sea plane tours, hot springs tours, Tonquin Beach, and buses to Nanaimo. Fifteen minutes' drive from golf and Pacific Rim National Park's beaches and rainforest trails. Guest sitting room with TV, books, piano, and CD player. Guest refreshment area with cookies and facilities for making coffee and tea. Guest rooms have sitting areas. Two of the guest rooms have fireplaces and private entrances. Pickup from bus and plane. One of the hosts is a Native artist. Coffee or tea is delivered to guest rooms before breakfast. Full breakfast is served in the dining room, which has a view of the inside waters of Duffin Passage. Reservations recommended. Cancellation notice seventy-two hours. Visa, MasterCard. Adult oriented. No pets; cat in residence. No smoking. **In the hosts' own words:** "We welcome you to our home with warm hospitality and invite you to share the extraordinary beauty of Tofino and Pacific Rim National Park in all seasons."

Ocean on the Beach Retreat—Ch-ahayis

Sandra Snetsinger
1377 Thornberg
Mail: Box 629
Tofino, BC V0R 2Z0
(250) 725-2710
Web site: http://www.islandnet.com/~chahayis/

• Three hours from Nanaimo.
• House (sleeps four). $150. Queen-sized bed, twin beds, and sofa bed. Private
bathroom. Three-bedroom house (sleeps six). $250. Two queen-sized beds,
twin beds, sofa bed. One and a half bathrooms.
Breakfast not included.
• Two two-storey houses on the ocean joined by a covered walkway and surrounded by two-hundred-year-old spruce trees. Both houses are a few steps from a beach and have ocean views, kitchens, wood stoves, laundry rooms, and outside deck showers. One house sleeps four and has a bath and a shower. The other house sleeps six and has a Jacuzzi tub. Five minutes from Tofino, Pacific Rim National Park, whale watching, kayaking, hotsprings, and hiking in a rainforest. Five minutes' walk from a restaurant. **In the hosts' own words:** "Cedar walls inside both our houses bring the West Coast experience into the comfort of the restful interiors. Our retreat on beautiful Chesterman Beach is ideal for weddings on the beach and surfers' holidays."

Mearesview B&B

Kathy Townsend and Judy Webster
607 Pfeiffer Crescent
Mail: Box 634
Tofino, BC V0R 2Z0
(250) 725-2961
Web site: http://www.bbcanada.com/1404.html

• From Tofino's town centre, take Campbell Street south for 250 metres. Turn right onto Lone Cone Road and right onto Pfeiffer.
• Room. $80. Double bed. Ensuite bathroom with shower.
Suite. $95. Queen-sized bed. Ensuite bathroom.
Extended stay rates. Open Easter to mid-October.
• A B&B with a view of Meares Island and Browning Passage, within walking distance of restaurants, galleries, and shops and of charters and tours for whale watching, kayaking, fishing, visiting a hot spring, and hiking on Meares Island and other islands. Near canoeing and saltwater and freshwater fishing. Ten minutes' drive from beaches, Pacific Rim National Park, walking and hiking trails, a golf course, and an airport. Guest rooms have coffee makers and coffee. Beds have down duvets. Suite has a private entrance. Guest sitting room with TV, fridge, and selection of teas. Continental breakfast of coffee, tea, juice, fresh fruit, cereal, and homemade granola and baked goods is served in the breakfast nook. Reservations recommended. Cancellation notice seventy-two hours. Cash, travellers' cheques. Adult oriented. No pets; small dog in residence. Smoke-free environment. **In the hosts' own words:** "Our B&B provides you with a home away from home while you experience the wonders of the west coast and Clayoquot Sound."

Paddler's Inn B&B

Dorothy Baert
320 Main Street
Mail: Box 620
Tofino, BC V0R 2Z0
The Tofino Sea-Kayaking Company
makes reservations for the B&B
and can be contacted as follows:
(250) 725-4222 Fax: (250) 725-2070
Toll-free: 1-800-863-4664
Toll-free fax: 1-800-863-4664
E-mail: paddlers@island.net
Web site: http://www.island.net/~paddlers

• In downtown Tofino.
• Rooms. Two people $58. Shared bathroom. Breakfast ingredients supplied.
Self-contained suite. Two people $80. Breakfast not provided.
Sea kayak tours, courses, and rentals available.
• A B&B on the ocean, with a view of Meares Island and Tofino harbour, in a building that was originally the Tofino Hotel. Guest rooms and suite are on the second floor. A store on the main floor sells kayaking equipment and camping items. Suite has a kitchen and a deck with a view of the harbour. Self-serve Continental breakfast is provided for guests staying in the rooms. **In the hosts' own words:** "We offer attractive and comfortable accommodation in a character building with a sea kayaking store, a bookstore, and an espresso bar."

Kitsilano Point B&B

Jennifer and Larry Barr
1936 McNicoll Avenue
Vancouver, BC V6J 1A6
(604) 738-9576

• Near Cornwall Avenue and Burrard Street.
• Two rooms. One person $70–80; two people $80–90. Twin beds. Washbasins and showers in the rooms and a shared guest toilet. Additional person $40.
Off-season rates $10 less, October to March.

• A 1911 house within walking distance of a beach and pool at Kitsilano Beach Park and Vanier Park's museums, planetarium, and observatory. The Vancouver Aquatic Centre and Granville Island market can be reached by a pedestrian ferry a couple of blocks from the B&B. Three to seven blocks from a store and restaurants. Three blocks from a bus stop. Five minutes' drive from downtown. One of the guest rooms has a fireplace. Living room with TV. Garden. Hot breakfast is served from 7:30 to 8:30 a.m. Check-in after 4:00 p.m. or earlier by arrangement; check-out until 10:30 a.m. Some French spoken. Not suitable for pre-school children or for pets. Nonsmokers preferred. **In the hosts' own words:** "Our friendly home is conveniently located for attending the annual fireworks competition, the children's festival, and the Bard on the Beach Shakespeare festival."

Jolie Maison

Dimka and Louis Gheyle
1888 West Third Avenue
Vancouver, BC V6J 1K8
(604) 730-8010 Fax: (604) 730-8045
E-mail: skelly@direct.ca

• One block west of Burrard Street. One block north of Fourth Avenue.
• Four rooms. One person $70–80; two people $85–135. King-sized bed; queen-sized bed. Ensuite, private, and shared guest bathrooms. Additional person $20.
Off-season and extended stay rates.

• A restored 1901 house in Kitsilano, four blocks from Kitsilano Beach Park and one block from shops and restaurants. Ten minutes' drive from downtown, Stanley Park, and Granville Island. Fifteen minutes' drive from the University of British Columbia. Around the corner from a bus stop. Sitting room with fireplace and TV. One of the guest rooms has a Jacuzzi tub and a walk-in shower. The other guest rooms have views of mountains. Breakfast is served in the dining room. Deposit of one night's rate required to hold reservation. Cancellation notice three days. French, Dutch, and German spoken. Smoking on the porch. **In the hosts' own words:** "We are located in Kitsilano, Vancouver's truly original and trendy neighbourhood. Put your feet up in front of the fire to read a book, watch TV, or visit with other guests. The relaxed and tranquil atmosphere of our charming B&B will make you feel right at home."

Maple House B&B

Fumi and Brian Pendleton
1533 Maple Street
Vancouver, BC V6J 3S2
(604) 739-5833 Fax: (604) 739-5877
E-mail: maplebb@portal.ca
Web site: http://www.vancouver-bc.com/MapleHouseBB/

• Five minutes from downtown Vancouver, across the Burrard Street bridge.
• Rooms. One person $70–110; two people $80–120. Queen-sized bed; double bed; twin beds. Ensuite, private, and shared guest bathrooms.
Suite. Four people $150–195. Queen-sized bed and double bed. Ensuite bathroom.
Off-season and extended stay rates.
• A restored 1900 house, one block from Kitsilano Beach Park and ten minutes' walk from Granville Island's shops and restaurants. Half a block from buses to downtown, Chinatown, and the University of British Columbia. Two blocks from cafés, bistros, and restaurants. Guest rooms have down duvets and either European antiques or contemporary West Coast–style furnishings. Breakfast is served in the dining room, which has antiques and a stained glass window. Cancellation notice seven days. Cash, traveller's cheques, JCB cards. Japanese spoken. Children over twelve welcome. No pets. Nonsmoking house. **In the hosts' own words:** "Our heritage house is in a great location—enjoy a stroll to the beach and then dinner and drinks at a nearby restaurant. Everything for the tourist or business traveller is at hand."

View of the Bay B&B

Helen Kritharis
2588 Cornwall Avenue
Vancouver, BC V6K 1C2
(604) 731-3290 Fax: (604) 739-1938

• In Kitsilano, at Cornwall Avenue and Trafalgar
Street.
• Room and one suite. $95–125. Double bed;
queen-sized bed and twin beds. Private bath-
rooms. Additional person $25.
• A B&B with a view of English Bay and Stanley
Park, across the street from an ocean beach and a park with an outdoor pool. A few minutes'
drive from the University of British Columbia and downtown. Within walking distance of
Granville Island, Stanley Park, Jericho Beach, restaurants in the Kitsilano Beach area, and
shopping and dining on West Fourth Avenue. Near the Vancouver Museum and Planetarium.
Suite is on the main floor and has a sitting area, a TV, a private entrance, a loft bedroom and
access to a roof patio that has a view of mountains, ocean, and city. Guest room is on the
second floor and has a deck with a view of mountains, ocean, and city. Nonsmoking house.
In the hosts' own words: "Enjoy our new, comfortable, contemporary house, tasty breakfasts, and gracious hospitality. When you stay here, Vancouver is at your doorstep."

Walnut House

Liz Harris and Mike Graham
1350 Walnut Street
Vancouver, BC V6J 3R3
(604) 739-6941 Fax: (604) 739-6942
E-mail: walnut@direct.ca
Web site: http://www.vancouver-bc.com/
  WalnutHouseBB/index.html

• An arts and crafts–style house modernized in
1996, on a quiet tree-lined street in Kitsilano
Point, a neighbourhood near downtown. Guest
rooms have ensuite bathrooms, books, TVs, and clock radios. Guest living room with fireplace. Fridge and microwave. Front porch. Two blocks from sandy beaches, tennis courts,
and a heated, outdoor swimming pool. Near walking, jogging, and biking paths. Near the
Vancouver City Museum, a planetarium, the Vancouver Maritime Museum, and the Vancouver School of Music. Thirty minutes by bus from the University of British Columbia. A
few blocks from four-star and fast-food restaurants. Within walking distance of shops, art
galleries, cinemas, and theatres. Thirty minutes' walk through a waterfront park from
Granville Island's public market. Thirty minutes' walk or ten minutes' bus ride from downtown. A foot-passenger ferry crosses the bay to downtown every day in the summer and on
weekends in the winter. Full breakfast. Cash, personal cheques, Visa, MasterCard. Adult oriented. No pets. Smoke-free house; smoking on the covered porch. **In the hosts' own words:**
"Our B&B is romantic, friendly, quiet, and convenient. We will be delighted to help you
relax and explore our city."

Heritage Harbour B&B

Debra Horner
1838 Ogden Avenue
Vancouver, BC V6J 1A1
(604) 736-0809 Fax: (604) 736-0074
E-mail: dhorner@direct.ca
Web site: http://www.vancouver-bc.com/HeritageHarbour

• Five minutes from downtown Vancouver.

• Two rooms. Two people $120–175. Queen-sized bed. Private bathrooms.

• A traditional-style house in Kitsilano Point across the street from a beach, with views of the ocean, heritage boats, mountains, and downtown. Five minutes' walk along the waterfront from tennis courts and a heated outdoor swimming pool. Two minutes' walk along the waterfront from Vanier Park's museum, planetarium, observatory, and moorage for heritage boats. Fifteen minutes' walk from Granville Island, boutique shopping, and fine dining restaurants on Fourth Avenue. Five minutes by bus, or fifteen minutes by small passenger ferry, or thirty minutes by foot from downtown, Stanley Park, and English Bay beaches. Fifteen minutes' drive from the University of British Columbia. One of the guest rooms has a view of the ocean, mountains, and downtown. The other guest room has French doors that lead to a private veranda overlooking a garden. Guest living room with oak wainscoting, TV, VCR, stereo, marble fireplace, and a view of the city and the ocean. Full breakfast is served in the dining room, which has a view of the harbour. Low-fat and low-cholesterol diets are accommodated. Check-in after 3:00 p.m.; check-out until 11:00 a.m. Visa. Not suitable for small children. Not suitable for pets. Smoking in front garden sitting area. **In the hosts' own words:** "We encourage guests to enter our home as visitors and to leave as friends. Enjoy our B&B's quiet, seaside location and the convenience of being near downtown."

Ogden Point B&B

Shirley and Karen Wheatcroft
1982 Ogden Avenue
Vancouver, BC V6J 1A2
(604) 736-4336 or (604) 738-2421
Fax: (604) 738-7461
E-mail: wheat@axionet.com
Web site: http://www.bbcanada.com/1890.html

• On Kitsilano Point, across the street from the
Vancouver Maritime Museum.
• Three rooms. One person $80–140. Two people
$90–180. Queen-sized bed; double bed. Ensuite and two shared guest bathrooms.
• A B&B with a view of the ocean, a few minutes by car or ten minutes by bus from down-town and across the street from the Vancouver Maritime Museum and Kitsilano Beach Park. Five minutes' walk from restaurants, the Vancouver Museum, and the Pacific Space Centre. Fifteen minutes' walk along the waterfront from Granville Island's public market, restau-rants, and boutiques. Guest rooms have TVs and telephones. Guest room with a queen-sized bed and ensuite bathroom has a balcony with a view of English Bay. Continental breakfast includes homemade muffins, scones, jam, and jelly. Adult oriented. No pets; black Labrador dog in residence. Nonsmoking. **In the hosts' own words:** "Enjoy our elegant heritage house, a few steps from Kitsilano Beach, in the heart of Vancouver."

Mickey's Kits Beach Chalet B&B

John Dewart
2142 and 2146 West First Avenue
Vancouver, BC V6K 1E8
(604) 739-3342 Fax: (604) 739-3342
Toll-free: 1-888-739-3342
E-mail: mickeys@direct.ca

• On West First Avenue, between Arbutus and
Yew.
• Six rooms. In summer, two people $95–130. In
winter, two people $75–120. King-sized bed and
pull-out couch; twin beds side by side with king-sized bedding and pull-out couch; queen-sized bed. Ensuite and shared guest bathrooms. Weekly and monthly rates.
• A B&B two blocks from Kitsilano Beach Park, with a garden, south-facing decks, and some guest rooms that have views of the North Shore mountains. Two of the guest rooms have views of the ocean. Five minutes' walk from Kitsilano Beach Park. Five minutes' drive from downtown. Two minutes' walk from restaurants on Yew Street. Three blocks from a shopping district on Fourth Avenue. Three minutes' walk from bus routes. Fifteen minutes' walk from a planetarium, a maritime museum, and Granville Island's public market. Ten minutes' drive from the University of British Columbia, Stanley Park, Vancouver General Hospital, city hall, and golf courses. Guest room with a king-sized bed has a fireplace. Each guest room has a TV and one or more of the following: a private garden, a south-facing deck, a view of the mountains, a private entrance, a pull-out couch, a fridge, or a coffee maker. Continental breakfast is served in the kitchen or in the garden at guests' convenience. Two-car garage and street parking. Smoking on patios. **In the hosts' own words:** "We have a spe-cial B&B in a special location, with beautifully landscaped private gardens and terraces. We are ideally situated for both business and pleasure travellers. After one stay, you'll want to come back many times."

Kenya Court Oceanfront Guest House

Dr. and Mrs. H. R. Williams
2230 Cornwall Avenue
Vancouver, BC V6K 1B5
(604) 738-7085

• Five self-contained suites. Two people $90–140. King-sized bed; queen-sized bed; twin beds. Ensuite bathrooms.

• A three-storey building across the street from Kitsilano Beach Park, which has an Olympic-sized outdoor heated saltwater swimming pool.

Seaside paths in Kitsilano Beach Park lead to Granville Island, a maritime museum, and a planetarium. One-thousand-square-foot self-contained suites have private entrances and views of water, city, and mountains. Five minutes' walk from tennis courts and ethnic restaurants. Ten minutes by bus from downtown. Near Jericho Beach, boutiques on Fourth Avenue, and the University of British Columbia's Museum of Anthropology. Full breakfast is served in a rooftop solarium that has a view. Check-in times are flexible. No smoking. **In the hosts' own words:** "We offer a heritage building in one of the best locations in Vancouver."

English Country Garden B&B

Carol Egan
3466 West Fifteenth Avenue
Vancouver, BC V6K 1X2
(604) 737-2526 Fax: (604) 737-2750
E-mail: english@uniserve.com

• Rooms. Queen-sized bed; twin beds (or twin beds side by side with king-sized bedding). Ensuite and private bathrooms.

• A B&B with a view of the North Shore mountains, the ocean, and the city skyline, on a tree-lined street in a residential neighbourhood. Near downtown, transit, beaches, parks, and the University of British Columbia. Antiques and art from around the world. Guest sitting room with TV and stereo. Guest rooms have sitting areas, TVs, and telephones. English garden and deck. Full breakfast includes an entrée cooked to order. Two cats and a dog in residence. **In the hosts' own words:** "Enjoy our English hospitality and home comforts while visiting our lovely city."

The Cherub Inn

Vivian Vasarajs and Alexandre Ravkov
2546 West Sixth Avenue
Vancouver, BC V6K 1W5
(604) 733-3166 Fax: (604) 733-3106
E-mail: cherub_inn@bc.sympatico.ca
Web site: http://www.vancouver-bc.com/ CherubInnBB/

• Ten minutes from downtown.

• Four rooms. In summer, one person $120–150, two people $135–165. In winter, one person $90–130, two people $99–145. Queen-sized bed; queen-sized bed and pull-out twin bed. Ensuite bathrooms.

• A restored and updated 1913 Craftsman-style house on a quiet residential street, with anaglyphic wallpaper, stained glass windows, high ceilings, and wood panelling. Belgian and English antiques, designer linen, feather beds, and Persian carpets. Fireplaces in guest living room and one of the guest rooms. One of the guest rooms has a sleigh-style bed and an ensuite bathroom with burgundy clawfoot tub. Some of the guest rooms have TVs and VCRs. Hair dryers available. Chocolates and morning papers provided. Covered front porch. Two blocks from fine dining restaurants and shopping on Fourth Avenue. Five minutes from beaches and Granville Island. Ten minutes from the University of British Columbia. Near bus route. Full breakfast is served on English bone china. Off-street parking. Children over twelve welcome; younger children by arrangement. **In the hosts' own words:** "We've combined our experience as an architect and as a former diplomat to create an elegant and inviting B&B. Our B&B is popular with international business travellers and as a romantic getaway and is suitable for memorable special occasion visits. Come and be pampered."

Penny Farthing Inn

Lyn Hainstock
2855 West Sixth Avenue
Vancouver, BC V6K 1X2
(604) 739-9002 Fax: (604) 739-9004
E-mail: farthing@uniserve.com
Web site: http://www.vancouver-bc.com/pennyfarthing

- Half a block west of MacDonald Street.
- Two rooms. In summer (May 15 to October 15), one person $85, two people $110. In winter (October 16 to May 14), one person $65, two people $95. Double bed; twin beds (or twin beds side by side with king-sized bedding). Ensuite and private bathrooms.
Two suites. In summer (May 15 to October 15), one person $105–125, two people $150–165. In winter (October 16 to May 14), one person $95–105, two people $125–135. Queen-sized bed and double sofa bed. Bathrooms in suites.
- A renovated 1912 house with stained glass windows, wood floors, and wood panelling. Within walking distance of Kitsilano Beach Park, cafés, tennis courts, shops, restaurants, and buses. Five minutes' drive from downtown and the University of British Columbia. Twenty minutes from the airport. Guest rooms and suites have telephones. Suites have gas fireplaces, fridges, stereos, CD players, and facilities for making tea and coffee. One of the suites is on the top floor and has skylights, a view of English Bay and mountains, a queen-sized brass bed, and a sitting room with sofa bed, TV, and VCR. The other suite is on the second floor and has a view of mountains, a pine four-post queen-sized bed, a sitting room with double sofa bed, a TV, a VCR, and a veranda overlooking the garden. One of the guest rooms has a pine four-post double bed and a porch overlooking the front garden. The other guest room has a view of the back garden. Guest living room with answering machine, books, games, TV, VCR, 150 videos, and CD player. Guest fridge. Guest business room with computer, scanner, printer, e-mail connection, fax machine, and photocopier. Refreshment area with tea, coffee, and cookies. Full breakfast, including baked goods, jam, jelly, fruit, and a hot entrée, is served in the dining room or on a brick patio in an English country garden. Cancellation notice fifteen days. Children over twelve welcome. Four cats in residence (the cats are not allowed in the guest rooms or suites). **In the hosts' own words:** "We offer warm hospitality and a delicious breakfast in a beautiful heritage setting."

Graeme's House

Ms. Graeme Elizabeth Webster
2735 Waterloo Street
Vancouver, BC V6R 3J1
(604) 732-1488
Web site: http://www.vancouver-bc.com/GraemesHouse

● Near West Broadway and Alma Street.
● Two rooms. One person $65; two people $75. Queen-sized bed; twin beds.
Shared guest bathroom. Additional person $20. Child under 12 $15. Additional
bed available. Rates are based on stays of two or more nights; additional charge
of $5 for one-night stays.
● A renovated 1926 cottage-style house with gardens and a deck, on a quiet street, one kilometre from Jericho Beach and a few minutes by bus or car from the University of British
Columbia, an aquatic centre, Granville Island, and downtown. Near shops on Broadway and
shops and services at Tenth Avenue and Sasamat Street. Within two blocks of restaurants,
shops, and a movie theatre. Living room with fireplace, kitchen/family room with TV, and
roof garden. Country décor. One of the guest rooms has a stained glass bay window. The
other room has access to a private deck. Due to the hosts' work schedules, guests sometimes
help themselves to breakfast. No pets; cat in residence. Smoking outdoors. **In the hosts' own
words:** "We welcome you to country-cottage charm in the city, great conversation, homemade muffins, and comfortable beds."

Collingwood Manor B&B

Stefanie and Howie Todd
1631 Collingwood Street
Vancouver, BC V6R 3K1
(604) 731-1107
Toll-free from within North America: 1-888-699-1631
E-mail: colmanor@direct.ca
Web site: http://www.bbcanada.com/1891.html

• In Kitsilano, between Alma and MacDonald streets.
• Two rooms. $110. Queen-sized bed. Shared guest bathroom.
Honeymoon suite. $165. King-sized bed. Ensuite bathroom.
• A restored 1912 house with a modern interior, one block from an ocean beach and three blocks from Jericho Park. Guest living room on the upper floor with hardwood floors, vaulted ceilings, a fireplace, two chesterfields, armchairs, hot and cold beverages, books, magazines, and a view of the ocean, mountains, and the city. Near kayak, bicycle, and windsurfing rental shops. Four blocks from public transit. Five minutes' drive from downtown. Guest rooms are on the main floor and have Egyptian cotton linen and down comforters. Honeymoon suite has a king-sized bed, a three-sided fireplace, and an ensuite bathroom with two sinks, a makeup table, and a two-person Jacuzzi. Breakfast includes fresh-squeezed juice, a fresh fruit plate, homemade muffins or scones, scrambled eggs with lox and cream cheese, French toast or pancakes, and coffee or tea; entrées change daily. Cancellation notice two days. Visa, MasterCard. Adult oriented; children welcome by arrangement. Smoke-free environment. **In the hosts' own words:** "Our beautifully restored heritage house, which has a sophisticated contemporary interior, is in one of Vancouver's most desirable and safe neighborhoods, a few blocks from first-class beaches and parks and a five-minute drive from major attractions—a B&B that is a delightful retreat."

B&B by Locarno Beach

Elke Holm
4505 Langara Avenue
Vancouver, BC V6R 1C9
Cel: (604) 341-4975

• Ten minutes from downtown.
• Rooms. One person from $55; two people from $65. Queen-sized bed and twin sofa bed. Ensuite bathrooms. Additional person $25.
• A B&B on a quiet side street in West Point Grey, across the street from a city park and a few minues' walk from a two-kilometre sandy ocean beach and seaside trail. The beach and trail have views of the North Shore and Howe Sound mountains, downtown, and Stanley Park. The B&B is within walking distance of tennis courts, boat rentals, and a beachside cafeteria. Five minutes' drive from the University of British Columbia and a public golf course. Near a bus route. Twenty minutes by bus or ten minutes by car from downtown. Guest rooms have TVs. Telephone in hallway. Full breakfast is served in the dining room. Cash, traveller's cheques. German and some French spoken. Nonsmoking guests. **In the hosts' own words:** "Enjoy our resortlike setting, within minutes of downtown Vancouver."

Dunbar Area B&B

3716 West Thirty-seventh Avenue
Vancouver, BC V6N 2V9
(604) 263-5428

• Half a block west of Dunbar Street, on the south side of Thirty-seventh Avenue.

• Two rooms. One person $65; two people $85. Twin beds (or twin beds side by side with king-sized bedding); double bed. Private and shared bathrooms. Rates are based on stays of two or more nights; additional charge of $5 for one-night stays.

Open June to September.

• A B&B on a tree-lined street, half a block from a bus stop and within walking distance of restaurants, a theatre, shops, riding clubs, golf courses, and the University of British Columbia Endowment Lands. Twenty minutes from the Vancouver International Airport, downtown, the University of British Columbia, Stanley Park, Queen Elizabeth Park, Dr. Sun Yat-Sen Classical Chinese Garden, the VanDusen Gardens, the Nitobe Japanese Gardens, the University of British Columbia Botanical Gardens, and ocean beaches. Guest rooms are on the main floor. Beds have cotton linen and heavy cotton spreads or down duvets. Guest room with a double bed has a private bathroom with skylight. Hardwood floors. Guest living room on the main floor has a fireplace, a piano, a games table, and a TV. Guests are requested to bring clean sports socks or slippers. Deck with view of English and organic gardens. Breakfast, including organic ingredients, free-range eggs, and homemade baked goods, is served in the dining room, which opens onto the deck. Diets are accommodated. Street parking in front of the B&B. Cash, traveller's cheques. Adult oriented; children over eleven welcome by arrangement. No pets. No smoking. **In the hosts' own words:** "Enjoy pleasant walks around the neighbourhood and the quiet comfort of our bright, beautifully renovated, classic bungalow."

Johnson Heritage House B&B

Sandy and Ron Johnson
2278 West Thirty-fourth Avenue
Vancouver, BC V6M 1G6
(604) 266-4175 Fax: (604) 266-4175
E-mail: johnsonBB@bc.sympatico.ca
Web site: http://www.vancouver-bc.com/JohnsonHouseBB/

• Near West Thirty-third Avenue and Arbutus Street.
• Three rooms. One person $65–135; two people $75–145. King-sized bed;
queen-sized bed; twin beds. Ensuite and shared guest bathrooms.
• A 1920s Craftsman-style house on a quiet tree-lined street, with interior woodwork and antique furniture including iron and brass beds, Persian carpets, carousel horses, and gramophones. Guest living room with oak floors, French doors, brick fireplace, TV, and VCR. Telephones, hair dryers, and toiletries in guest rooms. Guide books, maps, list of recommended restaurants, and a weekly-events calendar. Covered front porch with a partial view of Grouse Mountain. Rhododendron and rock garden with stone sculptures. Five minutes' walk from buses, restaurants, shops, and banks. Five to fifteen minutes from airport, downtown, ocean beaches, Stanley Park, Granville Island, Queen Elizabeth Park, the University of British Columbia, the Museum of Anthropology at UBC, and the VanDusen Gardens. Breakfast, including coffee, tea, juice, fruit, a hot entrée, and homemade muffins, scones, or cinnamon buns, is served from 8:15 to 9:30 a.m. Cash, cheques. Children over twelve welcome. No pets. Smoke-free. **In the hosts' own words:** "Our B&B offers comfortable beds, helpful hosts, satisfying breakfasts, and a wonderful neighbourhood—what you should expect from a quality B&B."

Heather Cottage

David and Moyra Turner
5425 Trafalgar Street
Vancouver, BC V6N 1C1
(604) 261-1442 Fax: (604) 261-7104
Web site: http://www.bcbandb.com

• Two rooms. One person or two people $85. Queen-sized bed; twin beds. Shared guest bathroom. Off-season rates.
Room. Two people $125; four people $150. Queen-sized bed and twin beds. Private bathroom. Crib and foam mattress available.

• A 1935 cottage-style house, on a quiet street, with leaded and stained glass, hardwood floors, family heirlooms, Scottish furnishings, and British India rugs. One of the guest rooms is the only room on the upper floor and has a skylight, a TV, a VCR, a washbasin in the room, and a double shower. Another guest room has a TV, a desk, and a walk-in closet. The third guest room has a Welsh wardrobe and dresser, stained glass, Wedgwood pottery, and a view of the front garden. Robes and turn-down service. Guest sitting room with fireplace, piano, books, TV, VCR, and telephone. Hot tub on a deck with flowers, chaises, umbrellas, and tables. Twenty-five minutes by bus from downtown. Within walking distance of restaurants, banks, churches, and stores. Near three botanical gardens and buses to the University of British Columbia. One of the hosts plays the piano, and guests are welcome to join in a singsong around the fireplace in the guest sitting room. Early morning tea or coffee and biscuits are served in guest rooms by request. Breakfast, including homemade bread and other baked goods, fresh-ground coffee, and a hot entrée, is served in the dining room, which has a fireplace. Diets accommodated. On Sundays in summer, an English breakfast, including sausages, bacon, eggs, champagne, and orange juice (or a choice of alternatives), is served at Spanish Banks, an ocean beach; the hosts bring kites and frisbees. Continental breakfast, including juice, fruit, muffins, and cereal, is served at the B&B before the guests and hosts leave for the beach at about 9:00 a.m. Street parking available. Pickup from plane or bus; $15 for guests staying less than three nights. Credit cards for reservations; cash (U.S. funds accepted), cheques. Smoking on the lower patio. **In the hosts' own words:** "We welcome you to our character house with a country atmosphere."

Chelsea Cottage B&B

Kim and Bob Jess
2143 West 46th Avenue
Vancouver, BC V6M 2L2
(604) 266-2681 Fax: (604) 266-7540
E-mail: chelsea@bc.sympatico.ca
Web site: http://www.vancouver-bc.com/chelseacottage

• Near West Forty-first Avenue and West Boulevard (Arbutus Street). Half a block west of West Boulevard.
• Four rooms. In summer, one person $85–110, two people $95–120. In winter, one person $65–90, two people $75–100. Queen-sized bed; twin beds. Ensuite and shared guest bathrooms. Additional person $20.
• A 1925 character house on a quiet tree-lined street in Kerrisdale, ten minutes' drive from downtown, the airport, ocean beaches, the University of British Columbia, Granville Island, and the VanDusen Gardens. Within walking distance of restaurants and shopping. Half a block from buses to downtown. Guest rooms have ceiling fans, telephones, TVs, and robes. Guest sitting room with fireplace, CD player, reading material, juice, soft drinks, and facilities for making coffee and tea. Full breakfast, including fresh fruit, homemade baked goods, and a cooked entrée, is served in the dining room. Street parking. Visa, MasterCard. Adult oriented; children over twelve welcome. No pets; pet boarding nearby. Smoke-free environment. **In the hosts' own words:** "We invite you to relax in the guest sitting room after your busy day and, in the morning, enjoy a gourmet breakfast."

Arbutus House B&B

Gus and Lani Mitchell
4470 Maple Crescent
Vancouver, BC V6J 4B3
(604) 738-6432 Fax: (604) 738-6433
E-mail: gumitche@unix.infoserve.net
Web site: http://www.triple1.com/ca/bc/cabc005.htm

- West of Granville Street, between Thirty-third Avenue and King Edward Avenue, at Twenty-ninth Avenue and Maple Crescent.
- Rooms. One person $85–130; two people $95–140. Queen-sized bed. Ensuite and shared guest bathrooms. Additional twin beds available.
Suite. One person $145; two people $155. Queen-sized bed and one twin bed. Ensuite bathroom.
Additional person $25. Off-season rates. May to October, minimum stay two nights. Open January 15 to November 30.
- A 1920s character house in Shaughnessy, with leaded windows, oak floors, cove ceilings, fireplaces, antiques, contemporary furnishings, and art. Guest living room with fireplace, antique pine armoire, and tourist information. Den with TV, VCR, books, and collection of old trains and toys. Guest rooms have sitting areas. One of the guest rooms has a private deck. Suite is six hundred square feet and has a TV, a sitting area with gas fireplace, and an ensuite bathroom. Decks and flower gardens. Fifteen minutes' drive from downtown shopping, Stanley Park, airport, beaches, the University of British Columbia, and General Motors Place. Two blocks from public transit. Within walking distance of the VanDusen Gardens, Queen Elizabeth Park, and restaurants. Tea, coffee, lemonade, and baked goods are served in the afternoon. Chocolates on the pillows, sherry, robes, hair dryers, and slippers. Full breakfast is served in a traditional dining room. Off-street parking. Cash, traveller's cheques. Children over twelve welcome. No pets; cat in residence. Smoking outdoors. **In the hosts' own words:** "Our B&B offers a great location, elegant interiors, fragrant gardens, delicious breakfasts, and smiling hosts. Come and share the experience."

A Tree House B&B

Barb and Bob Selvage
2490 West Forty-ninth Avenue
Vancouver, BC V6M 2V3
(604) 266-2962 Fax: (604) 266-2960
E-mail: treehouse@vancouver-bc.com
Web site: http://www.vancouver-bc.com/
  Treehouse

• Room and two suites. One person $80–130; two people $90–140. Queen-sized bed; queen-sized bed, double futon, and one twin futon; queen-sized bed and one twin futon. Ensuite and private bathrooms. Additional person $25.

• A multi-level house with contemporary art and sculpture, close to hiking, horseback riding, golf, tennis, swimming pools, and a community centre. A few minutes' drive from downtown, the University of British Columbia, the airport, and ferries to the islands. Near dining and shopping. One of the suites occupies the entire third floor and has private decks, a four-post queen-sized bed, a twin-sized futon, a skylit bathroom with Jacuzzi, and a sitting room with plants. The other suite is on the main floor and has a queen-sized bed, a sitting room with double futon and twin-sized futon, and an ensuite bathroom with Jacuzzi. The guest room has a queen-sized bed and a private bath, is decorated with Asian arts and crafts, and opens onto a Japanese courtyard garden. Guest living/dining room. Covered deck with a view of woodlands. Guest room and suites have telephones, TVs, VCRs, fridges, tea kettles, hair dryers, robes, slippers, toiletries, and chocolates on the pillows. Infants and children over ten welcome. Smoke-free environment. **In the hosts' own words:** "Our B&B provides a unique experience. Discover why our guests return year after year."

Balfour Inn B&B

Muni Nazerali
1064 Balfour Avenue
Vancouver, BC V6H 1X1
(604) 730-9927 Fax: (604) 732-4998
E-mail: balfourbb@aol.com
Web site: http://www.bbcanada.com/564.html

• North of King Edward Avenue, between Oak and Granville.

• Rooms. Two people $65–120. Ensuite and shared guest bathrooms. Off-season and weekly rates.

• A 1908 mansion surrounded by gardens, fifteen minutes from downtown, ocean beaches, the Vancouver Trade and Convention Centre, B.C. Place, the Queen Elizabeth Gardens, Stanley Park, Gastown, Vancouver General Hospital, and the Ford Centre for the Performing Arts. A few minutes' walk from the VanDusen gardens and synagogues on Oak Street. Near direct routes to the University of British Columbia, the U.S. border, the airport, and ferries to Vancouver Island and the Gulf Islands. One block from transit. Tours arranged, with pickup from the B&B. Small groups and weddings welcome. Guest sitting room. Full breakfast. Parking. Visa, MasterCard, American Express. No pets. Smoke-free environment. **In the hosts' own words:** "This is a green oasis in the city. Come and share it with us."

Marine Drive B&B

Margaret Healey
2520 South West Marine Drive
Vancouver, BC V6P 6C2
(604) 261-2327 Fax: (604) 261-2329
E-mail: 6048315106@msg.clearnet.com

• West of Arbutus.
• Rooms. One person $50; two people $65.
Shared guest bathrooms. One person or two people $90. Private bathroom.
• A B&B between McLeery and Marine Drive golf
courses, across the street from Maple Grove Park. Guest rooms face south and have views of the golf courses, the ocean, and Vancouver Island. Near hiking, horseback riding, golf, tennis, and swimming pools. A few minutes' drive from the University of British Columbia, Vancouver International Airport, and ferries to Vancouver Island. Pets welcome; cats in residence. Smoking in designated areas.

The Shamrock's Nook B&B

Heath and Loesha Manering
8234 Argyle Street
Vancouver, BC V5P 3M2
(604) 329-9535 Fax: (604) 327-6744
E-mail: Shamrock@istar.ca
Web site: http://www.vancouver-bc.com/
   ShamrocksNookBB

• Off South East Marine Drive, towards the
Fraser River, between the Knight Street bridge
and Victoria Drive.
• Two rooms. One person $75–85; two people $85–110. Double bed and one twin bed.
Ensuite bathrooms. Additional person $15–25.
• A B&B ten minutes from the Vancouver International Airport and near the U.S. border and ferries to Vancouver Island and the Gulf Islands. Within a block of buses to rapid transit and to downtown Vancouver. Five minutes from a golf course. A few minutes' walk from a promenade along the Fraser River. Natural water outdoor hot tub. Living room with TV, VCR, and grand piano. Deck. Cappuccino bar. Full breakfast. Adult oriented. Smoking on the deck. **In the hosts' own words:** "At our B&B, enjoy a unique combination of European hospitality and a healthy West Coast breakfast."

Shaughnessy Village B&B Guest House

Jan Floody
1125 West Twelfth Avenue
Vancouver, BC V6H 3Z3
(604) 736-5511 Fax: (604) 737-1321

• Between Granville and Oak streets, 5 minutes from downtown.
• Two hundred and forty rooms. One-room studio, one person from $39.95,
two people from $59.95; two-room suite, one person from $79.95, two people
from $93.95. Ensuite and private bathrooms. Additional person $10. Rates
include twelve video movies per day and health club membership. Weekly rates.
Monthly rate $595.
• A resort-style B&B with gardens, a heated swimming pool, a Jacuzzi, miniature golf, a
shuffleboard, and outdoor barbecues. Two blocks from shopping and buses. Five minutes'
drive from downtown. On direct route to the airport. Rooms and suites have Victorian décor,
private balconies, microwaves, fridges, TVs, clock radios, and thermostats for individually
controlled heat. Most rooms and suites have views either of Vancouver and False Creek or
of trees and Mount Baker. Health club with TV room, reading room, billiard room, exercise
room, sauna, indoor whirlpool, suntanning bed, and acumassage couch. Licensed restaurant,
hair salon, full-service and coin-operated laundry, housekeeping service, dry-cleaning service, and secretarial service. On-camera security and twenty-four-hour front desk securi-
ty/medicalert response system. Full breakfast is served all day. Visa, MasterCard. **In the
hosts' own words:** "Our resort-style residence is designed to accommodate B&B visitors to
Vancouver who require affordable, well-equipped, comfortable, furnished facilities. There is
lots for the visitor to do in a friendly city-country atmosphere."

Lillian Feist

896 West Thirteenth Avenue
Vancouver, BC V5Z 1P2
(604) 873-0842

• Near Oak Street and West Twelfth Avenue.
• Suites. Shared guest bathrooms. Off-season and monthly rates.
• A centrally located B&B near Oak Street and West Twelfth Avenue, one block from Vancouver General Hospital and four blocks from the Canadian Cancer Society. Ten minutes' drive from downtown. Near shops, restaurants, Granville Island, Queen Elizabeth Park, the VanDusen Gardens, Gastown, and Chinatown. Suites have TVs and kitchens and accommodate up to four people. Off-street parking. Controlled pets welcome. **In the hosts' own words**: "Our B&B is perfect for those who require an extended stay in Vancouver."

Columbia Cottage B&B

Susanna Sulzberger and Alisdair Smith
205 West Fourteenth Avenue
Vancouver, BC V5Y 1X2
(604) 874-5327 Fax: (604) 879-4547
E-mail: goobles@msn.com
Web site: http://www.vancouver-bc.com/
  ColumbiaCottage

• Twenty minutes from the airport. Ten minutes from downtown.
• Four rooms. $125–135. King-sized bed; queen-sized bed; double bed; twin beds. Ensuite bathrooms. Suite (sleeps up to four). Two people $150. Queen-sized bed and pull-out sofa. Ensuite bathroom. Additional person $20. Breakfast ingredients supplied.
• A 1929 Tudor-style cottage in the Mount Pleasant area of Vancouver, close to city hall. Five minutes' drive from Queen Elizabeth Park and Science World and ten minutes from Granville Island, downtown, Stanley Park, and cruise ships at Canada Place. Guest living room with fireplace. Suite accommodates up to four people and has a living room and a kitchen. Sherry is served in the main living room. Full breakfast is served in the dining room. Nonsmoking. **In the hosts' own words:** "Come enjoy our elegant accommodation, lush gardens, and gracious hospitality. We look forward to meeting you soon."

Albion Guest House B&B

Lise Caza and Richard Koroscil
592 West Nineteenth Avenue
Vancouver, BC V5Z 1W6
(604) 873-2287 Fax: (604) 879-5682
E-mail: albion@direct.ca

● At Cambie and Nineteenth. Fifteen minutes from Vancouver International Airport. Seven minutes from downtown.
● Four rooms. One person $110–$150; two people $125–170. Queen-sized beds. Ensuite and shared guest bathrooms. Additional person $25. Extended stay rates.
● A turn-of-the-century house, with antiques and contemporary furnishings, on a quiet residential street. Within walking distance of parks, shops, and restaurants. Half a block from public transit. Living room with fireplace. Garden. Guest rooms have queen-sized wrought-iron beds with cotton linen, feather mattresses, and duvets. One of the guest rooms has a balcony. Another guest room has a private entrance. Hot tub in a courtyard; robes provided. Tennis rackets and bicycles. Apéritif served when guests arrive. Full breakfast. French spoken. **In the hosts' own words:** "Enjoy a quiet conversation in front of the fireplace in the living room, and exchange Vancouver experiences with other guests over a gourmet breakfast. We offer great food and hospitality."

The Whitehead House B&B

Darlene Whitehead
901 West Twenty-third Avenue
Vancouver, BC V5Z 2B2
(604) 736-3050 Fax: (604) 736-3050

• One block east of Oak Street, on the corner of Laurel Street and Twenty-third Avenue. Ten minutes from downtown.
• Two rooms. In summer, one person or two people $85. In winter, one person or two people $70. Queen-sized bed; twin beds. Shared guest bathroom. Additional person $10. Cot available.
• A centrally located 1910 house within walking distance of Queen Elizabeth Park, the VanDusen Gardens, theatres, restaurants, and coffee bars. One block from bus route. Guest rooms have down quilts, feather pillows, and antiques. One of the guest rooms has a sitting area. Shared guest bathroom has a double shower. Guest entrance. Guest sitting room with table, chairs, and antique sideboard. Coffee, tea, and biscuits provided. Full breakfast. Visa. Children welcome. No smoking. **In the hosts' own words:** "Enjoy a healthy West Coast breakfast in our heritage house."

Peloquin's Pacific Pad

Janet Peloquin
426 West Twenty-second Avenue
Vancouver, BC V5Y 2G5
(604) 874-4529 Fax: (604) 874-6229

• Near King Edward Avenue and Cambie Street.
• Two rooms. One person $60–65; two people $70–85. Shared guest bathroom. Additional person $25. Child $15–20.
• A B&B in a residential neighbourhood, within walking distance of restaurants, shops, parks, and bus routes. A few minutes by car or bus from downtown, the University of British Columbia, General Motors Place, the Ford Centre for the Performing Arts, B.C. Place Stadium, and Vancouver General Hospital. Near the airport, ferries, and Highway 99 to the U.S. Host provides information about Vancouver. Guest rooms have private entrances and TVs. Guest common area with fridge, toaster, microwave, and dishes is stocked with coffee and tea. No cooking; the microwave is for warming food. Full breakfast, including homemade preserves, is served in a solarium-like kitchen. Check-in and check-out times are flexible. French and Ukrainian spoken. Children welcome. No pets. Nonsmokers welcome. **In the hosts' own words:** "Have a happy holiday."

Pillow 'n Porridge Guest House

Dianne Reader Haag
2859 Manitoba Street
Vancouver, BC V5Y 3B3
(604) 879-8977 Fax: (604) 879-8966
E-mail: pillow@uniserve.com
Web site: http://www.pillow.net

• From Cambie Street and Twelfth Avenue (city hall), go east on Twelfth for four blocks and turn right onto Manitoba Street. The B&B is the third house south of Twelfth Avenue.

• Two one-bedroom suites. $85–135 per night, $1400–2850 per month. Queen-sized bed and sleeping loft; king-sized bed, queen-sized bed, one twin bed, and sofa bed.

Two-bedroom suite (sleeps four). $130–160 per night, $2000–3500 per month. King-sized bed, double bed, and one twin bed.

Three-bedroom suite (sleeps six). $175–250 per night, $3000–4500 per month. Queen-sized bed and one twin bed. Two bathrooms.

Additional person $10. Minimum stay. Breakfast not included. Monthly rates include utilities and weekly maid service.

• Three colourfully painted houses built between 1906 and 1910, side by side, in the city hall area, within walking distance of fine dining and ethnic restaurants, shopping, Queen Elizabeth Park, Granville Island, Science World, and Vancouver General Hospital. Five minutes' drive from downtown, the Ford Centre for the Performing Arts, the Queen Elizabeth Theatre, General Motors Place, B.C. Place Stadium, and Chinatown. Three blocks from bus and rapid transit routes. Suites are decorated in themes and have bedrooms, bathrooms, kitchens, living rooms, dining areas, private entrances, microwaves, fridges, telephones, TVs, clock radios, and supplies for making coffee and tea. VCR available. Two of the suites have dishwashers. Two of the suites have washers and dryers. Three of the suites have fireplaces. One of the suites has a deck and a front porch. Robes provided. Smoking outdoors. **In the hosts' own words:** "Much more than just a room, we offer you your very own special Vancouver house in a heritage district."

Ambleside-by-the-Sea B&B

Kenneth Walters
763 Seventeenth Street
West Vancouver, BC V7V 3T4
(604) 922-4873

• Near Seventeenth Street and Marine Drive.
From Highway 1, take Fifteenth Street south.
Turn right onto Fulton. Turn left onto
Seventeenth Street.
From downtown Vancouver, go west on Georgia
Street. Continue through Stanley Park, over the
Lions Gate Bridge, and along Marine Drive. Turn right onto Seventeenth Street.
• Rooms. One person $45–55; two people $60–70; three people $80. Queen-sized bed;
double bed; twin beds; one twin bed. Shared guest bathrooms.
• A three-storey traditional house in a quiet residential area, two blocks from shops, parks, a
seawall walkway, and restaurants with West Coast and international cuisine. Solarium and
TV room. On bus route. Fifteen minutes from downtown Vancouver. Full breakfast is served
in the dining room. Off-street parking. Not suitable for children under ten or for pets.
Nonsmoking house. **In the hosts' own words:** "You will enjoy warm hospitality and friendship at our B&B."

The Palms Guest House

Heidi Schmidt
3042 Marine Drive
West Vancouver, BC V7V 1M5
(604) 926-1159 Fax: (604) 926-1451
Toll-free from within North America:
  1-800-691-4455
E-mail: hschmidt@alumni-ubc.ca
Web site: http://www.vancouver-bc.com/
  PalmsGuestHouse

• Rooms. In high season, $150–240. In low sea-
son, $120–180. Ensuite bathrooms. Additional person $30.
Honeymoon suite. King-sized bed.
• A house with antiques, near the ocean, within walking distance of shops, a seawall, and
restaurants. On bus route to downtown Vancouver and to ferries at Horseshoe Bay. Guest
rooms have TVs, telephones, and balconies with views of the city and the ocean.
Honeymoon suite has a canopied king-sized bed, a Jacuzzi, and a fireplace. Down duvets
and fine linen. Tea is served in a guest living room or on a terrace. Breakfast includes fresh-
squeezed orange juice, croissants, and a fruit plate and may include an entrée such as grave
lox with dill eggs. Visa, MasterCard. Spanish and German spoken. Adult oriented. No pets.
Smoking on balconies. **In the hosts' own words:** "Visit our B&B and experience unforgettable West Coast living."

Creekside B&B

Donna P. Hawrelko and John C. Boden, Sr.
1515 Palmerston Avenue
West Vancouver, BC V7V 4S9
(604) 926-1861 Fax: (604) 926-7545
Cel: (604) 328-9400

• From Highway 1, turn south onto Fifteenth Street. Turn right onto Palmerston
Avenue.
From Marine Drive in West Vancouver, turn north onto Fifteenth Street. Turn
left onto Palmerston Avenue.

• Room and honeymoon suite. $110–141. King-sized bed; queen-sized bed.
Ensuite and private bathrooms. Minimum stay two nights.

• A post-and-beam house on a wooded lot with a small stream, a bridge, and five waterfalls.
Garden with two-hundred-year-old cedar and spruce trees and four thousand flowering
plants. Near transit, parks, hiking, tennis courts, golf, fine dining restaurants, shopping,
ocean beaches, and skiing at Grouse Mountain and Mount Seymour. Guest room and honeymoon suite have balconies overlooking the stream and garden, dual showers, TVs, radio
alarm clocks, coffee makers, and fridges with wine, other beverages, and snacks. Robes, toiletries, and half-price coupons for dining, sightseeing, and entertainment. Honeymoon suite
is air-conditioned and has a gas fireplace and a two-person marble Jacuzzi tub; at night, stars
can be seen through a glass ceiling over the Jacuzzi. Guest room has a brass queen-sized bed
and a private bathroom with six-foot marble Jacuzzi tub and skylights. Full breakfast
includes cereal, fresh fruit, eggs, Canadian back bacon, English muffins, homemade bread,
juice, coffee, and tea. Deposit of half of one night's rate required to hold reservation. Cash,
Visa, MasterCard. Not suitable for children under ten. Small pets permitted by arrangement;
small poodle in residence. **In the hosts' own words:** "Our heritage house has recently been
renovated but retains its charm and serenity."

Dundarave Oceanview B&B

Vlasta Zverina
2635 Rosebery Avenue
West Vancouver, BC V7V 3A3
(604) 925-3531 Fax: (604) 925-3548
E-mail: vlastaz@axionet.com
Web site: http://www.vancouver-bc.com/DundaraveBB/

• Suite. Two people $120–160. Queen-sized bed.
Two-bedroom suite. Four people $240. Twin beds in each bedroom.
Additional person $25.

• A B&B with a garden and a view of the ocean, a few minutes from downtown Vancouver, Stanley Park, ocean beaches, Grouse Mountain, and the Capilano suspension bridge. Ninety minutes from Whistler. Suites have sitting rooms, TVs, kitchens, and private entrances. Breakfast is served in the dining room or on an adjacent patio with a view of the ocean. Adult oriented. No pets. No smoking. **In the hosts' own words:** "Our B&B is between the mountains and the ocean, in the peaceful tranquillity of West Vancouver. We offer well-appointed suites, modern comforts, and a true European ambience."

Beachside B&B

Gordon and Joan Gibbs
4208 Evergreen Avenue
West Vancouver, BC V7V 1H1
(604) 922-7773 Fax: (604) 926-8073
Toll-free from within Canada and the U.S.: 1-800-563-3311
E-mail: beach@uniserve.com

• From the Lions Gate Bridge, take Marine Drive west for 7 kilometres. Turn south onto Ferndale Avenue and continue for half a block. Turn left onto Evergreen Avenue. The B&B is at the end of the cul-de-sac.
• Three rooms. Two people from $145. Queen-sized bed. Ensuite bathrooms. Additional person $30. Off-season rates.
• A house on the ocean, at the end of a quiet cul-de-sac, with a sandy beach and a view of Vancouver and the Gulf Islands. Twenty minutes from downtown Vancouver, Stanley Park, the Horseshoe Bay ferry terminal, and North Shore attractions. Half a block from a bus route. Sunrises, sunsets, Alaska cruise ships, seals, sea otters, birds, and eagles can be seen from the beach. Near fishing, sailing, wilderness hiking, skiing, golf, parks, trails, tennis courts, antique stores, a convenience store, shopping, and fine dining restaurants. Guest sitting room with fireplace, videos, board games, puzzles, and books. Guest outdoor beachside Jacuzzi and beach patios. Indoor Jacuzzi. Guest rooms have fireplaces, TVs, VCRs, flowers, fruit baskets, fridges, coffee pots, hair dryers, and curling irons. Two of the guest rooms have ocean views. Antique stained glass, old brick, and hanging baskets throughout. One of the hosts is available as a tour guide. Full breakfast, including muffins, scones, fresh-ground coffee, and tea, is served in the dining room, which has a view of the ocean. Off-street parking. Deposit of 50 percent required to hold reservation. Cancellation notice fourteen days. Check-in 5:00 to 6:00 p.m. or by arrangement. Cash, traveller's cheques, Visa, MasterCard. No pets; dog in residence. Smoking on covered patios. **In the hosts' own words:** "We are well-travelled former teachers and can advise guests on local attractions. Relax, make new friends, and enjoy Vancouver's legendary scenery, cultural events, and attractions, in quiet seclusion just minutes from the city centre. We offer an ideal place for getaways and honeymoon retreats."

Union Steamship Company

Rondy and Dorothy Dike
Mail: Box 250
Bowen Island, BC V0N 1G0
(604) 947-0707 Fax: (604) 947-0708

• Fifteen minutes by ferry from the Horseshoe Bay ferry terminal. The B&B cottages are next to the ferry landing on Bowen Island.

• Two two-bedroom cottages. In summer (May 1 to October 15), two people $100. In winter (October 16 to April 30), two people $85. Queen-sized bed and two sets of bunk beds with double-width lower bunks.

One-bedroom float house. In summer (May 1 to October 15), two people $90. In winter (October 16 to April 30), two people $75. Queen-sized bed. Private bathroom.

Two-bedroom house. Two people $140. King-sized bed and one twin bed; bunk beds with double-width lower bunk.

Breakfast not included.

Additional beds $10. Discount of 15 percent on stays of five or more nights.

Minimum stay two nights on summer weekends.

• A B&B with a two-bedroom house and two of the original cottages of the Union Steamship Company, in a resort village in Snug Cove on Bowen Island, with views of mountains and Howe Sound. Bald eagles can be seen. Each cottage has two bedrooms, a living room with wood stove, a TV, a kitchen, and a porch. Remodelled float house on a dock has a bedroom, a living room, a kitchen, a TV, and a futon sofa. Two-bedroom Victorian-style house has a view of Snug Cove, stained-glass windows, a clawfoot tub, a living room with fireplace, and a kitchen with wood stove. One block from a bakery, a deli, and a restaurant. A few minutes from private coves, public beaches, parks, and hiking and biking trails. Bowen Island's port has boutiques, boardwalks, and turn-of-the-century buildings. Breakfast not included. Credit cards. Children and pets welcome. **In the hosts' own words:** "There's no place in the world like the B.C. coast, and there's no better way to see its scenery and natural sights than seated on the front porch of one of our rustic cottages."

Cedar Hill B&B

Jean and Adolph Olson
1095 West Keith Road
North Vancouver, BC V7P 1Y6
(604) 988-9629 Fax: (604) 990-8966
E-mail: cedarhil@citywidenet.com
Web site: http://www.bbcanada.com

• One and a half blocks from Marine Drive, near
Capilano Road.
• Rooms. $65–85. Queen-sized bed; double bed;
one twin bed. Private and shared guest bathrooms.
Suite. $95. King-sized bed. Bathroom in suite. Adjoining room with double bed for additional $65.
Twin bed available.
Additional person $30. Child $15.
• A B&B at the foot of Grouse Mountain, with cedar trees and a garden, fifteen minutes from downtown Vancouver. Views of downtown Vancouver and cruise ships entering the harbour. Flowers throughout. Suite has a private entrance, a patio, and a sitting room with fireplace, TV, VCR, bar, and piano. Guest rooms have private entrances. One of the guest rooms is upstairs and has a sitting room with TV. Another guest room is at ground level and has a patio. Large yard with garden. Chairs, benches, and mats on lawn and patios. Within walking distance of public transit, Capilano Mall, restaurants, and shopping. Near the Capilano suspension bridge, the Grouse Mountain gondola, the Royal Hudson steam train, Stanley Park, ocean beaches, hiking trails, and a passenger ferry to downtown Vancouver. Breakfast is served in the dining room, which has a bay window, or on the patio. Parking. Wheelchair accessible. Suitable for families and groups. Children welcome. Smoking outdoors. **In the hosts' own words:** "The comfort of our guests is our first concern. We are located in quiet, secluded Pemberton Heights. Our B&B is a North Shore treat."

Pacific View B&B

Sylvia and Gerhard Gruner
139 West St. James Road
North Vancouver, BC V7N 2P1
(604) 985-4942 Fax: (604) 985-4942

• From Highway 1, take exit 18 to Lonsdale
Avenue. Go north on Lonsdale and turn left onto
St. James. The B&B is in the first block.
• One person $50; two people $65–80. Queen-
sized bed. Ensuite and private bathrooms.
• A B&B with a view of the ocean and the city, in
a residential neighbourhood, twenty minutes from downtown Vancouver, Stanley Park, and the Horseshoe Bay ferry terminal. Fifteen minutes' drive from Grouse Mountain. Ten minutes' drive from the Royal Hudson steam train, the Capilano River fish hatchery, the Capilano suspension bridge, and a passenger ferry to downtown Vancouver and a rapid transit station. Two minutes' walk from a bus stop. Suites have TVs. Guest living room is on the upper floor and has a balcony with a view. Full breakfast is served in a heated sun room overlooking a garden. German and Polish spoken. No pets; small bird in residence. Nonsmokers welcome. **In the hosts' own words:** "Our house is your home away from home."

Ocean Breeze B&B

Margaret Gradowska
462 East First Street
North Vancouver, BC V7L 1B7
(604) 988-0546 Fax: (604) 988-0546
Toll-free from within Canada and the U.S.: 1-800-567-5171

• From downtown Vancouver, cross the Lions Gate Bridge and take the North Vancouver exit onto Marine Drive. Turn right onto Lonsdale. Turn left onto First Street.
From the Upper Levels Highway, take the Lonsdale exit. Turn left onto First Street.
• Rooms and one self-contained suite. Two people $115-195. King-sized bed; queen-sized bed; queen-sized bed and twin beds. Ensuite, private, and shared bathrooms.
• A gingerbread-style house with views of the harbour, cruise ships, and downtown Vancouver from most guest rooms and patios. Near Grouse Mountain, the Capilano suspension bridge, Gastown, and Chinatown. Within walking distance of restaurants, shops, and entertainment. Twenty minutes from the Horseshoe Bay ferry terminal. Ninety minutes from Whistler. Guest rooms have TVs and keyed doors. Some of the guest rooms have fireplaces. Private telephone available. Brochures and maps are provided. Full breakfast. Parking. Cancellation notice seventy-two hours. Cash, traveller's cheques, Visa, MasterCard. Children welcome in suite. Smoking outdoors in designated areas. **In the hosts' own words:** "I am a former flight attendant, and I offer European hospitality."

Norgate Parkhouse B&B

Vicki Tyndall
1226 Silverwood Crescent
North Vancouver, BC V7P 1J3
(604) 986-5069 Fax: (604) 986-8810

• Fifteen minutes from downtown Vancouver. From the Lions Gate Bridge, turn right onto Marine Drive, right onto Tatlow, and right onto Silverwood Crescent. The B&B is on the right.

• Three rooms. In summer, one person $75–95, two people $95–115. In winter, one person $65–85, two people $85–105. King-sized bed; queen-sized bed; twin beds. Ensuite and shared guest bathrooms. Minimum stay two nights on holiday weekends.

• A contemporary ranch-style house with a separate wing for guests and a West Coast–style garden, fifteen minutes from downtown Vancouver and ten minutes from wilderness hiking. Three blocks from public transit. Five minutes from B.C. Rail station. Three to five blocks from restaurants and car rentals. Guest rooms have telephones. Two of the guest rooms open onto the back garden. The third guest room has a private deck. Guest sitting room with fireplace, books, tourist brochures, and TV. Full breakfast. Deposit required to hold reservation. Not suitable for small children. Two resident cats and, at times, a family of raccoons. Smoking outdoors. **In the hosts' own words:** "We invite you to experience Vancouver's friendly hospitality. Relax in our large West Coast garden, have a quiet sleep, and enjoy a delicious breakfast."

Laburnum Cottage B&B

Delphine Masterton
1388 Terrace Avenue
North Vancouver, BC V7R 1B4
(604) 988-4877 Fax: (604) 988-4877

• From Vancouver, take Georgia Street (Highway 99) across the Lions Gate Bridge. Turn right onto Marine Drive, left onto Capilano Road, right onto Paisley Road, right onto Philip, right onto Woods, and left onto Terrace.
From the U.S. border, take Highway 15 north. Take Highway 1 west to North Vancouver. Take exit 14 north to Capilano Road. Turn right onto Paisley, right onto Philip, right onto Woods, and left onto Terrace.
From the Horseshoe Bay ferry terminal, take Highway 1 east. Go north on Capilano Road. Turn right onto Paisley, right onto Philip, right onto Woods, and left onto Terrace.
• Rooms. Queen-sized bed. Private bathrooms.
Two self-contained cottages. King-sized bed and children's loft; double bed. Private bathrooms.
• A B&B with Victorian antiques and an English garden, on half an acre surrounded by old-growth forest, fifteen minutes from downtown Vancouver and from Horseshoe Bay. Ninety minutes from Whistler. Five minutes from Grouse Mountain. Two blocks from bus route. Covered porch with a view of the garden and a creek. Cottages have fireplaces and kitchens. Afternoon tea. Breakfast includes homemade jam, biscuits, and pancakes. Parking. Deposit of one night's rate, $15 of which is nonrefundable, required to hold reservation. Cancellation notice seven days. Check-in times are flexible. Visa, MasterCard. Smoking outdoors. **In the hosts' own words:** "We invite you to enjoy restful, peaceful seclusion. Our charming B&B has a Victorian air and beautifully appointed guest rooms. We hope you will find a few moments to relax on the covered porch overlooking the gardens and the meandering creek."

Capilano B&B

Soledad Lu
1374 Plateau Drive
North Vancouver, BC V7P 2J6
(604) 990-8889 Fax: (604) 990-5177
E-mail: capilano@direct.ca
Web site: http://www.vancouver-bc.com/capilanoBB

• From downtown Vancouver, cross the Lions Gate Bridge and turn right, to North Vancouver. At the first intersection, turn left onto Capilano Road. Turn right onto the road that leads to Highway 1. Before Highway 1, turn right onto West Keith Road. Turn left onto 22nd Street, left onto Bridgman Avenue, and left into the back lane at the end of Bridgman. Continue to the B&B's parking lot.

• Three rooms. One person or two people $65–125. Queen-sized bed, shared bathroom; twin beds side by side with king-sized bedding (or twin beds), shared bathroom; queen-sized bed and two bunk beds, ensuite bathroom. Self-contained one- or two-bedroom suite. One-bedroom suite (sleeps up to four), two people $125. Two-bedroom suite (sleeps up to eight), four people $175. Rooms booked separately, two people $95–$125 per room. Two double beds. Private bathrooms.

Additional person $20.

Open May to October.

• A B&B with three guest rooms and a fourteen-hundred-square-foot self-contained suite, a few minutes' drive from Stanley Park, ocean beaches, Grouse Mountain, the Capilano suspension bridge, Capilano River Regional Park, and the Royal Hudson steam train to Squamish. Ten minutes from downtown Vancouver and Chinatown. Fifteen minutes from the Horseshoe Bay ferry terminal. Thirty minutes from Vancouver International Airport. Self-contained suite can be booked as either a one- or a two-bedroom suite, accommodates up to eight people, and has a private entrance, a patio, a living/dining area, a kitchen, a TV, a telephone, and two double beds in each bedroom. Guest rooms have TVs, small fridges, telephones, and coffee makers. Full breakfast. Cancellation notice seven days. Traveller's cheques, Visa, MasterCard. Mandarin, Cantonese, German, and Dutch spoken. Children welcome in one of the guest rooms and in the suite. No pets. Smoking outdoors.

Summit View B&B

Sherri Amirkia
5501 Cliffridge Place
North Vancouver, BC   V7R 4S2
(604) 990-1089 Fax: (604) 987-7167

• From Highway 1, take the Capilano Road exit and go north on Capilano Road. Turn right onto Prospect Road, left onto Cliffridge Avenue, and left onto Cliffridge Place. The B&B is the first house on the left.
From Marine Drive, turn north onto Capilano Road.

• Rooms and one honeymoon suite. One person from $55; two people from $110. Queen-sized bed; double bed; twin beds. Ensuite bathrooms, private bathrooms, shared guest bathrooms, and shared bathrooms. Extended stay rates.

• A B&B with mountain and forest views, close to hiking, skiing, swimming, and tennis courts. Bicycles and table tennis. Near Grouse Mountain, Cleveland Dam park, the Capilano suspension bridge, the Capilano River fish hatchery, and public transportation. A few minutes from shopping and restaurants. Formal dining room and family room. Balcony. Guest rooms have keyed doors. Some of the guest rooms have TVs. Honeymoon suite has a queen-sized bed, a dormer window area with twin bed, an ensuite bathroom with skylight, and a walk-in closet. Pickup from plane or ferry for a fee. Full breakfast. Dinner on request. Diets are accommodated. Suitable for families or groups. Smoke-free environment. **In the hosts' own words:** "We offer a gourmet breakfast. Come as a guest and leave as a friend."

The Nelson's B&B

Roy and Charlotte Nelson
470 St. James Road West
North Vancouver, BC V7N 2P5
(604) 985-1178 Fax (604) 985-1178

• From Highway 1, take exit 17 north onto
Westview. Turn right onto Windsor and continue
for one block. Turn left onto St. James.
• Rooms. One person $50; two people $65–80.
Queen-sized bed and one twin day bed; two dou-
ble beds; one twin bed. Ensuite and private bath-
rooms. Child under 6 $5. Child 6 to 12 $10. Child 13 to 16 $15.
Open April to November.
• A B&B on a quiet tree-lined street, three blocks from buses and ten minutes from restau-
rants, parks, sports facilities, beaches, and shopping. Ten minutes from Grouse Mountain,
Cleveland Dam, the Capilano suspension bridge, a fish hatchery, par three golf, and
Lonsdale Quay. Twenty minutes from Stanley Park, Gastown, an Imax theatre, downtown
Vancouver, and ferries to Vancouver Island. Sitting room with TV and VCR. Deck, garden,
and heated swimming pool. Breakfast includes homemade jam and muffins. Deposit of one
night's rate required to hold reservation. Check-in 2:00 to 6:00 p.m.; check-out until 11:00
a.m. No pets; cat in residence. No smoking. **In the hosts' own words:** "Your satisfaction is
our pleasure."

Poole's B&B

Doreen and Arthur Poole
421 St. James Road West
North Vancouver, BC V7N 2P6
(604) 987-4594 Fax: (604) 987-4283
E-mail: rapoole@lightspeed.bc.ca

• From Highway 1, take exit 17 north onto
Westview. Turn right onto Queens and left onto
Stanley, which leads to St. James.
• Three rooms. One person $45; two people $60.
Queen-sized bed; double bed; twin beds. Shared
guest bathrooms. Additional person $10. Child 6 to 12 $5. Children under 6 free. Crib and
cot available.
Off-season and weekly rates.
• A colonial-style house in a residential district, twenty minutes' drive from downtown
Vancouver and two blocks from a bus stop. Within walking distance of restaurants, shop-
ping, parks, and an indoor public swimming pool. Ten minutes by car or bus from the
Capilano suspension bridge, the Grouse Mountain skyride, and a passenger ferry to downtown Vancouver. Twenty minutes' drive from Stanley Park and ferries to Vancouver Island.
Deck and garden. Guest room with twin beds has a TV. Breakfast is served at a candlelit dining table with flowers from the garden. No pets. No smoking. **In the hosts' own words:** "We
are retired and are happy to help with directions and information about our beautiful city and
surrounding areas. We welcome guests to share our quiet, relaxed B&B."

Gazebo in the Garden B&B

Monika and Jack Rogers
310 St. James Road East
North Vancouver, BC V7N 1L2
(604) 983-3331 Fax: (604) 980-3215
E-mail: mrogers@direct.ca
Web site: http://www.vancouver-bc.com/gazebo

• From Vancouver, cross the Lions Gate Bridge and take the exit to North Vancouver. Turn left onto Capilano Road. Take the turnoff to Highway 1 east. From Highway 1, take exit 18 to Lonsdale Avenue. Turn left onto Lonsdale and right onto St. James.

• Four rooms. One person $55–65; two people $75–105. Twin beds; queen-sized bed. Private and ensuite bathrooms.

Two-bedroom suite (sleeps six). $215. Double bed, queen-sized bed, and queen-sized hide-a-bed. Bathroom in suite.

• A house built in 1910, fifteen minutes from downtown Vancouver and the Horseshoe Bay ferry terminal. Two-bedroom suite accommodates up to six people and has a patio, a private entrance, a TV, a VCR, and access to a cooking area with microwave, fridge, toaster, coffee maker, and dishes. Guest room with queen-sized bed has a sitting area, a TV, and an ensuite bathroom. Guest room with twin beds has a southwest view of Stanley Park, the Lions Gate Bridge, and Vancouver Island. A few minutes from Grouse Mountain, Capilano suspension bridge, a shopping mall, and a passenger ferry to downtown Vancouver. Living room with stone fireplace. Garden. Continental breakfast. Cancellation notice seven days. Deposit of one night's rate required to hold reservation. Cash, traveller's cheques, Visa, MasterCard. No pets. Nonsmoking. **In the hosts' own words:** "Our heritage house is a fine example of Frank Lloyd Wright's prairie-style architecture. Relax by our massive stone fireplace; enjoy a stroll in the garden, where you may find the resident master gardener; or enjoy morning coffee in the gazebo. We offer friendly hospitality in a private setting."

Sue's Victorian Guest House

Jen Lowes and Gail Fowler
152 East Third Street
North Vancouver, BC V7L 1E6
(604) 985-1523
Toll-free: 1-800-776-1811

• Half a block east of Lonsdale Avenue.
• Three rooms. One person $60–75; two people $70–85. Ensuite and shared
guest bathrooms. No showers. Additional person $25. Breakfast not included.
Seventh night free in the off-season. Extended stay rates.
• A 1904 house with original exterior finish, authentically framed double-glazed windows, original staircases, antiques, soaker tubs, and a full-width front veranda. Guest rooms have TVs, VCRs, heaters, fans, telephones (for short local calls), and keyed doors. Four blocks from the harbour and Lonsdale Quay. Near a fitness centre, the Royal Hudson steam train, Grouse Mountain, two suspension bridges, and Stanley Park. Twelve minutes across the harbour by passenger ferry from Gastown, a conference centre, an Imax theatre, downtown Vancouver, and connections to rapid transit, buses, and Alaska cruise ship departures. Breakfast is not provided; there is a guest fridge, and there are restaurants and stores nearby. Off-street parking behind the house and behind 158 East Third. Nonrefundable deposit of first night's rate required to hold reservation. Visa for reservations only. Cancellation notice eight days. Cash, traveller's cheques. Adult oriented. Nonsmoking guests. **In the hosts' own words:** "Years of love and effort have gone into restoring our charming heritage house in North Vancouver. Why have so many guests stayed here? Because the price is right."

Kings on Kings B&B

Marjie and Ron Houlden
260 East Kings Road
North Vancouver, BC V7N 1H6
(604) 987-7886 Fax: (604) 987-7886

• From Highway 1 in North Vancouver, take exit 18 onto Lonsdale Avenue and continue for five blocks. Turn right onto Kings Road.
• Self-contained one-bedroom suite (sleeps four). Two people $90–125. Queen-sized bed and two sofa beds. Ensuite bathroom. Additional person $20. Extended stay rates.
• A ground-level suite that accommodates up to four people and has a kitchen, a living room with fireplace, TV, and two fold-out loveseats, a bedroom with queen-sized four-post bed, and an ensuite bathroom. Five minutes from Capilano and Lynn Canyon suspension bridges, the Capilano River fish hatchery, salmon fishing, the Royal Hudson steam train, Lonsdale Quay, and a twelve-minute passenger ferry that crosses the harbour to downtown Vancouver. The downtown terminal is near Gastown, a conference centre, an Imax theatre, Stanley Park, Alaska cruise ship departures, and connections to buses and rapid transit. The B&B is at the foot of Grouse Mountain. Near skiing at three ski areas—Grouse Mountain, Mount Seymour Provincial Park, and Cypress Provincial Park. Ninety minutes from Whistler. Coffee and tea available. Full breakfast. Cash, traveller's cheques. No pets. Smoke-free accommodation. **In the hosts' own words:** "Our B&B is a gem, with a breakfast fit for a king."

Mavis's B&B

Mavis Walkley
1—269 East Keith Road
North Vancouver, BC V7L 1V4
(604) 986-9748

• From Highway 1, take exit 18 to Lonsdale Avenue. Go south on Lonsdale and turn left onto Keith Road. The B&B is between St. Georges and St. Andrews avenues.
• Two rooms. One person from $45; two people from $70. Twin beds; queen-sized bed. Private and ensuite bathrooms. Child 2 to 6 $5. Child 7 to 12 $10.
• A B&B within walking distance of restaurants, Lonsdale Quay, and a passenger ferry to Vancouver. On bus route to Capilano Canyon and Grouse Mountain. Ten minutes' drive from Stanley Park, the Royal Hudson steam train, and Lynn Canyon. Twenty minutes' drive from the Horseshoe Bay ferry terminal. Guest rooms have TVs. One of the guest rooms has a queen-sized bed, an ensuite bathroom with Jacuzzi bathtub, and a private patio. Sitting room and family room. Full or Continental breakfast is served in the dining room. Children welcome. No pets; cats in residence. No smoking indoors. **In the hosts' own words:** "Enjoy your stay in an attractive, clean, comfortable house with us as your friendly hosts."

Gloria's B&B

Gloria and Tim Enno
6191 Madrona Crescent
Richmond, BC V7C 2T3
(604) 277-7097 Fax: (604) 277-7097

• Near Westminster Highway and Gilbert Road.
• Two suites. Two people $60–65. Queen-sized bed and sofa bed. Ensuite bathrooms. Additional person $15. Minimum stay two nights.
• A B&B in the city of Richmond, twenty minutes from downtown Vancouver, ten minutes from Vancouver International Airport, and thirty minutes from the U.S. border. Each suite accommodates up to four people and has a separate entrance, a sitting room, an ensuite bathroom, a TV, a fridge, and facilities and supplies for making coffee. Full breakfast includes home-made bread and fresh-ground coffee. Children over nine welcome. No pets. No smoking indoors. **In the hosts' own words:** "We offer a central location, private suites, and an enjoyable stay at our well-established B&B."

The Corner House—Sue's B&B

Sue and Norm Richard
11220 Second Avenue
Richmond, BC V7E 3K5
(604) 275-0913 Fax: (604) 275-0962
Cel: (604) 220-3740
E-mail: srichard@lynx.bc.ca
Web site: http://www.bbcanada.com/858.html

• From Highway 99, exit west onto Steveston Highway. Cross Number One Road and take the first left onto Second Avenue. The B&B is on the southeast corner of Second Avenue and Hunt.
• Two rooms. One person $50–60; two people $55–65. Double bed, private bathroom; queen-sized bed and sofa bed, ensuite bathroom. Additional person $15. Child 2 to 14 $1 per year of age. Children under 2 free. Off-season rates.
• A new house in a historical fishing village, ten minutes' drive from Vancouver International Airport and twenty minutes' drive from ferries to Vancouver Island and the Gulf Islands. On bus route to Richmond and downtown Vancouver. Near restaurants, shopping, and Garry Point Park. In the area are bicycle rentals, dike trails to walk on, and shops on the quay that sell local fresh fish. Guest rooms have TVs and facilities for making coffee and tea. Guest sitting room. Reservations recommended. Children welcome. No pets. No smoking. **In the hosts' own words:** "We really enjoy meeting such interesting people as our guests. We look forward to meeting you and sharing with you the magic of Steveston."

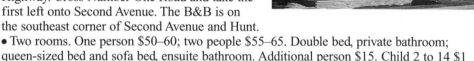

Brigadoon B&B

Tom Hamilton
4180 Lancelot Drive
Richmond, BC V7C 4S3
(604) 271-7096 Fax: (604) 271-7099
E-mail: brigadoon@vancouver-bc.com
Web site: http://www.vancouver-bc.com/
  BrigadoonBB

• From Highway 99, take the Steveston Highway
westbound exit. Turn right onto Gilbert Road.
Turn left onto Francis Road and continue past
Railway Avenue to the next road, Lancelot Gate, and turn right.
• Three rooms. One person $60–75; two people $75–100. Queen-sized bed; double bed;
twin beds. Ensuite, private, and shared guest bathrooms.
• A B&B ten minutes from Vancouver International Airport and close to ferries and the U.S.
border. A block from direct buses to downtown Vancouver. Five minutes from cycling, an
ocean dike to walk on, shops, boardwalk restaurants, and a historical fishing village at
Steveston. Guest sitting room with TV, VCR, and books. Terrace garden. Reservations recommended. Visa, MasterCard, American Express. Adult oriented. Corgi dog in residence.
Smoke-free environment. **In the hosts' own words:** "We invite you to enjoy our hospitality
and a delicious breakfast served in the guest dining room."

The Ranch House B&B

Jon and Margaret Taylor
7061 Ladner Trunk Road
Delta, BC V4K 3N3
(604) 946-1553

• On Highway 10 (Ladner Trunk Road),
between Highway 17 and Highway 99.
• Three rooms. One person $75; two people
$85. Queen-sized bed; double bed. Two shared
guest bathrooms. Crib available.
• A ranch-style house on a small hobby farm
with horses. Deck and outdoor hot tub with views of farmland and the North Shore mountains. Near the George C. Reifel Migratory Bird Sanctuary, bicycling and hiking trails on
dikes, sandy beaches, golf courses, restaurants, shopping, water slides, Boundary Bay
tidal flats, Deas Island Regional Park, and Burns Bog. Guest living room with gas fireplace, TV, stereo, and books. Covered front porch. Twenty minutes from Vancouver
International Airport. Ten minutes from ferries to Victoria. Fifteen minutes from the U.S.
border. Thirty minutes from downtown Vancouver. Forty minutes from skiing at Grouse
Mountain ski area. Guests can pet the horses. Bicycles available. Transportation from and
to the Boundary Bay airport. Reservations recommended. Check-in 3:30 to 9:00 p.m.;
check-out until 10:00 a.m. or by arrangement. Visa. Children welcome. Smoking outdoors. **In the hosts' own words:** "We offer country-style hospitality and friendliness.
Relax on our spacious deck or soak in the hot tub with captivating views of the North
Shore mountains."

Duck Inn Cottage

Jill and Allen York
4349 River Road West
Ladner, BC V4K 1R9
(604) 946-7521 Fax: (604) 946-7521
Web site: http://www.bbcanada.com/1671.html

• In Ladner, 20 minutes south of the Vancouver International Airport.
• Self-contained one-bedroom cottage. Two people $120–150. King-sized bed.
Ensuite bathroom. Breakfast ingredients supplied. Extended stay, off-season,
and weekly rates.
• A cottage on pilings at the edge of the Fraser River, with views of the Ladner Reach and
the North Shore mountains. Ducks and other marine birds can be seen on the river below.
Ten minutes from the Tsawwassen ferry terminal's ferries to Victoria, Nanaimo, and the Gulf
Islands. Near the George C. Reifel Migratory Bird Sanctuary. Living and dining area with
waterfront views, fireplace, TV, VCR, CD player, telephone, and French doors that lead to a
balcony. Bathroom with jetted tub. Private twelve-by-twelve-foot floating dock. Canoe,
bikes, hammock, and patio with barbecue. Sherry and snacks provided. Kitchen is stocked
with smoked salmon and other breakfast items. Visa, MasterCard, American Express. Smoking on the balcony. **In the hosts' own words:** "Enjoy a romantic riverfront escape and explore the waterways of the Fraser delta at your leisure."

Villa del Mare

Ulrike Baecker
486 Centennial Parkway
Tsawwassen, BC V4L 1L2
(604) 943-0386 Fax: (604) 943-2861

• Two rooms. Two people $130–155. Queen-sized bed. Ensuite bathrooms. Additional person $30.

• A Tuscany-style house on the ocean, on Boundary Bay, one block from Boundary Bay Park. Boundary Bay is known for its many species of birds. Swimming, canoeing, and, at low tide, beach walking. A short walk on trails through Boundary Bay Park from shopping and a bus stop. Ten minutes' drive from the Tsawwassen ferry terminal. Twenty minutes from Vancouver International Airport. Thirty minutes from downtown Vancouver. Sunsets over Mount Baker can be seen from the beach and from a courtyard with grape vines next to a goldfish pond. One of the guest rooms has a Jacuzzi tub and a view of the ocean. Full breakfast is served in the dining room or on a patio that faces the beach. Cash, traveller's cheques, Visa. Adult oriented. No pets. No smoking. **In the hosts' own words:** "Fall asleep to the rhythm of the waves and awaken to the sound of seagulls. Our B&B is in an area that is a photographer's paradise. Come and enjoy some time with us and you won't want to leave."

Ingrid's on Twelfth European B&B

Ingrid and Helmut Becker
5447 Twelfth Avenue
Tsawwassen, BC V4M 2B2
(604) 943-4378 Fax: (604) 943-4378
E-mail: hbecker@uniserve.com
Web site: http://www.vancouver-bc.com/
    Ingrids

• In the centre of Tsawwassen.

• Three rooms. In summer, one person $80–90, two people $110–120. Queen-sized bed; two queen-sized beds and hide-a-bed. Private bathroom and ensuite bathroom with shower.

• A B&B near golf courses, ocean beaches, tennis courts, and dike walks for birdwatching. Five minutes from the Tsawwassen ferry terminal. Thirty minutes from Vancouver International Airport. Forty minutes from downtown Vancouver. Guest rooms have antiques, TVs, VCRs, down duvets, robes, and slippers. Deck. One of the guest rooms is self-contained, and the other two rooms have fridges. Room with two queen-sized beds has a hide-a-bed in the sitting room and a Jacuzzi tub. Mountain bikes for exploring the area. The hosts operate a beauty salon; beauty services available. Breakfast is served in a formal dining room or on the deck. Reservations required. **In the hosts' own words:** "Our philosophy is that whatever we do in whatever endeavour, we aim for perfection. Our guests experience our careful attention to detail. Your stay with us will be a most comfortable and memorable one. We are a convenient stop-over point for guests visiting Vancouver Island."

Southlands House B&B

Lyla-Jo and Bruce Troniak
1160 Boundary Bay Road
Tsawwassen, BC V4L 2P6
(604) 943-1846 Fax: (604) 943-2481
E-mail: btron@bc.sympatico.ca
Web site: http://www.vancouver-bc.com/SouthlandsHouseBB/

• From Vancouver, take Highway 99. Turn right onto Highway 17. Turn left onto Fifty-sixth Avenue and left onto Twelfth Avenue. Boundary Bay Road is at the end of Twelfth Avenue.

• Four rooms. One person or two people $110–155. Two extra-long twin beds side by side with king-sized bedding (or extra-long twin beds); queen-sized bed. Ensuite bathrooms.

Two-bedroom suite. One person or two people $155; three people $200; four to six people $250. Two queen-sized beds. Bathroom in suite.

Group and seniors' rates.

• A West Coast–style house with a view of the ocean and mountains, next to Boundary Bay Regional Park. The park, which is part of the Pacific flyway bird migration route, offers bird-watching, wildlife viewing, walking and biking trails, and beachcombing. Guest rooms, suite, guest living room, and two dining rooms have ocean and mountain views. Guest living room with stone fireplace, TV, VCR, CD player, and adjoining sitting rooms. Guest rooms are in a carriage house and have fireplaces. Two of the guest rooms have dressing rooms. Two-bedroom, two-storey suite is in a tower and has a living room with fridge, bar, TV, and VCR and a deck with a view of the ocean and the park. Guest rooms and suite have feather beds with duvets and private decks or patios. Two dining rooms have French doors that open onto patios with a view of the park. Library in an enclosed walkway that connects the main section of the house to the tower suite. Ten minutes from ferries. Twenty minutes from Vancouver International Airport. Thirty minutes from downtown Vancouver. Near private clubs for golf, squash, and fitness. TVs and telephones. Fax service and Internet access available on request. Full West Coast breakfast. Nonsmoking environment. **In the hosts' own words:** "Let us show you our hospitality at our West Coast country estate, in the sun belt of Greater Vancouver. Our B&B is perfect for a romantic retreat or a corporate getaway. The large number of migratory birds along the seashore in front of our house makes our B&B a paradise for birdwatchers."

Leah-Anne's Ancient Willow B&B

Leah-Anne Arbers
5520 Parker Street
Burnaby, BC V5B 1Z7
(604) 299-4070 Fax: (604) 294-8540
E-mail: leah-anne_arbers@bc.sympatico.ca

• From Highway 1 or Highway 1A/99A (Kingsway), turn north onto Willingdon Avenue. Turn right onto Parker Street.
• Rooms and suite. Queen-sized bed, private bathroom; two double beds, shared guest bathroom. Two people $55–85. Additional person $15. Off-season rates.
• A Tudor-style house, close to Burnaby Mountain and Simon Fraser University and twenty minutes' drive from downtown Vancouver. Across the street from a bus stop. Suite accommodates up to four people and has a kitchen area and a gas fireplace. Guest rooms and suite have telephones and TVs. Full breakfast is served in a solarium. Wheelchair accessible. Off-street parking. Visa, MasterCard. French, German, Dutch, Spanish, and Ukrainian spoken. Children welcome. Nonsmoking house. **In the hosts' own words:** "We welcome you with genuine hospitality."

Moldovanos B&B

John and Anne Moldovanos
6869 Sussex Avenue
Burnaby, BC V5J 3V1
(604) 430-2123 Fax: (604) 430-2123
Toll-free from within North America:
  1-888-430-2123

• Rooms. One person $75–85; two people $85–95. Queen-sized bed; twin beds. Ensuite and shared guest bathrooms.
Self-contained two-bedroom suite.
• A B&B within walking distance of rapid transit, a shopping mall, theatres, restaurants, a library, and Central Park. The park has trails, ponds, golf, tennis, and cycling. Living room with gas fireplace, books, and TV. Breakfast is prepared and served by one of the hosts, who is a restaurateur. Parking on the premises. Visa, MasterCard, American Express. Smoking on a covered porch.

Tall Cedars B&B

Dwyla and Ed Beglaw
720 Robinson Street
Coquitlam, BC V3J 4G1
(604) 936-6016 Fax: (604) 936-6016
E-mail: tallcedars_bnb@bc.sympatico.ca

• In Coquitlam, bordering on North Burnaby.
From Seattle, take the Bellingham-Lynden
route to the Aldergrove border crossing. Take
Highway 1 west to exit 37 (Cariboo). Phone or
e-mail for further directions.

• Three rooms. One person or two people $45–75. Queen-sized bed; double bed; twin
beds. Private and shared bathrooms. Weekly rates.

• A B&B with tall fir and cedar trees and a lighted, covered balcony with flowers. Near
Simon Fraser University. Twenty minutes from downtown Vancouver. Down comforters.
Sitting room with TV and books. Full or Continental breakfast includes homemade
muffins and biscuits. **In the hosts' own words:** "It's not just a business for us; we enjoy
having guests visit us from around the world."

Woodside B&B

Helen Wood
100 College Park Way
Port Moody, BC V3H 1S4
(604) 939-3718 Fax: (604) 939-3718
E-mail: woodside_bb@hotmail.com
Web site: http://www.bbcanada.com/
**   1798.html**

• Two rooms and one honeymoon suite. One
person $45–60; two people $60–85. Queen-
sized bed; double bed; twin beds.

• A B&B on a quiet, tree-lined residential street, across the street from a large park with
forest trails and a swimming pool. Near Burnaby and Simon Fraser University. A bus that
stops in front of the B&B connects to rapid transit and a commuter train that reaches
downtown Vancouver in twenty minutes. Five minutes' drive from cafés, movie theatres,
and malls. Sitting room with grand piano and fireplace. Den with TV, VCR, stereo, and
reading chairs. Dining room with antique mahogany table and buffet and adjacent patio
that looks out onto a flower garden and trees. Honeymoon suite has a view of the forest,
a pine queen-sized bed, pine dressers, a TV, a VCR, a telephone, and a bathroom with
soaker tub and shower. One of the guest rooms has a double antique brass bed, a TV, and
a telephone. Rooms and suite have flowers from the garden, duvets, and antiques. Full,
three-course breakfast is served in the dining room or on the patio. Hosts provide directions and information on places to see in the Vancouver area. Cat in residence. Smoking
on the patio. **In the hosts' own words:** "Enjoy your stay in our attractive, clean, comfortable house, with us as your friendly hosts."

Terraces on the Waterfront B&B

David Rhodes and Laurie Ann Bone (Rhodes)
936 Alderside Road
Port Moody, BC V3H 3A6
(604) 469-3678 Fax: (604) 469-4893
E-mail: TerracesBB@aol.com
Web site: astronweb/terraces.com

- On Burrard Inlet, thirty minutes east of Vancouver.
- Three rooms. One person or two people $99–189. King-sized bed; queen-sized bed. Ensuite bathrooms. Additional person $25. Twin beds available.
Off-season and mid-week rates.
Luxury and romance packages.
- A B&B on the ocean, with decks that have views of the ocean and with a private boat dock that has deepwater moorage. Guest rooms, a guest sitting area with fireplace, and a guest dining room have decks with views of the ocean. Canada geese, bald eagles, otters, and seals can be seen year round. Guest rooms have TVs, VCRs, and small fridges. Coffee and tea provided in guest rooms. Terry robes and bath products provided. Videos. Deck chairs. Hot tub on lower deck. Canoe, kayak, and sixteen-foot dinghy. Secretarial services available. Hosts offer personalized tours of Vancouver and outlying areas and can arrange harbour cruises and fishing. Fifteen minutes' walk along a shoreline trail from Noons Creek salmon hatchery. Five minutes from restaurants, shopping, and a commuter train that provides morning service to Vancouver and late afternoon service from Vancouver. Fifteen minutes from Belcarra Regional Park, Buntzen Lake, White Pine Beach, golf, and horseback riding. Pickup and drop-off for guests travelling by plane, ferry, train, or cruise ship by arrangement. Continental breakfast includes fruit in season and baked goods. Deposit and cancellation policy; call for information. Visa, MasterCard. Adult oriented. Pets in residence, in the hosts' living quarters. Smoking on the lower deck. **In the hosts' own words:** "Come to our B&B for an unforgettable experience. Our spectacular waterfront location and attractive accommodation provide a friendly, comfortable, and private environment."

Gunilda's Guest House B&B

Patricia Gunilda Drew
26683 Dewdney Trunk Road
Mail: RR 4
Maple Ridge, BC V2W 1N9
(604) 462-7509

• Eleven kilometres east of downtown Maple Ridge.
• Suite. Two people $85. King-sized bed, twin beds, and two day beds. Private bathroom.
Additional person $15.
• A B&B with a view of Blue Mountain, on nine and a half acres of farmland and woods. Suite has high open ceilings, a cedar interior, a separate entrance, and a kitchen/dining area with two chesterfields, sink, fridge, and microwave. The upper floor of the suite has a bedroom with king-sized brass bed, a TV, a writing area, and an ensuite bathroom with soaker tub and shower. French doors in the dining area of the suite lead to a sun room, which has a sitting area, two twin beds, and two day beds for up to four additional guests. The ground floor of the suite has a living room with wood-burning stove and TV, a laundry room, and a bathroom. Hot tub in gazebo. In the area are hiking, nature, and horseback riding trails. Fifteen minutes' drive from Whonnock, Alouette, and Rolley lakes. The hosts, who have lived on the property for thirty-eight years, share their knowledge of the area. Coffee, a bottle of wine, and an evening snack provided. Full breakfast is served on a candlelit table in the dining area of the suite. Check-in times negotiable. Cash, traveller's cheques. No pets. No smoking indoors. **In the hosts' own words:** "Perfect for a romantic getaway or for relaxing after a day of sightseeing and outdoor activities."

Riverside B&B

Wilma and Alan Wilson
21868—132nd Avenue
Maple Ridge, BC V4R 2T1
(604) 463-3167 Fax: (604) 463-7351

● Fifty-five minutes from Vancouver. Five minutes from downtown Maple Ridge. From Vancouver, take Highway 7 (Lougheed). Turn left onto 216th Street. Turn right onto 132nd Avenue.

● Two suites. One person $55; two people $75. Two double beds; double bed and double sofa bed. Ensuite bathrooms. Additional person $20.

● A hand-built log house with antiques, on two acres along the South Alouette River. Near hiking in Golden Ears Park, boating, swimming, and golf courses. Walking, biking, and horseback riding trails from the B&B. Across the street from an equestrian centre and restaurant. Veranda with a view of the river and wildlife. One of the suites is upstairs and has two antique brass double beds, a sitting area with loveseat, armchair, desk, and TV, and a balcony with a view of the river. The other suite has a view of the river, a private wheelchair-accessible entrance, an antique brass double bed, a double sofa bed, a loveseat, a dining table, a TV, and access to the veranda. Full breakfast, including a hot entrée, juice, fruit, homemade muffins, scones, and rolls, is served in the suites, in the dining room, or on the veranda. Cash, cheques, Visa. No pets; dog in residence. Smoking on the veranda. **In the hosts' own words:** "We look forward to welcoming you and ensuring that you have a pleasant stay in beautiful Maple Ridge."

The Counting Sheep Inn

Virginia C. Edwards
8715 Eagle Road, RR 3
Mission, BC V2V 4J1
(604) 820-5148 Fax: (604) 820-5149
E-mail: vcesheep@universe.com
Web site: http://www.vancouver-bc.com/CountingSheep/

• Ninety minutes from Vancouver. Five minutes from Mission, off Highway 7 (Lougheed).
• Three suites. $90–125. King-sized bed; queen-sized bed; twin beds. Ensuite and private bathrooms. Additional person $25.
Knitting and spinning classes.
• A B&B on a six-acre working sheep farm, bordering on Hatzic Lake and a wetland preserve with trumpeter swans. Stalls and pastures for guests' horses. Rose and other flower gardens. Fifteen minutes from the U.S. border. Berry and apple picking in season. Children can attend lambs' births in spring and help with farm chores such as collecting eggs. The host spins wool and knits. Wool and craft shop on the property. Knitting and spinning classes can be arranged. Guest rooms have sitting areas, fireplaces, antique furnishings, TVs, VCRs, duvets, and robes. One of the bathrooms has a double-jetted Jacuzzi. Some of the guest rooms have sofa beds. One of the guest rooms has a private entrance and garden. Another guest room has a private deck and garden. Guest rooms are separate from the hosts' living quarters. In the area are birdwatching, golf, horseback riding, swimming, skiing, fishing, lakes, hiking trails, stores, and restaurants. Bicycles available for exploring neighbouring farms and antique stores. Picnic baskets available. Breakfast, including homemade baked goods, preserves, and eggs (which guests can collect from the hens), is served in the guest suites, in the garden, or on the veranda. Kosher and vegetarian diets accommodated. Kennels for pets; sheepdog in residence. Babysitting available with advance notice. Smoking outdoors. **In the hosts' own words:** "Relax in the garden with a book, watch the sheep grazing in the fields, or take a stroll to the lake with a picnic lunch. The best of new and old—modern luxury in a country setting."

Fence Post Lane B&B

Fran and Martin Perdue
8575 Gaglardi Street
Mission, BC V4S 1B2
(604) 820-7009 Fax: (604) 820-4974
E-mail: cherbert@van.hookup.net
Web site: http://www.bbcanada.com/
** bb_show_web_page.cfm?htmlnum=906**

• Eight kilometres west of Mission. From
Mission, take Highway 7 (Lougheed). Turn right
onto Chester Street, left onto Silverdale Avenue,
and right onto Gaglardi Street.

• One person $45–50; two people $60–75. Queen-sized bed; double bed. Private bathrooms.

• A new thirty-six-hundred-square-foot ranch-style house in the country, on landscaped
acreage with a creek and a bridge. Eight minutes from restaurants, shops, golf, Mission
Raceway, and Westminster Abbey. Forty-five minutes from Harrison Hot Springs. Twenty
minutes from Abbotsford and the U.S. border. An hour from Vancouver. Hiking in Mission,
Whonnock Lake, Hayward Lake, and Rolly Lake. Entertainment room and patios. Full
breakfast with homemade baked goods; diets accommodated. Cat in residence. No smoking.
In the hosts' own words: "Come and enjoy our country hospitality—it's quiet and you'll
love it."

Shalynne-by-the-Lake B&B

Marlene and David Johnston
29487 Silver Crescent, RR 2
Mission, BC V2V 4H9
(604) 826-3161

• From the junction of highways 11 and 7 in
Mission, take Highway 7 west for 7 kilometres
and turn right onto Hayward Street. Take the
first left onto Silver Crescent.

• Two rooms. In winter, $40–55. In summer,
$55–70. Queen-sized bed; double bed and one
twin bed. Two shared guest bathrooms. Additional person $20. Roll-away bed available.

• An all-cedar house on a lake, an hour from Vancouver and ten minutes from Mission City
and a commuter train that reaches downtown in seventy minutes. Hot tub and private beach
with beach chairs. Near swimming, fishing, canoeing, sailing, paddle-boating, biking, and
hiking. Water skiing is available by arrangement, as are picnic lunches for biking and hiking
on local trails. Guests can have fires on the beach. Living room with stone fireplace, TV,
VCR, books, and a view of the lake. Guests can play board games and cards at the kitchen
table, by a second stone fireplace. Portable fireplace on patio. Full or Continental breakfast
is served in the dining room, which has a view of the lake, or on the patio. Cash, Visa, traveller's cheques. Children over five welcome. No pets. Smoking outdoors. **In the hosts' own
words:** "Enjoy outstanding hospitality in a wonderful setting. Be our special guests. Come
as strangers, leave as friends."

Harrison Mills Country House

Fred and Betty Block
828 Kennedy Road
Mail: Box 59
Harrison Mills, BC V0M 1L0
(604) 796-0385 Fax: (604) 796-2214
Toll-free from within Canada and the U.S.: 1-800-551-2511

• Ninety minutes east of Vancouver. Thirty minutes from Mission. Take Highway 7 (Lougheed) east through Mission. (Alternatively, take Highway 1 to the Abbotsford-Mission turnoff (Highway 11), go north to Highway 7 (Lougheed), and turn right.) Take Highway 7 (Lougheed) east to School Road, just over the Harrison Bridge. The B&B is a yellow farmhouse.

• Four rooms. Two people $125–150. Queen-sized bed. Ensuite bathrooms. Additional person $20. Off-season rates.

• A Victorian farmhouse on a seventeen-acre Christmas-tree farm in the Fraser Valley, ninety minutes from Vancouver. Antiques and views of mountains and rivers. Guest rooms have antiques, terry robes, and views of surrounding farms. Coffee and tea are set at guest room doors in the morning. Library with books, magazines, games, and puzzles. Family room with pool table, TV, and fireplace. Movies in a sixteen-seat theatre. Indoor hot tub and sauna. Near skiing at Hemlock Valley and boating and swimming at Kilby Park. Two minutes from a new golf course. Fishing for cutthroat trout and coho and spring salmon in the Harrison River. Eleven hundred bald eagles winter in the area; some can be seen in the trees around the house. Near Harrison Mills, a historical sawmill town with a turn-of-the-century heritage store and museum. Fifteen minutes' drive from hot springs pool at Harrison Hot Springs. Small weddings and reunions accommodated. Full breakfast, including fresh fruit, cereal, baked goods, and a hot entrée, is served in the dining room. No pets; English setter in residence. Smoking outdoors. **In the hosts' own words:** "Enjoy a brisk walk around our acreage, meander along country roads, or pick some luscious blackberries. Our home is your home, and we encourage our guests to relax and live on country time for a while."

Historic Fenn Lodge

Diane Brady and Gary Bruce
15500 Morris Valley Road
Mail: Box 67
Harrison Mills, BC V0M 1L0
(604) 796-9798 Fax: (604) 796-9274
Toll-free from within Canada and the U.S.: 1-888-990-3399
E-mail: fennlodg@dowco.com
Web sites: http://www.tbc.gov.bc.ca/chamber/fenn.html
http://www.vancouver-bc.com/FennLodgeBB

• Ninety minutes from Vancouver. Three hours from Seattle. Thirty minutes from Mission.

• Six rooms and one suite. $85–105. Ensuite and shared guest bathrooms. Additional person $25.

• An eight-thousand-square-foot house built in 1903, on ninety acres with forest trails that lead to a half mile of riverfront and a two-hundred-foot waterfall. Sixty-by-twenty-foot swimming pool with patio. Covered porch with tables and chairs. Guest library/sitting room and guest living room with fireplace are on the main floor. The suite, which accommodates up to six people, is on the ground floor and has a fireplace and doors that lead to the pool. Hammocks, swings, benches, picnic tables, and garden furniture. Twenty minutes from Harrison Hot Springs and skiing at Hemlock Valley. Fifteen minutes from Weaver Creek spawning channels, Agassiz-Harrison Historical Museum, and an agricultural research station. Ten minutes from Kilby historical store and farm. Five minutes from a golf course. Near hiking, biking, downhill and cross-country skiing, canoeing, kayaking, birdwatching, horseback riding, hang-gliding, paragliding, and year-round fishing for steelhead, sturgeon, trout, and salmon; guides and gear available. Full breakfast. Lunch and dinner by arrangement, for an extra fee. Reservations recommended. Cash, traveller's cheques, Visa, MasterCard, Interac. Phone for information on children and pets. Smoking outdoors. **In the hosts' own words:** "Our beautifully restored 1903 house extends a warm invitation to relax and revitalise. We offer an ideal setting for a workshop, retreat, or reunion. The Chehalis River curls around the property from northwest to south, providing deep fishing pools and pleasant paths for strolling. Share a healthy and delicious breakfast with us, and then set out to explore the surrounding towns and countryside or just relax and enjoy the B&B."

Little House on the Lake

Arla and Wayne Swift
6305 Rockwell Drive
Mail: Box 492
Harrison Hot Springs, BC V0M 1K0
(604) 796-2186 Fax: (604) 796-2186
Toll-free from within Canada and the U.S.: 1-800-939-1116
Toll-free fax from within Canada and the U.S.: 1-800-939-1116
E-mail: littlehouse@vancouver-bc.com
Web site: http://www.vancouver-bc.com/LittleHouse/

• Ninety minutes from Vancouver. From Highway 1, turn north onto Highway 9. At the four-way stop in Harrison Hot Springs, turn right. Continue for 3 kilometres to the B&B.

• Four rooms. One person $130–150; two people $155–175. Queen-sized bed. Ensuite bathrooms. Additional person $25. Extended stay rate for two nights or more, $10 less per night.

• A hand-hewn log lodge with a private beach on the shore of Harrison Lake. Guest rooms have fireplaces, sitting areas, balconies, skylights, CD players, small TVs with VCRs, and flowers. Lake, mountain, and forest views. Hand-carved mahogany four-post or iron and brass beds with down comforters (alternatives to down available). Guest living room with stone fireplace, billiards, games table, upright grand piano, TV, VCR, conversation area, and washroom with utility sink for artists to use. Guest fridge with complimentary soda and juice. Books, videos, and CDs. Hot tub with a view of the lake. Robes provided. Dock and canoe. Roof-top and lower decks with views. In the area are skiing, swimming, windsurfing, sailing, kayaking, hiking, mountain biking, golf, art and music festivals, and country fairs. Near fine dining restaurants. Afternoon tea and evening snack by request. Morning coffee and muffins delivered to guest rooms. Full breakfast is served in a lakeside library/dining room. Reservations recommended. Visa, MasterCard. Young people over sixteen welcome. No pets; German shepherd, hamsters, and squirrels in residence. Nonsmoking establishment. **In the hosts' own words:** "A warm welcome in a beautiful setting awaits you with an invitation to retreat, relax, and renew. Permission to do absolutely nothing is gladly given."

Abbeydale House B&B

Mary and Colin Rankin
17346—27A Avenue
Surrey, BC V4P 9P8
(604) 531-9768 Fax: (604) 531-8756
E-mail: abbeydale@vancouver-bc.com
**   mcrankin@axionet.com**
Web sites: http://www.islandnet.com/
**   ~pixsell/ bcbbd.htm**
http://www.vancouver-bc.com/
http://www.virtualcities.com

• Five minutes from the U.S. border. Forty-five minutes from Vancouver. Four kilometres from White Rock.
• Two rooms. One person $60; two people $70. Queen-sized bed. Shared guest bathroom.
• A house on an acre of landscaped grounds, with English-style décor. Slate floors, oak furnishings, and formal guest dining and living rooms. Lawn for playing croquet and badminton. Heated pool. Hosts direct guests to nearby golf, tennis, nature walks, beaches, and fine dining restaurants. English breakfast is served in the dining room or by the pool. **In the hosts' own words:** "We pride ourselves on detail. We are committed to your enjoyment, and we want you to return."

White Heather Guest House

Glad and Chuck Bury
12571 Ninety-eighth Avenue
Surrey, BC V3V 2K6
(604) 581-9797

• Ten minutes from Highway 1. Twenty-five minutes from the U.S. border.
• Two rooms. One person $45–55; two people $55–65. Queen-sized bed; double bed. Ensuite half bathroom and shared guest bathroom. Children's rates negotiable.
• A house with mountain views, in a quiet suburb close to rapid transit, near the highway to downtown Vancouver. Guest rooms, breakfast room, TV, and living rooms are on the main floor. Patio, deck, and guest TV room. Hosts share their knowledge of the area and Vancouver Island. Pickup from plane, ferry, train, and rapid transit. Full English breakfast with homemade bread is served in a sun room that has a view of the mountains on the north shore. Children welcome. No pets. No smoking. **In the hosts' own words:** "We are well travelled and enjoy sharing our home with you."

B&B on the Ridge

Dale and Mary Fennell
5741—146th Street
Surrey, BC V3S 2Z5
(604) 591-6065 Fax: (604) 591-6059
E-mail: fennell@planeteer.com
Web site: http://www.vancouver-bc.com/BBRidge

• From Highway 1, take exit 66 or exit 53 onto Highway 15 (Pacific). Turn right onto Highway 10 (Fifty-sixth Avenue). Turn right onto 146th Street.
From Vancouver, take Highway 99. Take exit 16 onto Highway 10. Turn left onto 146th Street.
From the Victoria ferry, take exit 17 onto Highway 10. Turn left onto 146th Street.
From the U.S., take Highway 5. Take exit 265 (truck crossing) onto Highway 15 (Pacific). Turn left onto Highway 10 (Fifty-sixth Avenue). Turn right onto 146th Street.

• Three rooms. One person $45–60; two people $50–80. Queen-sized bed; queen-sized bed and day bed; twin beds. Ensuite and private bathrooms. Additional person $10. Two cots, pull-out couch, and crib available.

• A B&B on half an acre in a quiet country setting, with skylights, antiques, and a wrap-around deck. Ten minutes' drive from beaches, shopping, golf courses, rapid transit, a race track, antique shops, restaurants, and the U.S. border. Twenty-five minutes from ferries and Vancouver International Airport. Thirty-five minutes from downtown Vancouver. Ten minutes from the Northview Golf and Country Club, which holds a PGA Open Golf Tournament. Guest sitting area with TV and VCR. Full breakfast. **In the hosts' own words:** "We offer a warm welcome with a relaxed and tranquil atmosphere. Our light is always on, and our door is always open."

Dorrington B&B

Pat Gray
13851—19A Avenue
White Rock, BC V4A 9M2
(604) 535-4408 Fax: (604) 535-4409
E-mail: grayp@direct.ca
Web site: http://www.bbcanada.com/508.html

• In Surrey, take Highway 99A (south of Highway 99) south to exit 10. Take Crescent Beach Road. Turn left onto 140th Street. Turn right onto 19A Avenue.
• Three rooms. One person $65–80; two people $75–90. Queen-sized bed; double bed. Ensuite bathrooms. Off-season rates.
Minimum stay two nights.
• A B&B on half an acre of gardens, with an outdoor tennis court and hot tub, five minutes from White Rock's beach promenade, cafés, specialty shops, art galleries, antiques, and restaurants. Thirty minutes from ferries to Victoria and the Gulf Islands. Sitting room with twelve-foot ceilings, a river rock fireplace, and a view of the gardens. Guest rooms are decorated in themes. Towels, robes, slippers, scented soap, and tennis rackets and balls provided. The hosts provide menus and recommendations to local restaurants and picnic baskets for outings to Stanley Park. Full breakfast is served indoors or on the patio. Deposit of one night's rate required to hold reservation. Cancellation notice seven days. Check-in 2:00 to 9:00 p.m.; check-out until 11:00 a.m. Visa. Adult oriented. No pets; miniature dachshund in residence. No smoking. **In the hosts' own words:** "Luxury and elegance in a peaceful setting."

Fisher's B&B

Jill Fisher
5033—209th Street
Langley, BC V3A 5Y4
(604) 534-1104

• Two rooms. $55. Double bed; twin beds.
Shared guest bathroom. Extended stay rates.
• A B&B two blocks from a golf course, two and
a half blocks from a swimming pool, and within
walking distance of Langley. Fifteen minutes
from the U.S. border. Easy access from the high-
way. One block from a bus stop. Living room, TV, VCR, fireplace, sun room, deck, and
enclosed yard. Breakfast includes juice, fruit, cereal, toast, and homemade muffins and jam.
Full hot breakfast for a fee. Off-street parking with space for RV. Small well-behaved pets
welcome. No smoking. **In the hosts' own words:** "Relax, put your feet up, and enjoy the
friendly warmth of our home-style hospitality."

The Goose Green B&B

Lynn Moore and Chris Mion
7047—210th Street
Langley, BC V2Y 2R8
(604) 533-3456 Fax: (604) 533-3453
Toll-free: 1-877-533-3456
E-mail: Chris_Mion@bc.sympatico.ca
Web site: http://www.bestinns.net/canada/bc/
  goosegreen.html.

• Five minutes from Highway 1. Take 200th
Street exit southbound. Turn left onto Seventy-
second Avenue. Turn right onto 210th Street and look for the B&B's sign.
• Rooms and one suite. One person $55–65; two people $65–75. Queen-sized bed; queen-
sized bed and queen-sized hide-a-bed. Ensuite and private bathrooms.
• A ranch-style house on an acreage with a landscaped garden, a hot tub, a sauna, and an outdoor pool. Near the original trading post at Fort Langley. Fifteen minutes' drive from six golf
courses, horseback riding, and hot air ballooning. Less than an hour from Vancouver, ferries,
Vancouver International Airport, and the U.S. border. Guest rooms have queen-sized brass
beds and TVs. Suite has a queen-sized bed, a queen-sized hide-a-bed, a fireplace, a VCR, a
fridge, and a garden patio and can accommodate an extra bed. One of the guest rooms has a
private bathroom with clawfoot tub. Full breakfast includes eggs from the B&B's free-range
chickens. Special diets accommodated with advance notice. Wheelchair accessible. Children
over seven welcome. No pets; cat and dogs in residence. No smoking indoors. **In the hosts'
own words:** "Whether you are on business, on a journey, or celebrating an event, we look
forward to making your stay special in our private, quiet house."

Cedaridge Country Estate

Lucille Johnstone
9260—222nd Street
Langley, BC V1M 3T7
(604) 882-8570 Fax: (604) 888-7872
Web site: http://www.vancouver-bc.com

• From Highway 1, take exit 58 onto 200th Street. Go north over the freeway and continue to the end of 200th street. Turn right onto 96th Avenue and continue for 5 kilometres. Turn right onto 222nd Street and continue for 1 kilometre. The B&B's sign is on the left.

• Three rooms. $60–75. King-sized bed; queen-sized bed; twin beds. Ensuite bathrooms.

Group rate for the three rooms. Off-season rates.

• A B&B on fifty acres by the Salmon River, an hour from Vancouver, with an eastern view that extends 120 kilometres, to the mountains in the Hope area, and a southern view that extends 120 kilometres, into the state of Washington. Guest indoor swimming pool, sauna, games room, library, sitting rooms, tennis court, lawns, and patios. Trails for walking, jogging, and cycling on the property and in the immediate area. On site equestrian centre; training lessons and accommodation for guests' horses available for additional fees. Riding on the property and on eight kilometres of off-site riding trails. Five minutes from three golf courses. Fifteen minutes from a shopping centre. Near historical Fort Langley, a winery, restaurants, ice rinks, and a bowling alley. Guest rooms are on the top floor. One of the guest rooms has a king-sized bed with duvet, a gas fireplace, a covered balcony, two vanity areas, and a sunken tub. Afternoon coffee or tea provided. Full breakfast. Deposit of one night's rate required to hold reservation. Check-in 1:00 to 6:00 pm.; check-out until 11:00 a.m. Cash, traveller's cheques, Visa, MasterCard. Adults only. Smoking outdoors. **In the hosts' own words:** "You will enjoy our scenic, spacious, spectacular, and secluded retreat."

Big Sky B&B

Cindy and Rob Kugel
21333 Allard Crescent , RR 16
Langley, BC V1M 3H8
(604) 888-8102
Toll-free from within North America:
 1-888-881-2889

• Ten minutes from Fort Langley. Ten minutes
from Highway 1. An hour from downtown
Vancouver.
• Two rooms. One person $50; two people $55.
Queen-sized bed. Private or shared guest bathroom. Hot tub heated for a $5 fee.
• A B&B in the country, with a heated indoor swimming pool, a sauna, a hot tub, and a deck
with a view of meadows, mountains, and the Fraser River. Near Fort Langley's Hudson's Bay
Fort historical site. On bicycle route. Guests can walk to the Fraser River through meadows
behind the house. Antique stores and gift shops in Fort Langley. One kilometre from fish-
ing, picnicking, and camping at Derby Reach regional park. Five minutes' ride across the
Fraser River on the Albion ferry from Fort Langley to hiking at Golden Ears Provincial Park.
Within thirty minutes of three golf courses. Birdwatching in the area. Guest living room with
fireplace. Jacuzzi. Use of kitchen by arrangement. Hot tub heated for a $5 fee. Full break-
fast includes homemade jam and farm-fresh eggs. Reservations recommended. Exotic birds,
rabbits, chickens, and dogs on the premises. **In the hosts' own words:** "We offer a very
casual, friendly, and relaxed B&B and an animal lovers' paradise. Surround yourself with
the peace of our pastoral setting and the comforts of a luxurious house. The sunsets are spectacular—remember to leave time to enjoy the big sky."

Traveller's Joy B&B

Sylvia and Alan Schwertner
59 Wagonwheel Crescent
Langley, BC V2Z 2R1
(604) 533-2696 Fax: (604) 533-3480
Web site: http://www.vancouver-bc.com/
 TravellersJoyBB/

• From Highway 1, take exit 66 south to 232nd
Street. Turn left onto Fifty-sixth Avenue, right
onto Clovermeadow, and left onto Wagonwheel.
• Two rooms. One person $40; two people $60.
Queen-sized bed and sofa bed; queen-sized bed. Ensuite and private bathrooms.
Additional person $15. Weekly and off-season rates.
• A B&B in a quiet residential area, a few minutes' drive from Fort Langley, parks, restaurants, and shopping. An hour from Vancouver. Five minutes from Highway 1. Ten minutes
from the U.S. border. Near golf, cycling and walking trails, beaches, a race track, Langley
Airport and flight museum, equestrian centres, horseback riding trails, farms, and a winery. Guest living room. Country-style garden. Guest rooms have private balconies. One of
the guest rooms has a sitting area with sofa bed. English or Continental breakfast with
garden produce and seasonal fruit. Reservations recommended. Deposit of one night's rate
required to hold reservation. Cancellation notice seventy-two hours. Check-in between
4:00 and 6:00 p.m. or by arrangement; check-out until 11:00 a.m. Cash, cheques, traveller's cheques. Not equipped for children under five. Pets welcome; two cats in residence.
Smoking outdoors. **In the hosts' own words:** "We invite you to enjoy our friendly, infor-
mal hospitality. We are happy to provide you with information on local, Vancouver, and
Fraser Valley attractions and to direct you to a variety of day trip options."

Everett House B&B

Cindy and David Sahlstrom
1990 Everett Road
Abbotsford, BC V2S 7S3
(604) 859-2944 Fax: (604) 859-9180

• From Highway 1, take exit 92. Go north on Sumas Way for two blocks. Turn right onto Marshall and continue for about six blocks. Turn right onto Everett Road. The B&B is the first house on the left.

• Two suites and one room. Two people $70–105. King-sized bed; queen-sized bed. Ensuite and private bathrooms. Additional person $15.

• A Victorian house in the central Fraser Valley, with a view of Sumas Prairie and Mount Baker. Suites have clawfoot bathtubs, private decks, double-head showers, and Victorian décor. Beds have Battenburg lace linen. In the area are shopping, golf, horseback riding, hiking, fishing, skating, and swimming. Forty minutes from skiing at Mount Baker. Guest hot tub in the garden. Home theatre and movies. Breakfast is served in guest rooms, in the dining room, or outdoors. Cash, Visa, MasterCard. Smoking outdoors. **In the hosts' own words:** "Our B&B is an ideal retreat from the world or a romantic getaway. When you are our guest, we want you to feel special."

The Manse B&B

Yoko and Dick Goold
4314 Wright Street
Abbotsford, BC V2S 7Y8
(604) 853-7984 Fax: (604) 853-3753
Web site: http://www.faximum.com

• In the town of Clayburn, off Highway 11 between Abbotsford and Mission.

• Three rooms. One person $60; two people $65. Queen-sized bed and sofa bed, ensuite bathroom; double bed, shared guest bathroom; twin beds, shared guest bathroom. Additional person $20.

• A 1912 house built originally for ministers of the village church, with a garden and a patio. Near hiking, cycling, and trail riding. Clayburn has a general store, a tea shop, a brick church, an old schoolhouse, and turn-of-the-century buildings. Two of the guest rooms have French doors that lead to a balcony that overlooks the garden. Guest sitting room on the main floor with fireplace, grand piano, and French doors that lead to the patio and garden. Bicycles available. Full breakfast is served in guests' rooms, in the dining room, or on the patio. Traveller's cheques, Visa, MasterCard. Children welcome.

Glacier View B&B

Beryl and Mike Murrell
40531 Thunderbird Ridge
Mail: Box 3786
Garibaldi Highlands, BC V0N 1T0
(604) 898-1630 Fax: (604) 898-1630
E-mail: glacierv@mountain-inter.net
Web site: http://www.bbcanada.com/1574.html

• In Squamish (halfway between Vancouver and Whistler).
• Two rooms. One person $60; two people $75. Double bed; queen-sized bed. Private and shared bathrooms. Additional person $15. Fold-up bed available.
• A modern house in the Garibaldi Highlands area of Squamish, with views of coastal mountains. Near trail walks, valley and alpine hiking, rock climbing, golf, fishing, river rafting, and eagle viewing in winter. Guest sitting room with private entrance, TV, and small fridge. Full breakfast is served in the dining room or on the deck. Children welcome by arrangement. Small pets may be accommodated; dog and cat in residence. Smoking on the deck. **In the hosts' own words:** "From our B&B high in the Garibaldi Highlands, enjoy warm hospitality and spectacular coast mountain views while you share a delicious full breakfast with us."

Hummingbird Pension

Abe and Yoko Kushida
Mile 18.5 Upper Squamish
Mail: Box 3653
Garibaldi Highlands, BC V0N 1T0
(604) 898-2809 Fax: (604) 898-2809
Web site: http://www.mountain-internet.net/hummingbird

• Ninety minutes from Vancouver. Forty-five minutes from Whistler. Twenty
minutes from Brackendale.

• Five rooms. One person $70–85; two people $140–170. Queen-sized bed. Ensuite and shared bathrooms. Dinner $15 per person.

• A B&B on six and a half acres with flower gardens, fruit trees, a pond, and views of mountains and a small waterfall. Guest living room with river rock fireplace, counter with stools,
and balcony. Four of the guest rooms have balconies. Picnic tables. Barbecue. Indoor seven-
person Jacuzzi. Near horseback riding, river rafting, and sightseeing flights. Wedding ceremonies accommodated. Full breakfast. Dinner with Canadian and Japanese cuisine available. Check-in 2:00 p.m.; check-out until 10:00 a.m. Dog and chickens on the property. **In
the hosts' own words:** "Come and join us—relax at our silent place."

Brew Creek Lodge

Peter and Susan Vera
1 Brew Creek Road
Whistler, BC V0N 1B1
(604) 932-7210 Fax: (604) 932-7223

• Fifteen minutes south of Whistler Village. At the lodge's signpost on Highway 99, turn west onto Brew Creek Road and continue for 1 kilometre.

• Six rooms in a lodge. One person or two people $85. Ensuite bathrooms. Additional person $25.

Two-storey guest house (sleeps thirteen). One to six people $450. Two private bathrooms. Additional person $75.

Three-storey guest house (sleeps eight). One to six people $450. Two private bathrooms. Additional person $75.

Cabin. One to four people $200. Private bathroom.

Breakfast not included; Continental breakfast provided for a fee.

• A lodge, a two-storey guest house, a three-storey guest house, a meeting house, and a cabin on two landscaped acres in a wilderness setting, fifteen minutes south of Whistler. Lodge has six guest rooms, a dining area, and a sitting area with stone fireplace. Two-storey guest house, which accommodates up to thirteen people, has a kitchen, a dining room, a living room, a Jacuzzi, and a suite with king-sized bed, fireplace, bathroom, and private entrance. Three-storey guest house, which accommodates up to eight people, has a kitchen, a dining room, a dry sauna, a Jacuzzi, and a living room that has a stone fireplace and opens onto a deck. Log meeting house, built over Brew Creek, has a stone fireplace and a view of the surrounding forests and mountains and accommodates meetings of up to thirty people. On the grounds are a six-person guest outdoor hot tub, a volleyball court, and a natural swimming pond. Near hiking and biking trails. Near tennis, golf, horseback riding, and river rafting.

Haus Landsberg B&B

Heinz and Donna Wango
3413 Panorama Ridge
Whistler, BC V0N 1B3
(604) 932-5233 Fax: (604) 932-5233
E-mail: haus@uniserve.com
Web site: http://www.bbcanada.com/167.html

• From Vancouver, go north on Highway 99 to Whistler. In Whistler, go through two traffic lights and turn right onto Panorama Ridge. The B&B is the fourth house from the end of Panorama and has a sign.
• Three rooms. In winter, one person $120, two people $130. In summer, one person $85, two people $95. Queen-sized bed and one twin bed; double bed and twin bunk beds. Ensuite bathrooms. Additional person $30.
• A quiet house with a view of Alta Lake, Blackcomb ski runs, and mountains. Fifteen minutes' walk from Whistler Village via the Valley Trail, which is lit at night. Guest rooms have TVs, down comforters, and ensuite bathrooms with Jacuzzi tubs. Pickup from bus and train. Hosts provide transportation to ski lifts. Full, varied breakfast includes a hot entrée, fresh fruit, granola with yogurt or milk, homemade bread, jam, juice, coffee, and tea. Parking. Bicycle and ski storage. Check-in after 4:30 p.m.; check-out until 10:00 a.m. Cancellation notice thirty days. Visa. No smoking. **In the hosts' own words:** "We offer a European and truly Canadian high alpine experience."

Golden Dreams B&B

Ann and Terry Spence
6412 Easy Street
Whistler, BC V0N 1B6
(604) 932-2667 Fax: (604) 932-7055
Toll-free: 1-800-668-7055
E-mail: goldendreams@whistlerweb.net

• From Vancouver, take Highway 99 for 111
kilometres to Whistler. At Whistler's fourth traffic light, turn left onto Lorimer. Go down the
hill past the school and turn right onto Balsam
Way. Take the first left onto Easy Street. The B&B is the third house on the left; enter
through the separate arched guest entrance.

• Rooms. In winter, one person or two people $85–115. In summer, one person or two
people $75–95. Queen-sized bed; two double beds. Private and shared guest bathrooms.
Additional person $25. Child over 5 $10.

• A B&B with mountain views, one mile from ski lifts, restaurants, and village shops. Bike
rentals at the B&B. On the Valley Trail, which leads to several golf courses, Rainbow Beach,
and a sports centre. Guest rooms are decorated in Victorian, Asian, and Aztec themes and
have down comforters and sherry decanters. Guest living room with fireplace and mountain
view. Guest kitchen. Outdoor hot tub. Breakfast includes homemade bread, waffles, homemade preserves, and cappuccino. Vegetarian diets are accommodated. Visa, MasterCard.
Children welcome. No smoking indoors. **In the hosts' own words:** "We invite you to be surrounded by nature's beauty and enjoy a wholesome breakfast at our B&B."

Stancliff House B&B

Stan and Shirley Langtry
3333 Panorama Ridge
Mail: Box 995
Whistler, BC V0N 1B0
(604) 932-2393 Fax: (604) 932-7577
Web site: http://www.bbcanada.com/
    264.html

• From Vancouver or the Horseshoe Bay ferry
terminal, take Highway 99 north. Go through the
Whistler Creek area and continue to the Brio
area. Turn right onto Panorama Ridge.

• Two rooms. In summer, two people $75–95. In winter, two people $85–120. Queen-sized
bed; twin beds. Additional person $20.

• A house on the side of Whistler Mountain, with a view of a valley. Near lakes, a golf
course, tennis courts, and the seventeen-kilometre Valley Trail. Within walking distance of
Whistler Village. Guest hot tub, TV room, microwave, sink, and fridge. Piano, small art collection, wood stove, and patio. Pickup from bus and train can be arranged. Hosts help guests
plan activities. Tea and coffee supplies provided. Full breakfast. Parking and ski/bike storage. Smoking on decks. **In the hosts' own words:** "Welcome to our home. Enjoy warm hospitality and hearty Canadian breakfasts in our contemporary-style house."

The Inn at Clifftop Lane

Sulee and Alan Sailer
2828 Clifftop Lane
Whistler, BC V0N 1B2
(604) 938-1111 Fax: (604) 938-9880
Toll free: 1-888-281-2929
E-mail: cliffinn@direct.ca
Web site: http://www.whistler.net/resort/accomodations/cliffinn

• One kilometre from Whistler Creekside and 4 kilometres from Whistler Village. Approaching from Vancouver, turn right at the Bayshores sign and right onto Cheakamus Way. At the end of Cheakamus Way, bear right onto Clifftop Lane.

• Five rooms. In winter, two people $130–175. In summer, two people $105–125. Twin beds side by side with king-sized bedding (or twin beds); queen-sized bed; double bed and pull-out sofa bed. Ensuite bathrooms. Additional person $30.

Ski and golf packages.

• A West Coast–style house of log pier and beam construction, with mountain and forest views. Guest rooms have French or Asian antiques, down duvets, TVs, radios, and ensuite bathrooms with Jacuzzi tubs, hair dryers, and toiletries. Guest room with a double bed and pull-out sofa bed has a balcony. VCR and selection of videos. Guest sitting room with stone floor, Oriental carpets, fireplace, books, phone, and long distance phone line. Guest patio with covered hot tub. Guest entrance. Daily housekeeping services. Full breakfast includes fresh juice and fruit, homemade bread and pastry, and a hot entrée. Dinner is available several days a week. Parking. Ski and equipment storage. Deposit of one night's rate required to hold reservation. Cancellation notice thirty days. Check-in after 3:00 p.m.; check-out until 10:30 a.m. Smoking outdoors. **In the hosts' own words:** "Our inn blends the best qualities of a small European hotel and the traditional hospitality of a B&B; enjoy our quiet location, well-decorated rooms, and warm and comfortable surroundings."

Chalet St. Anton

Jan Lowe
3016 St. Anton Way
Mail: Box 1414
Whistler, BC V0N 1B0
(604) 938-9868 Fax: (604) 938-4797

• From Vancouver, go north on Highway 99.
One kilometre south of Whistler Village, turn
left onto Blueberry and immediately left onto
St. Anton Way. The B&B is the third house on
the left.

• Three rooms. In winter, two people $75–125. In summer, two people $70–95. King-
sized bed; queen-sized bed; twin beds. Ensuite bathrooms. Additional bed $20–25.

• A new chalet in a quiet location, close to Whistler Village, ski lifts, and a golf course.
Near a lake and the Valley Trail. Guest sitting room with TV and VCR. Tea and coffee.
Outdoor hot tub among trees. English breakfast. Parking. Bicycle and ski storage. No
smoking. **In the hosts' own words:** "Enjoy our charming chalet at beautiful Whistler
Mountain."

Lorimer Ridge Pension

Eva and Stan Plachy
6231 Piccolo Drive
Whistler, BC V0N 1B6
(604) 938-9722 Fax: (604) 938-9155
Web site: http://www.whistlerinns.com/
   LorimerRidge

• Eight rooms. In winter, one person $90–170,
two people $100–180. In summer, one person
$80–120, two people $90–130. Queen-sized bed;
extra-long twin beds. Ensuite bathrooms.
Five-day and seven-day skiing packages. Summer packages.

• A West Coast–style mountain lodge within walking distance of Whistler Village and ski
hills, with views of Blackcomb, Fissile, and Rainbow mountains. Near golf and hiking.
Guest room beds have duvets. Two of the guest rooms have gas fireplaces. Guest living room
with TV and VCR. Guest living room and billiards room have river rock fireplaces. Heated
floors throughout. Guest outdoor whirlpool, deck, and sauna. Full breakfast. Ski lockers and
storage for sports equipment. Daily housekeeping. Parking. Deposit of one night's rate
required to hold reservation; full payment required thirty days before arrival. Cancellation
notice thirty days. Check-in 3:00 to 10:00 p.m.; check-out until 10:00 a.m. Visa, Master
Card. No pets. No smoking. **In the hosts' own words:** "Our mountain lodge, with its spectacular surroundings and our Canadian hospitality, will make the perfect setting for your holiday."

Edgewater Lodge

Jay Symons
8841 Highway 99
Mail: Box 369
Whistler, BC VON 1B0
(604) 932-0688 Fax: (604) 932-0686
E-mail: jays@direct.ca
Web site: http://www.whistler.net/resort/edgewater

• Three kilometres north of Whistler village, at the intersection of Highway
99 and Alpine Way.
• Twelve rooms. Two people $105–255. King-sized bed; twin beds. Additional
pull-out twin and/or queen-sized bed in each room. Additional person $25–35.
Retreat packages.
Lunch and dinner available.
• A lodge on a lake, with views of Whistler and Blackcomb mountains, on forty-five acres
of forested land on Green Lake, beside the Nicklaus North golf course, the River of Golden
Dreams, the Valley Trail, and Wedge Park. A few minutes from Whistler Village. Guest
rooms and licensed guest lounge/dining room have views of the lake and of Whistler and
Blackcomb mountains. Spa and horseback riding on the property. Canoeing and kayaking
on the lake. Across the street from a recreation centre with a pool, a spa, exercise equipment,
ice skating, raquetball, tennis, and conference room facilities. Lodge staff organizes art
classes, cooking classes, float plane tours, biking, hiking, golf, sailing, swimming, summer
and winter skiing, cross-country skiing, parapenting, rock climbing, and horseback riding.
Six of the guest rooms have living rooms with queen-sized sofa beds and private decks. The
lounge/dining room has seating for up to forty-five guests; more seating is available outdoors in the summer. Lakeside patio and grass area. Meeting space is available in a nearby
private meeting facility, which has audio-visual equipment and accommodates up to twelve
people, or in the lounge, which accommodates up to twenty-five people. Lodge staff organizes itineraries for groups, including inviting experts to teach sessions. Breakfast includes
fruit salad, yogurt, homemade granola, and homemade croissants. Other meals available.
Diets are accommodated at all meals.

Idylwood Inn B&B Chalet

Lily Antunes
8725 Idylwood Place
Mail: Box 797
Whistler, BC VON 1B0
(604) 932-4582 Fax: (604) 932-4556
E-mail: gbsa@whistler.net

• From Whistler Village, take Highway 99 north for 3.5 kilometres. At Alpine Meadows, turn left onto Alpine Way. Take the fourth left, onto Idylwood Place.

• Three rooms separate from the hosts' living quarters. In summer, two people $95–115. In winter, two people $125–145. King-sized bed; queen-sized bed; twin beds. Ensuite and shared guest bathrooms.

Suite separate from the hosts' living quarters. In summer, from $150. In winter, from $200.

The entire B&B. In summer, from $250. In winter, from $300. For guests renting the suite or the entire B&B, breakfast is available for an additional fee.

• A B&B on a quiet cul-de-sac a few minutes' drive from Whistler Village, with a view of Blackcomb and Whistler mountains. Within walking distance of a sports complex, tennis courts, a playground, the Valley Trail, and the Nicklaus North golf course. The B&B is separate from the hosts' living quarters. One of the guest rooms has an ensuite bathroom with Jacuzzi. Another guest room has an ensuite bathroom with steam room. Guest outdoor hot tub. Barbecue, fireplace, stereo, selection of CDs, TV, VCR, selection of videos, and laundry room. Guest room rates include breakfast. For guests renting the suite or the entire B&B, breakfast is available for an additional fee. Double garage with ski tune-up bench. Bike and ski storage. Suitable for families and small groups. Smoking outdoors. **In the hosts' own words:** "Stay in the lap of luxury and soak up the spectacular mountain view from our outdoor hot tub."

Rainbow Creek B&B

Heidi Lieberherr
8243 Alpine Way
Mail: Box 1142
Whistler, BC V0N 1B0
(604) 932-7001

• From Highway 99, 3.5 kilometres north of Whistler Village, turn left at Alpine Meadows onto Alpine Way and continue for three blocks. The B&B is on the right.

• Three rooms. In summer, two people $75–85. In winter, two people $90–105. Ensuite and private bathrooms. Additional person $20.

• A log house surrounded by evergreens, five minutes' drive from Whistler and Blackcomb ski lifts. A few minutes' walk from an ice rink, a swimming pool, a playground, tennis courts, picnic areas, and riding and walking trails at Meadow Park. Living room with fireplace and TV. Guest rooms have mountain views; one has a balcony. Full breakfast is served in the dining room. Afternoon tea. Visa, MasterCard. German spoken. No smoking. **In the hosts' own words:** "Nothing is more spectacular than a Whistler winter—except perhaps a Whistler summer. Enjoy our Swiss hospitality at this great year-round escape."

Alta Vista Chalet B&B Inn

Tim and Yvonne Manville
3229 Archibald Way
Whistler, BC V0N 1B3
(604) 932-4900 Fax: (604) 932-4933
E-mail: avcb_b@direct.ca

• Two kilometres north of Whistler South
(Creekside). Turn left onto Hillcrest Drive,
immediately right onto Alpine Crescent, and left
onto Archibald Way.
• Eight rooms. In summer, one person from $79,
two people from $89. In winter, one person from $120, two people from $135. Queen-
sized bed; twin beds. Ensuite bathrooms. Additional person $20–25. Child 3 to 10 $10.
• A B&B on a treed lot on the Valley Trail, with a view of Alta Lake, two kilometres from
the ski centres of Whistler Village and Whistler South. Fifteen minutes' walk via the Valley
Trail from Whistler Village. Near Lakeside Beach, which has swimming, picnic tables, barbecues, and canoe, kayak, and windsurfer rentals. Two of the guest rooms are larger than the
other six, have TVs, and can accommodate up to four people; one of these rooms has a fireplace. Antiques. Guest living room opens onto a deck with Jacuzzi. Adjoining games room
with TV, VCR, and guest fridge. Sauna. Afternoon tea. Breakfast is served in the dining
room. Off-street parking and ski storage. No smoking.

The Pemberton Valley Inn

Heather and Patrick Bradner
1427 Collins Road
Mail: Box 817
Pemberton, BC V0N 2L0
(604) 894-5857 Fax: (604) 894-5857
E-mail: bradner@whistlerweb.com
Web site: http://www.workfire.com/
    pemberton

• In the Pemberton Valley, 34 kilometres north
of Whistler. Cross the railway tracks and turn
right at the Bank of Nova Scotia. Continue for 1 kilometre and turn right onto Collins
Road. The B&B is the fourth house on the left, set back 250 metres from the road.
• Three rooms. $79–99. King-sized bed; queen-sized bed. Private bathrooms. Additional
person $20. Extended stay rates. Group rates.
• A log house on a seven-acre farm and vineyard, with a view of Mount Currie. Guest
rooms have mountain views, separate entrances, decks, and fireplaces. Hot tub. Breakfast
includes eggs from the farm. Reservations recommended. No pets. No smoking. **In the
hosts' own words:** "Come and enjoy the ambience, stargaze from the secluded hot tub,
and savour a gourmet breakfast. We offer a private, relaxing, and very peaceful setting."

Marina House B&B

Sue and Gordon Bailey
546 Marine Drive
Mail: Box 1696
Gibsons, BC V0N 1V0
(604) 886-7888
Web site: http://www.bcbandb.com:80/
  whis/marina.htm

• Four kilometres from the Langdale ferry terminal.
Seventy-seven kilometres from the Earls Cove ferry terminal.
• Three rooms. One person $80; two people $90. Queen-sized bed, ensuite bathroom; twin beds (or twin beds side by side with king-sized bedding), private bathroom. Additional person $20. Cots available.
• A house on the ocean, with moorage and beach access, a short walk from Gibsons Landing and Molly's Reach. A base for cross country skiing, hiking, trout fishing, golf, canoeing, and sailing day trips. A few minutes' walk from restaurants, a pub, a bookstore, antique shops, art galleries, pottery and jewelry shops, a government dock, and kayak and canoe rentals. Pebble beach. Near a sandy beach for swimming. Guest rooms are on the top floor and have ocean views of Shoal Channel and Lions Bay. Guest entrance. Sitting room with TV and books. Covered porch. Breakfast includes homemade baked goods and local products. Cancellation notice seven days. Visa, MasterCard. Not suitable for children under twelve. No smoking indoors. **In the hosts' own words:** "Enjoy our heritage house in Gibsons Landing."

Fern Creek Cottage

Ellen and Bill Gregg
896 Joe Road
Roberts Creek, BC
Mail: RR 2 Site 40 C–2
Gibsons, BC V0N 1V0
(604) 886-8750 or (604) 922-9749
E-mail: tgregg@direct.ca

•From the Langdale ferry terminal, take Highway 101 through Upper Gibsons for 9 kilometres. Turn left onto Lower Road. Go 3.5 kilometres and turn right onto Joe Road. The B&B is the first cottage on the right. Accessible by bus.
• One-bedroom cottage. Two people $85. Queen-sized bed. Extended stay rates. Open May to September.
• A cottage with a small veranda, on five acres with an English garden, a creek, and a forest. Near beaches, a golf course, parks, and towns. Continental breakfast includes homemade bread and jam. **In the hosts' own words:** "Relax and enjoy our spacious and cheerful cottage and our private, rural setting."

SeaGarden B&B

Marilyn Marshall and Vera Wall
1247 Gower Point Road
Mail: RR 4 Site 15 C–30
Gibsons, BC V0N 1V0
(604) 886-4643 Fax: (604) 886-4619
E-mail: m_marshall@sunshine.net
v_wall@sunshine.net
Web site: http://www.bbcanada.com/2079.html

• From the Langdale ferry terminal, turn left at the lights. In Gibsons, just past Molly's Reach, turn left onto Gower Point Road. At the stop sign before the post office, turn right. At the next stop sign, turn left. Continue for 3 kilometres. The B&B is on the left. A sign giving the B&B's address points down the driveway.

• Two rooms. One person $120; two people $135; three people $185; four people $200. Queen-sized bed. Ensuite or shared guest bathrooms. The second room is rented only to additional travellers in the same group. Minimum stay two nights. Extended stay rates.

• A two-storey house on the ocean, on a high bank, with a garden. Guest rooms, sitting room, and deck on the lower level have a view of mature gardens sloping down to the Strait of Georgia esplanade, with Vancouver Island visible across the strait. Deer graze in the garden. A heron can often be seen. Large fir trees are habitat for eagles. Stone walkway and stairs lead from a guest entrance to a hot tub, a sauna, and a shower in a cedar-sided room among trees. Guest bathroom with Jacuzzi. One of the hosts is a registered polarity practitioner and is available for massage/polarity sessions. Five minutes from shopping, sightseeing, and boating in Gibsons. Three minutes from walking, swimming, and beachcombing at Bonniebrook Beach and Secret Beach. Ten minutes from rainforest hiking at Cliff Gilker Park. Breakfast is served on the deck or in the cedar-sided room. Visa, MasterCard. Adults only. No pets. No smoking. **In the hosts' own words:** "You will be our only guests in our beautiful and very private facility, which provides a special opportunity for self-care, reflection, and relaxation.

Lookout B&B

Günter and Franziska Rebele
318 Shoal Lookout
Mail: Box 1323
Gibsons, BC V0N 1V0
(604) 886-1655 Fax: (604) 886-1655
E-mail: lookout@sunshine.net
Web site: http://www.sunshine.net/lookout

• In Gibsons, a 40-minute ferry ride from the
Horseshoe Bay ferry terminal, which is 30 min-
utes from Vancouver.
• Two rooms. One person $75; two people $85. Two queen-sized beds; queen-sized bed
and one twin bed. Ensuite bathrooms.
Suite (the room with the queen-sized bed and one twin bed and a living room with dou-
ble sofa bed). One person or two people $110. Ensuite bathroom.
Additional person $15. October to March, discount of 20 percent.
Customized guided tours and holiday packages available.
RV parking and hook-up.
• A new house on the ocean, on a bluff with a view of islands and mountains. In the area
are beaches, parks, hiking in the rainforest, sailing, fishing, kayaking, diving, golf, horseback riding, tennis, sightseeing, and shopping. One kilometre from the town of Gibsons,
where there are shops, restaurants, and a harbour. Guest entrance, fitness room, small eating area, fridge, TV, VCR, telephone, bicycles, and RV parking and hook-up. Guest rooms
are decorated in themes and have sliding doors that lead to a balcony. One of the guest
rooms can be rented with a living room to form a suite. Hosts give customized guided
tours of the area. Breakfast is served in a breakfast room that has a skylight. No pets. No
smoking indoors. **In the hosts' own words:** "We are looking forward to your visit."

Sunshine Coast Country Hide-Away

Günter and Marcelina Beyser
1148 Reed Road
Mail: RR 4 Site S1B C–17
Gibsons, BC V0N 1V0
Cel: (604) 740-2960 Fax: (604) 886-7261

• Two kilometres from the upper town centre of
Gibsons.
• Two suites. One person $50; two people $60.
Queen-sized bed and double bed; twin beds.
Ensuite bathrooms. Additional person $15.
• A B&B on a quiet parklike acreage with fir and
cedar trees. One of the suites has twin beds and a fridge. The other suite accommodates two
to four people and has a queen-sized bed and a double bed in an adjoining room. Suites have
TVs, VCRs, and private entrances. Garden and wooded parts of the acreage to walk in. Full
breakfast is served in the dining room or on the deck. German spoken. **In the hosts' own
words:** "Enjoy a getaway from the city, in a country setting on the beautiful Sunshine Coast,
or plan to make your stay with us part of the Vancouver Island circle tour. Relax in our attrac-
tively decorated rooms."

Ocean-View Cottage B&B

Dianne and Bert Verzyl
1927 Grandview Road
Mail: RR 2 Site 46 C–10
Gibsons, BC V0N 1V0
(604) 886-7943 Fax: (604) 886-7943
Toll-free from within North America: 1-800-231-9122
Web site: http://www.bbcanada.com/436.html

• From the Langdale ferry terminal, take Highway 101. Turn left onto Lower Road, left onto Pine Road, and right onto Grandview Road. The B&B is 9 kilometres from the ferry terminal.

• Two rooms. One person $70; two people $80–85. Queen-sized bed; twin beds. Ensuite bathrooms.

Self-contained cottage (sleeps six). Two people $115. Queen-sized bed, two sofa beds, and cot. Private bathroom. Additional person $20. Child under 12 $10.

• A B&B on three acres, with views of the Strait of Georgia and Vancouver Island. Guest rooms have sliding glass doors that lead to a guest deck. Self-contained cottage has a bedroom, a four-piece bathroom with soaker tub, a kitchen, a TV, a fireplace, skylights, and a deck with tables and chairs. Near shopping and restaurants. Afternoon coffee or tea is served. Full breakfast is served in the dining room or the sun room. Cash, traveller's cheques, Visa, MasterCard. French and Dutch spoken. No pets. No smoking. **In the hosts' own words:** "Relax at our B&B and enjoy the Sunshine Coast's spectacular ocean and mountain views and beautiful sunsets."

Bonniebrook Lodge B&B

Karen and Philippe Lacoste
1532 Ocean Beach Esplanade
Mail: RR 4 Site 10 C–34
Gibsons, BC V0N 1V0
(604) 886-2887

• Take the ferry from Horseshoe Bay to Langdale. From the Langdale ferry terminal, take Highway 101. Turn left onto Pratt Road, continue to the bottom, and turn right onto Gower Point Road. The B&B is at the foot of Gower Point Road.

• Four rooms. Two people $80–100. Queen-sized bed; extra-long double bed; extra-long double bed and sofa bed. Private and two shared guest bathrooms with showers.
Additional person $25.
Three suites. Two people $130.

• A 1920s oceanside lodge with a restaurant. Guest rooms are on the upper floor. Guest deck. Guest entrance. Patio with a view of sunsets over the Strait of Georgia. Three of the guest rooms face the ocean. One of the guest rooms has a sitting area with two wing-backed chairs and an antique wardrobe. Another guest room has a queen-sized canopied bed and a sitting area with a sofa. A third guest room has a sitting area with sofa bed and coffee table. Terry robes. Suites have fireplaces and swirl tubs. Full breakfast, including omelettes, hash browns, homemade baked goods, fresh fruit, toast, homemade jam, juice, and coffee or tea, is served in the dining room between 8:30 and 10:00 a.m. For guests leaving early, a Continental breakfast tray is provided. Check-in after 2:00 p.m.; check-out until noon. Cancellation notice three days. No smoking in the guest rooms.

Country Cottage B&B

Philip and Loragene Gaulin
1183 Roberts Creek Road
Mail: Box 183
Roberts Creek, BC V0N 2W0
(604) 885-7448

• From the Horseshoe Bay ferry terminal (30 minutes from Vancouver), take the Sunshine Coast ferry (40 minutes). Take Highway 101 (Sunshine Coast) and continue for 25 minutes. Past the golf course, turn left onto Roberts Creek Road.
• Self-contained cottage. One person $99; two people $115. Queen sized bed. Private bathroom.
Self-contained lodge (sleeps six). One person $105; two people $135. Three queen-sized beds. Private bathrooms. Additional person $50.
• A farmhouse, a cottage, and a lodge, five minutes' walk from Roberts Creek, a beach, swimming, golf, parks, and fine dining at a French restaurant. Hosts help plan and book day trips for hiking, kayaking, scuba diving, fly fishing, and cross-country skiing. The self-contained cottage has a wrought iron queen-sized bed, a kitchen, antiques, and a wood stove. The self-contained lodge has views of an acre of cedars and a grassy pasture and is decorated in Adirondack style, with a river rock fireplace, fly-fishing memorabilia, Navaho rugs, and arts and crafts antique furniture. Lodge has a kitchen, a wood-fired sauna, a campfire circle, and a loft with two queen-sized beds. Separate cottage connected to the lodge by a walkway has a queen-sized bed and a private bathroom. The lodge accommodates up to six people and is rented to one couple or group at a time. English country gardens, croquet equipment, and bicycles. Guests can feed the chickens and sheep. One of the hosts is a spinner and weaver. The other host is a wood worker and antique car and motorcycle enthusiast. Tea and scones are served at 4:00 p.m. on the lawn or in the living room in front of a fire. Full breakfast is cooked on a 1927 Etonia wood-burning stove in an antique-furnished kitchen and is served in the hosts' farmhouse. Adults only. No pets. Nonsmokers. **In the hosts' own words:** "We offer quality service, hospitality, and attention to detail. A visit to our B&B is like staying with friends at their country house."

Pacific Shores B&B

Dorothy Dolphin
5853 Sunshine Coast Highway (Highway 101)
Mail: Box 614
Sechelt, BC V0N 3A0
(604) 885-8938

• From Langdale, take Highway 101 through Sechelt. One hundred metres past the end of town and the T junction, turn into the second driveway on the left.
From Earls Cove, take Highway 101 to Sechelt. Before the T junction and immediately before a highway sign for Highway 101 South, turn right into the driveway.

• Two rooms. $100–125. Queen-sized bed. Ensuite bathrooms. Extended stay rates.

• A B&B on an acre of level waterfront, five minutes' walk from Sechelt. Garden-level guest room has a private entrance, a fireplace, and picture windows with views of the garden and the ocean. Birds, marine life, herons, eagles, seals, and deer are often seen. Across the lawn from a pebble swimming beach. Five minutes' drive from an eighteen-hole golf course. Full breakfast is served in guest rooms or on the patio, which has a view of Trail Bay and the Strait of Georgia. Deposit of one night's rate required to hold reservation. Visa, MasterCard. Adult oriented. No pets. No smoking. **In the hosts' own words:** "Our B&B offers independent serenity, seclusion, and a romantic aspect with direct beach access."

Four Winds B&B

David Fedor and Brenda Wilkinson
5482 Hill Road
Mail: RR 2 Black's Site C–33
Sechelt, BC V0N 3A0
(604) 885-3144 Fax: (604) 885-3182
Toll-free from within North America: 1-800-543-2989
E-mail: fourwinds@sunshine.net
Web site: http://www.sunshine.net/fourwinds

• From Langdale, take the Sunshine Coast Highway (101) to Sechelt. Five kilometres past Sechelt, turn left onto Hill Road, a non-through road. Keep left and continue to the end of the cul-de-sac.
From Earls Cove, on Highway 101, watch for Hill Road on the right, 1 kilometre past the second entrance to Redrooffs Road and 5 kilometres before Sechelt.

• One person $75–120; two people $90–135. Queen-sized bed; twin beds. Ensuite and private bathrooms.

• A B&B on a rocky point jutting out into the ocean. Guest living room surrounded by water on three sides. Guest rooms have window seats that are six metres from the water. Winter storms. Heavy quilts and wool mattress covers. One of the hosts is a registered massage therapist and takes advance bookings. Pickup can be arranged for guests coming by bus from Vancouver and Powell River. Hot tub on a deck. Breakfast is served on the deck or in the dining room; seals and a resident heron are often seen during breakfast. Visa, MasterCard. No children. No pets. No smoking. **In the hosts' own words:** "Celebrate a special occasion or plan a healthy weekend retreat at our B&B."

Diane Mazzei/93

Summer Hill House B&B

Christa Rost
6282 Norwest Bay Road
Mail: RR 2 Drapers Site C–32
Sechelt, BC V0N 3A0
(604) 885-6263 Fax: (604) 885-0196

● From the Langdale ferry terminal, take Highway 101 to Sechelt. Just past
Sechelt, turn right onto Norwest Bay Road and continue for 1 kilometre.

● Three rooms. Two people $45–60. Queen-sized bed, ensuite bathroom; double
bed or twin beds, shared guest bathroom.

● A B&B on a wooded property, with a view of the Strait of Georgia and Vancouver Island.
A few minutes' drive from the village of Sechelt, a beach, shops, and restaurants. One of the
guest rooms has a private balcony and a view of the ocean. Living room with fireplace, TV,
and reading material. Breakfast is served in the dining room or on the deck. Reservations
recommended. German spoken. Children welcome. No smoking. No pets. **In the hosts' own
words:** "Welcome to our B&B on the Sunshine Coast. We offer a variety of delicious breakfasts."

SUMMER · HILL · HOUSE   SECHELT

Mason Road B&B

Joyce Rigaux and John Rayment
5873 Mason Road
Mail: RR 2 TLC Site C–73
Sechelt, BC V0N 3A0
(604) 885-3506 Fax: (604) 885-3506
E-mail: john_rayment@sunshine.net

• From Highway 101, just north of Sechelt, turn right onto Norwest Bay Road. Turn right onto Mason Road and continue for 1 kilometre.
• Two rooms. One person $50; two people $75. Queen-sized bed; twin beds. Ensuite bathrooms. Additional person $25.
Adventure travel tours.
• A new timber-frame house on a forty-acre farm, a few minutes' drive from Sechelt Inlet and the Strait of Georgia. Horses, chickens, and border collies on the property. Horse boarding available. A few minutes' drive from Porpoise Bay Provincial Park, which has a beach, a children's play area, and barbecue pits. Sechelt Inlet has reefs and a sunken destroyer for scuba divers to explore. A few minutes' drive from hiking, cycling, golf, tennis, horseback riding, and backcountry skiing. Hosts arrange adventure travel tours for scuba diving, salmon fishing, kayaking, canoeing, sailing, hiking, and cycling. Guest rooms have separate entrances, private decks, and wool duvets. Eight-person guest hot tub on a cedar deck. Breakfast, including farm-fresh eggs, berries in season, bread baked in a wood stove, and homemade muffins, is served on a cedar deck or in the guest sitting/dining room. Cancellation notice seven days. Children welcome. No pets. No smoking.

Davis Brook Retreat

John and April MacKenzie-Moore
7079 Sechelt Inlet Road
Mail: RR 3 Sandy Hook Site C–17
Sechelt, BC V0N 3A0
(604) 885-9866

• Eight kilometres northwest of the village of
Sechelt.
• Two suites. One person $70; two people
$80–100. Queen-sized bed; queen-sized bed and
sofa bed. Bathrooms in suites. Additional person
$15. Weekly rates.
• A B&B on four wooded acres, with a swimming pool, a hot tub, and a fish pond on parklike grounds. Suites have fireplaces, private decks, and private entrances. The larger suite has
a kitchen and a private yard. Two minutes from kayak and canoe rentals and lessons on
Sechelt Inlet. Five minutes from Porpoise Bay Provincial Park. Twenty minutes from
Tetrahedron recreation plateau. Continental breakfast with fruit is served at guests' convenience. No pets. No smoking. **In the hosts' own words:** "Relax and refresh yourself in our
beautiful surroundings."

Inlet View Guest House

Gloria and David Pye
6937 Porpoise Drive
Mail: Box 1873
Sechelt, BC V0N 3A0
(604) 885-4490 Fax: (604) 885-4490

• Four rooms. $90. Queen-sized bed; double bed
and one twin bunk bed; double bed; two futons.
Two shared guest bathrooms.
Self-contained four-bedroom house (sleeps up to
ten). Breakfast by arrangement. Group rates.
• A post-and-beam-style house near Sechelt, a few metres from a secluded beach for swimming. Open-plan kitchen, dining room, and living area. All rooms have views. Stone fireplace. Solarium with views of Sechelt Inlet and of bald eagles roosting in nearby Douglas
firs. One of the bathrooms has a Jacuzzi tub. Fifteen minutes from shopping, hiking, bicycling, diving, golf, horseback riding, windsurfing, fishing, boating, and skiing. **In the hosts'
own words:** "At our B&B, awaken to the sounds of nature and enjoy the solitude and the
ever-changing mountain sunsets."

Burchill's B&B by the Sea

Jack and Millie Burchill
5402 Donley Drive
Mail: RR 2 Donley Site C–17
Halfmoon Bay, BC V0N 1Y0
(604) 883-2400
Web site: http://www.bbcanada.com/
  478.html

• Off Highway 101, 24 kilometres north of
Sechelt.
• Self-contained cottage. One person or two peo-
ple $90. Double bed and two double bunk beds. Private bathroom. Breakfast ingredients
supplied. Additional person $40. Child $25.
• A self-contained cottage a few steps from the ocean, with a view of Malaspina Strait and
Texada Island. Cottage accommodates eight people and has a master bedroom with double
bed, two bedrooms with double bunk beds, a kitchen, a deck, and a living room with fireplace. Rowboats available. Swimming in the ocean and in a saltwater swimming pool.
Breakfast supplies, including homemade bread, muffins, and jam, are provided in the cottage kitchen. Children welcome. No pets. No smoking. **In the hosts' own words:** "There is
always a lot to see and do on the Sunshine Coast, or you can just relax at the beach or on the
deck by our pool."

Seawind B&B

Pat and George Larsen
9207 Regal Road
Mail: RR 2 Curran Site C–17
Halfmoon Bay, BC V0N 1Y0
(604) 885-4282
Toll-free from within North America:
  1-888-999-5993
E-mail: seawind@sunshine.net

• From the Langdale ferry terminal, take Highway
101 for 42 kilometres. Past Sechelt, turn left onto
Curran. At the second intersection, turn left onto
Regal Road.
From Earls Cove, take Highway 101 for 40 kilometres to Curran Road.
• Two rooms. One person $80; two people $90. Queen-sized bed. Ensuite bathrooms.
Additional person $25.
• A contemporary West Coast–style house among Douglas fir and cedar trees, with a view
of Halfmoon Bay and the Strait of Georgia. Guest rooms have ocean views, covered decks,
and private entrances. Guest sitting room with games, books, TV, VCR, sink, fridge, and
microwave. Near fishing, sea kayaking, cycling, swimming, golf, birdwatching, and summer
and winter scuba diving. Multi-course breakfast is served in the dining room, which has a
view of the ocean, or in the guest living room. Deposit of one night's rate required to hold
reservation. Cancellation notice seven days. Cash, Visa, MasterCard. Adult oriented. No
pets. Smoking on the deck. **In the hosts' own words:** "Our B&B is a place for a romantic
getaway or a retreat from the workday world—let us pamper you with elegant comfort and
gourmet breakfasts."

Beaver Island Inn

Diane and Chris Kluftinger
4726 Webb Road and 4678 Francis Peninsula
  Road
Mail: RR 1 Site 4 C–6
Madeira Park, BC V0N 2H0
(604) 883-2990

• From Langdale, take Highway 101 north. Turn
onto Francis Peninsula Road and continue for 2
kilometres. The B&B's driveway is the first on
the left after the intersection of Francis Peninsula
and Webb roads.

• Five rooms in two cottages. One person $40–65; two people $85. Cottage (sleeps six)
$150. Variety of bed combinations available. Private and shared guest bathrooms.
Additional person $15. Corporate and group retreats. Tugboat charters.

• A B&B on one of Pender Harbour's original homesteads, with a private beach, a 130-foot
dock, and a view of Bargain Harbour and the Thormanby Islands. Orchard and garden with
flowers and shrubs. Farmyard with dogs, cats, pygmy goats, potbellied pigs, and chickens.
One of the guest rooms has a fridge, a microwave, a sink, a toaster, a coffee maker, dishes,
and cutlery. Cottage has a living room, a sun room, and a fireplace. Canoe and rowboat.
Vintage 1920 tugboat available for charters. Five minutes from village centre. Five to fifteen
minutes from hiking, swimming, fishing, diving, and water sports. Moorage available.
Licenced dining room. Breakfast, including ingredients from the farm, is served in the dining room or on the deck, which has a view of the ocean. Dinner available in summer, at an
extra cost. Visa, MasterCard. German spoken. No pets. **In the hosts' own words:** "Let our
Swiss chef pamper you in spectacular country surroundings."

Hotel Lake B&B

June and Barry Leech
4661 Hotel Lake Road
Mail: RR 1 Site 12 C–9
Garden Bay, BC V0N 1S0
(604) 883-9133

• In Pender Harbour. From the Langdale ferry
terminal, take Highway 101 north for an hour
and a quarter. Turn left onto Garden Bay Road
(gas station on the corner) and continue for 5.3
kilometres. Turn onto Irvines Landing Road
and follow signs to Hotel Lake Road.

• Three rooms, one self-contained suite, and one self-contained A-frame cabin. One person or two people $50–75. Queen-sized bed; twin beds; double bed. Ensuite and shared
guest bathrooms. Cabin with shower and outhouse. Additional person in suite or cabin
$25. Weekly rates.
Charters on 40-foot boat.

• A B&B on a lake, on a hobby farm. Swimming, fishing, and rowboating on the lake.
Lakefront fire pit and barbecue. Near golf, diving, hiking, beachcombing, saltwater fishing, shopping, and fine dining restaurants. Forty-foot boat for saltwater boat charters.
Cabin has a fireplace and a loft. Full breakfast. Cash, traveller's cheques. No pets; dog in
residence. Smoking areas. **In the hosts' own words:** "Come and enjoy warm hospitality
and the simple pleasures of life in our idyllic, peaceful lakefront setting."

Owl's Nest Guest House

Sieg and Lucy Grohs
13282 Keelson Road
Irvine's Landing, BC
Mail: RR 1 Site 9 C–4
Garden Bay, BC V0N 1S0
(604) 883-2294 Fax: (604) 883-9855

• Ninety minutes from the Langdale ferry terminal. Twenty minutes from the Earls Cove ferry terminal. From the Sunshine Coast Highway (via Sechelt to Kleindale), turn left onto Garden Bay Road and follow the signs to Irvine's Landing (8 kilometres). Turn right onto Crosstree Road and right onto Keelson Road.

• Suite. Two people $65. Twin beds. Ensuite bathroom.
Two self-contained one-bedroom suites. Two people from $65. Queen-sized bed and queen-sized hide-a-bed. Bathrooms in suites.
Alternatively (with connecting door unlocked), self-contained two-bedroom suite. Two queen-sized beds and two queen-sized hide-a-beds. Two ensuite bathrooms. Six people $150.
Breakfast not provided.

• A guest house on one acre, at the entrance to Pender Harbour and near the Strait of Georgia and Lee Bay. Deer and other animals are often seen. Two blocks from a marina and a pub. Suites have patios or decks, private entrances, and TVs. Two of the suites have fireplaces. Barbecue in a picnic area. Breakfast not provided. Credit cards. Smoking outdoors. **In the hosts' own words:** "We are surrounded by many freshwater lakes and the ocean. Our guests can enjoy many forms of outdoor activities from their comfortable and friendly home away from home."

Beacon B&B

Roger and Shirley Randall
3750 Marine Avenue
Powell River, BC V8A 2H8
(604) 485-5563 Fax: (604) 485-9450

• On Marine Avenue, 2.2 kilometres south of the Comox ferry (the Westview ferry terminal). Thirty kilometres north of the Sechelt ferry (the Saltery Bay ferry terminal). Take Highway 101 and watch for the B&B's sign.

• Two rooms and one suite. One person $75–125; two people $85–125. Queen-sized bed; queen-sized bed and one twin bed; queen-sized bed, one twin bed, and queen-sized murphy bed. Ensuite and private bathrooms. Additional person $20.

• A modern house on the ocean with a view of the Strait of Georgia and snowcapped mountains on Vancouver Island. Half a block from beach access. Thirty minutes from an eighteen-hole golf course, hiking trails, lakes, canoe rentals, a canoe route, and a diving area. Five minutes' drive from fishing. Suite has a sitting room with queen-sized murphy bed. Hosts arrange advance bookings for charters, diving, and sightseeing at Desolation Sound. Indoor hot tub with ocean view. One of the hosts offers massage. Full breakfast is served between 7:00 and 9:00 a.m. Suite is wheelchair accessible. Cash, traveller's cheques, Visa, MasterCard. Adult oriented; children over twelve by arrangement. Cat in residence. Smoking outdoors. **In the hosts' own words:** "If you are trying to get away from all the hustle and bustle of city life, you will truly enjoy our modern house and waterfront setting."

Cranberry Comfort B&B

Deborah and Paul McIsaac
5357 McGuffie Street
Powell River, BC V8A 3T6
(604) 483-4047 Fax: (604) 483-4039
E-mail: paul@pr.mala.bc.ca
Web site: http://www.prwebs.com/b&b

• On the outskirts of Powell River, midway between the Westview and Townsite areas. Three kilometres north of the Comox ferry (the Westview ferry terminal). Thirty-five kilometres north of the Sechelt ferry (the Saltery Bay ferry terminal). The B&B is at the corner of Manson and McGuffie.

• Two rooms. One person or two people $60. Double bed. Shared bathroom. Suite. One person or two people $75. Queen-sized bed and fold-up cot. Ensuite bathroom. Additional person $15. Charters.

• A West Coast–style house with French doors and guest rooms that have balconies. A short walk or drive from restaurants, shopping, a recreation complex, ocean beaches, lakes, and trails for hiking and biking. Bicycles available. Suite has an ensuite bathroom with Jacuzzi tub. The hosts operate a sailing school and charter business in Desolation Sound and arrange fishing and diving charters, sightseeing flights, kayak and canoe rentals, theatre and musical event tickets, and cultural tours. Breakfast includes cranberry baked goods and a selection of coffee and tea. Cash, traveller's cheques. Children welcome by arrangement. Pets welcome in yard; dog in yard. Smoking outdoors and on balconies. **In the hosts' own words:** "Our B&B, located between town and country, offers delicious food and tranquil surroundings, minutes away from a variety of relaxing and exciting activities for individuals and families."

Ocean Beach Lodge B&B

Barbara and Roger Canzian
RR 3 C–9
12297 Scotch Fir Point Road
Powell River, BC V8A 5C1
(604) 487-9299 Fax: (604) 487-9299

• From Powell River's Westview ferry terminal, go 17 kilometres south. Turn right onto Loubert Road.
From the Saltery Bay ferry terminal, go 10 kilometres north to Roberts Road and turn left.
• Rooms. One person $55–80; two people $65–90. Queen-sized bed; twin beds. Ensuite bathrooms. Additional person $15. Extended stay rates.
• A quiet lodge on the ocean, with a pebbled beach and with guest rooms that face Frolander Bay and Malaspina Strait. Bald eagles, Bohemian waxwings, loons, seals, deer, and black bears can be seen. Ten kilometres from an eighteen-hole golf course. Three kilometres from a dive site. Kayak, canoe, and bicycles available. Near fly fishing and canoe route on Lois Lake. Near fishing for salmon and cutthroat and steelhead trout. Barbecue. Outdoor swimming pool with deck. Sauna. Guest sitting room with fireplace. Guest entrance. Full breakfast. Wheelchair accessible. German, French, and Italian spoken. Cash, Visa, MasterCard. Smoking outdoors. **In the hosts' own words:** "Our secluded B&B is on a beach with cool, clear water and oysters and prawns. Grill your own catch on the barbecue."

Savary Island Summer House

Janice and Doug Dalzell
Vancouver Boulevard
Savary Island
Mail: 5305 Sprucefield Road
West Vancouver, BC V7W 3B1
Savary Island number: (604) 483-4727
Vancouver number for messages and faxes: (604) 925-3536

• On Savary Island, at the mouth of Desolation Sound, 140 kilometres north of Vancouver. Accessible by water taxi from Lund, boat, or float plane. The B&B is 1 kilometre from the wharf, by land taxi.
Five-day packages. One person $599.
• Two rooms. One person $125; two people $250. Queen-sized bed. Ensuite half bathrooms and shared guest bathroom. Rates include all meals. Open June to October.
• A log house centrally located on Savary Island, with fireplaces in the living room and dining room. Sandy beaches and wooded trails for hiking. Wildlife in the area. Hosts provide phone numbers and information on flights and water taxis. Picnic lunches available. Meals with local seafood, organically grown vegetables, and desserts are served by candlelight in the dining room. Full breakfast, including fresh-squeezed orange juice, fruit salad, and homemade bread, buns, and jam, is served in the dining room or on the patio. Deposit of one night's rate required to hold reservation. Visa. Not suitable for small children. No pets; dog in residence. Smoking outdoors.

Rainbow Lake Lodge

Karen Soule
Highway 40, RR 1 S1
Princeton, BC V0X 1W0
(250) 295-7988 Fax: (250) 295-4138
E-mail: pcastle@mail.netshop.net

• Near Princeton, at Princeton Castle Resort.
•Seven rooms. Two people $65–125. Private bathrooms. Additional person $20.
Cabins. Seasonal rates. Breakfast not provided.
RV campsite with hookups. Breakfast not provided.
• A log house on 110 acres with a creek and lake, adjacent to the Kettle Valley Railway bed, which has hiking and biking trails. Walking trails along the creek and around the lake. A few minutes' drive from Princeton. Each guest room is individually decorated and has a TV, a VCR, and a private bathroom with Jacuzzi tub. Exercise room, games field with bocci, horseshoe pits, and sandlot volleyball. Guest hot tub. Birds in the area. Near golf and lake fishing. A base for day trips along the Similkameen River and Valley and to wineries in the Okanagan Valley. Near cement ruins from the early 1900s. In winter, snowmobiling, cross-country skiing, and skating on the lake. RV campsite with hookups on the property. Full breakfast for guests staying in the guest rooms. Guest rooms are wheelchair accessible. No pets. Smoking outdoors. **In the hosts' own words:** "Sit back and enjoy the warm country décor. Savour our breakfast creations. You may see a doe with her fawns or a coyote with her pups or hear the warning slap of a beaver as it wanders its way down the creek—all in natural surroundings."

Mountain Valley Ranch

Franz and Janet Bergendahl
RR 1, Johnstone Creek Road West
Rock Creek, BC V0H 1Y0
(250) 446-2805 Fax: (250) 446-2805

• From Osoyoos, take Highway 3 east for 40 kilometres. Take the turnoff for Conkle Lake Provincial Park and continue for 1.2 kilometres.

• Three self-contained suites. One person $50; two people $65. Queen-sized bed and one twin bed. Additional person $15. Children under 7 free. Weekly rates.

• A guest log house at eleven-hundred-metre elevation, with a veranda and a view of forests, hills, and wildflowers. Birds and wildlife can be seen. Authentic log barn and outbuildings. Barn and bale for guests' horses. Suites have kitchens. Near cross-country skiing, tobogganing, and trails for hiking and horseback riding. Fire pit and barbecue. Swimming, fishing, gold panning, river floating, and mountain biking on adjacent crown land, in Kettle River Provincial Park (fifteen minutes away), and in Conkle Lake Provincial Park (thirty-five minutes away). Breakfast includes farm-fresh eggs, fruit, and homemade baked goods.
In the hosts' own words: "We love to serve you."

Fossen's Bar 7 Ranch

Louise and Ed Fossen
Highway 3 West , RR 1
Rock Creek, BC V0H 1Y0
(250) 446-2210 Fax: (250) 446-2210
Web site: http://www.bbcanada.com/186

• On Highway 3, 40 kilometres east of Osoyoos and 8 kilometres west of Rock Creek.

• Two rooms. One person $50; two people $60. Queen-sized bed; double bed. Shared guest bathroom.

Guest log house (sleeps up to five). One person $60; two people $80. Double beds and one twin bed. Private bathroom. Additional person $20. Child $10.

Open April to October.

• A five-hundred-acre working cattle ranch with trails for horseback riding, hiking, and cross-country skiing. Guest rooms are on the lower floor of the hosts' house and have an adjoining solarium and hot tub. Guest log house accommodates five people and has two bedrooms, a living room, a dining room, a bathroom, a kitchen, a TV, a microwave, a woodstove, a covered porch, and electric heat. Landscaped yard with lawnchairs, picnic tables, and children's play area. Breakfast includes farm-fresh eggs and homemade baked goods. Guests staying in the guest house are provided with breakfast supplies or have breakfast in the main house. No smoking indoors. **In the hosts' own words:** "Enjoy fresh air, open vistas, a friendly atmosphere, and the animals and wildlife of our working cattle ranch."

Lake Osoyoos Guest House

Italia Sofia Grasso
5809 Oleander Drive
Mail: Box 1323
Osoyoos, BC V0H 1V0
(250) 495-3297 Fax: (250) 495-5310
Toll-free, for reservations: 1-800-671-8711

• Near downtown Osoyoos.
• Rooms. One person $50; two people $75–95. King-sized bed; queen-sized bed; twin beds. Ensuite bathrooms.
Self-contained suite. Two people $125–150. Queen-sized bed and queen-sized sofa bed. Bathroom in suite.
Off-season rates November to March. Discount of 10 percent on stays of six or more nights.
• A guest house on a lake, with a garden, on a quiet street, ten minutes' walk from downtown. Self-contained ground-floor suite has a kitchen and sliding glass doors that lead to a rose garden. Guest rooms and suite have private entrances. Swimming in the lake. Paddle boats available. Fire pits and gas and briquet barbecues. Full breakfast. Off-street parking. Cash, traveller's cheques. No pets. Smoking in the garden. **In the hosts' own words:** "Our B&B has a luxurious European atmosphere and is an ideal location for a special vacation. If you are celebrating an anniversary, are on a second honeymoon, or are simply having a quiet, relaxing holiday, look no further. We take pleasure in pampering guests."

Wagon Wheel Guest Ranch

Annina and Jörg Hoffmeister
Highway 3
Mail: RR I
Bridesville, BC V0H 1B0
(250) 446-2309 Fax: (250) 446-2309

• On Highway 3, 25 kilometres east of Osoyoos
and 25 kilometres west of Rock Creek.
• Three rooms. Two people $60. Shared guest
bathrooms.
Two cabins. Two people $60. Private bathrooms.
Additional person $5.
Accommodation for horses.
• A 320-acre farm with trails for horseback riding and cross-country skiing. Fallow deer,
wild boar, sheep, horses, and cows on the property. Stocked lake for fishing. Thirty minutes
from skiing at Mount Baldy. Full breakfast includes farm-fresh eggs and homemade baked
goods. Children welcome. **In the hosts' own words:** "Enjoy our Swiss hospitality."

Lindale Farm Guest House

Roger and Linda Lebert
10932—337th Avenue
Mail: Box 1056
Oliver, BC V0H 1T0
(250) 498-4196 Fax: (250) 498-4197

• From Highway 97, turn west onto 350th, left
onto 121st, and left onto 337th.
• Two rooms. One person $60; two people $80.
Double bed, private bathroom; twin beds,
shared bathroom.
Suite. One person $80; two people $100. Queen-sized bed. Ensuite bathroom.
Weekly rates.
• A Cape Cod–style guest house in a quiet vineyard setting, a few minutes' drive from
Oliver, wineries, and golf courses. Guest rooms and suite have sitting areas. Patio with a
view of a nine-acre vineyard, Mount Baldy, and surrounding hills. Front veranda with a
view of a golf course, hills, and neighbouring orchards. Sitting room with TV and fire-
place. Air conditioning. Near wine tastings, water sports, winter skiing, and the Kettle
Valley Trail for hiking and biking. Thirty-seven kilometres from Mount Baldy. Farm-style
breakfast is served in the dining room. Off-street parking. Reservations required. No pets.
No smoking indoors. **In the hosts' own words:** "We invite you to enjoy our B&B, in a
quiet location in the hub of wine country, with fruit trees and a lovely landscaped garden."

Login B&B

Helen Falkenberg
RR 1 Site 27 C–1 Highway 3 West
Keremeos, BC V0X 1N0
(250) 499-2781 or (250) 499-2664
E-mail: loginbnb@keremeos.com

• On Highway 3, 5 kilometres west of
Keremeos.
Four hours east of Vancouver.
• Three rooms and three overflow rooms. One
person $55; three or four people $90. Queen-
sized bed. Shared guest bathrooms. Roll-away beds and queen-sized sofa beds available.
Discount of 10 percent on reservations made 48 hours in advance. Group rates. Family
rates including housekeeping.
• A log house in the country, a short walk from the Ashnola River. Hiking trails from the
B&B. Swimming in the river. Forty-five minutes from Apex Alpine ski hill, Penticton, and
the U.S. border. A short drive from Cathedral Lakes Park and Fairview wilderness area.
Guest rooms have air conditioning and views and are separate from the hosts' living quar-
ters, the house is a duplex, with three guest rooms in one unit and the hosts' living quarters and three additional guest rooms in the other unit. Two bathrooms in each unit. Guest
living room with fireplace, guest kitchen, and guest video lounge. Laundry facilities.
Breakfast includes homemade bread. Visa, MasterCard. Horses and leashed pets welcome.
No smoking.

Riordan House B&B

John and Donna Ortiz
689 Winnipeg Street
Penticton, BC V2A 5N1
(250) 493-5997 Fax: (250) 493-5997
Cel: (250) 490-7017

• Two blocks from downtown, at the corner of
Winnipeg and Eckhardt.
• Two people $55–75. Additional person $15.
• A 1920 arts and crafts house known locally as
"the house that rum built," within walking distance of a beach, galleries, and restaurants. Near
estate wineries. Guest rooms have sitting areas, antique furnishings, TVs, VCRs, robes, slippers, glasses of lemon water when guests arrive, and treats on the pillows. One of the guest
rooms has a fireplace and two bay windows. Antique shop on the property. Breakfast
includes fruit dishes, juice, tea or coffee, and homemade croissants, scones, and muffins.
Visa, MasterCard. Children over twelve welcome. No pets; small dog in residence. No
smoking. **In the hosts' own words:** "We are in the heart of wine country."

Eagle's Point Manor B&B

Barry and Verla Wilson
3145 Juniper Drive
Penticton, BC V2A 7T3
(250) 493-6555
Toll-free from within Canada: 1-888-658-8444

• Four rooms. $75–85. Queen-sized bed. Ensuite bathrooms.

• A ten-thousand-square-foot house with turrets, on a mountain face above Penticton. Five minutes from the city centre. Near golf courses, beaches, lakes, wineries, and fine dining restaurants. Guest rooms have TVs, decks, and views of orchards, vineyards, lakes, and the city. Library. Metal toy collection and sports room. Full breakfast. Nonsmoking house. **In the hosts' own words:** "We welcome you and offer a tranquil place to renew your energy. Your stay will be memorable."

Paradise Cove B&B

Ruth Buchanan
3129 Hayman Road
Naramata, BC
Mail: Box 699
Penticton, BC V2A 6P1
(250) 496-5896 Fax: (250) 496-5896

• From Westminster and Main in Penticton, take
Naramata Road and continue for 13 kilometres.
Turn left onto DeBeck Road (firehall on the cor-
ner) and continue for 1 kilometre. Turn right onto
Hayman Road.
• Two rooms. In summer, two people from $75. In winter (November to March), two people
from $70. Queen-sized bed. Ensuite bathrooms.
Self-contained suite. In summer, two people from $115. In winter (November to March),
two people from $95. Queen-sized bed and sofa bed. Bathroom in suite.
Additional person $15.
• A modern two-storey house above Manitou Beach, among orchards and vineyards, with a
view of Okanagan Lake. Twenty minutes from downtown Penticton. Near swimming, hiking
along the historical Kettle Valley Railway, five wineries, a wharf, two fine dining restaurants,
and a pub. Forty-five minutes from skiing at Apex. Self-contained suite has a queen-sized bed,
a sofa bed, a five-person hot tub, a fireplace, laundry facilities, and a kitchen. Suite and guest
rooms have lake views, private decks, telephones, TVs, fridges, and beverages. Suite and one
of the guest rooms have private entrances. Full breakfast is served in the dining room or on
the deck. One of the guest rooms is wheelchair accessible. Cash, Visa, MasterCard. Adult oriented. No pets. No smoking indoors. **In the hosts' own words:** "Our B&B offers idyllic surroundings with a lake view, friendliness, and comfort."

Lakeshore Memories B&B

Betty Raymond
12216 Lakeshore Drive
Mail: RR 1 Site 14 C–9
Summerland, BC V0H 1Z0
(250) 494-5134 Fax: (250) 494-5134
E-mail: gary_raymond@bc.sympatico.ca

• From Highway 97, at the bottom of the hill at
the south end of Summerland, turn onto
Lakeshore Drive and continue for two blocks.
The B&B is on the left, on a corner.
• Three rooms. One person $55–70; two people $65–80. Queen-sized bed; double bed;
twin beds. Ensuite and shared guest bathrooms.
• A restored turn-of-the-century house, a few steps from Lake Okanagan, on the original
Summerland townsite. A few minutes' walk from beaches, sailing, and a fish hatchery. Near
golf courses, wineries, a restaurant, art galleries, museums, orchards, the gardens of an agricultural research station, hiking on the Kettle Valley Railway line, and downhill and cross-
country skiing. Host shares knowledge about the local arts scene. Information on local fishing is available. Living room, sun room, and gardens. Air-conditioned. Full breakfast
includes homemade baked goods and local products. Adults only. No smoking indoors. **In
the hosts' own words:** "We invite you to relax in a lovingly restored heritage house. Each
room has been furnished to provide an atmosphere of comfort and romance."

Heidi's B&B

Heidi and Lyle
4510 Gartrell Road
Mail: RR 4 Site 86 C–16
Summerland, BC V0H 1Z0
(250) 494-0833 Fax: (250) 494-4428

• In the Okanagan Valley, 400 kilometres from
Vancouver. Forty-five minutes south of
Kelowna. Fifteen minutes north of Penticton.
Half an hour south of the Coquihalla Connector
at Peachland. Five minutes from Summerland.

• Room. One person $45; two people $55. For two or more nights, one person $40, two
people $50. Queen-sized bed. Private bathroom.
Llama cart tours and rides.

• A B&B on a five-acre hobby farm with a cherry orchard, birds, dogs, cats, horses, llamas,
and wildlife. Lake and mountain views from an east-facing patio. View of Giant's Head
Mountain from a west-facing patio. Fifteen minutes' drive from golf courses, swimming
beaches, boat and sailboat launches and rentals, the historical Kettle Valley Railway, and
winery and vineyard tours. Forty-five minutes' drive from trail rides, hiking, and Apex
Alpine and Crystal Mountain ski areas. Living room. Chinese energy massages available.
Full breakfast is served on the patio, weather permitting. Patio dinners available by arrangement. Reservations required. German spoken. Pets and horses welcome. No smoking. **In the
hosts' own words:** "There is so much to say about our place that we just don't know where
to begin. Please pay us a visit and we'll share it with you."

Augusta View B&B

Kurt and Edith Grube
998 Augusta Court
Kelowna, BC V1Y 7T9
(250) 763-0969 Fax: (250) 763-0969
Toll-free from within Canada and north
     western U.S.: 1-800-801-2992

• Two rooms. One person $65; two people $75.
Queen-sized bed; queen-sized bed and one twin
bed. Ensuite bathrooms.
Suite. One person $79; two people $89. Queen-
sized bed, one twin bed, and double hide-a-bed. Ensuite bathroom.
Additional person $20. Child under 12 $10. Off-season rates.

• A quiet, centrally located B&B with gardens, fruit trees, and a view of the Kelowna Golf
and Country Club. Five minutes' drive from shopping, restaurants, golf, and wineries. An
hour from Penticton, Vernon, and three ski hills. Near cross-country skiing, horseback riding, and boating, fishing, and lake cruises on Okanagan Lake. Air-conditioned rooms have
views of the city, lake, mountains, and golf course. Guest sitting room with antiques, TV,
VCR, telephone, library, wood stove, and fridge. Suite has a TV and a private entrance
through the garden. Two of the guest rooms share an entrance through the guest sitting room.
Guest patio with wicker furniture leads to the gardens. Full breakfast is served on a garden
deck, weather permitting. German spoken. No pets. No smoking. **In the hosts' own words:**
"Sonora B&B has become Augusta B&B. Experience a peaceful retreat in our spacious
house, decorated with antiques and an artist's touch. You'll enjoy our warm hospitality."

Bluebird Beach House B&B

Bernie Breitkreuz and Bettina Voigt-Breitkreuz
3980 Bluebird Road
Kelowna, BC V1W 1X6
(250) 764-8992 Fax: (250) 764-8992
Web site: http://www.bbcanada.com/571.html

• From Highway 97, turn east onto Pandosy, which becomes Lakeshore Road. Turn right onto Bluebird.

• Three rooms. One person $85; two people $95–120. Queen-sized bed; two double beds. Ensuite bathrooms. Additional person $20. Extended stay rates. In high season, minimum stay two nights.

• A custom-built two-storey modern house on Okanagan Lake, with a thirty-metre private beach and a dock, ten minutes from downtown. Near golf courses, hiking trails, boat rentals, and a boat launch. Guest rooms have southwest lake views and private balconies facing the lake. Patio, backyard, and sandy beach. Swimming. Walking along Bluebird Beach Bay and Mission Creek. Within walking distance of shopping, fine dining restaurants, wineries, and a bus stop. Guest rooms have sitting areas, TVs, and fridges. Full breakfast is served at a beach cabana on the lake. Kitchen facilities and barbecue in the cabana are available for guests to prepare other meals. Parking. Check-in 3:00 to 6:00 p.m. or by arrangement. Deposit of two nights' rate required to hold reservation. Cash, traveller's cheques, Visa. German spoken. Children over ten welcome. No pets. Smoking outdoors. **In the hosts' own words:** "Relax on a beach chair at the beach and enjoy the ambience. At sunset, sip a glass of local wine on the dock, and later sleep well with the soothing sound of the waves. We are world travellers and truly enjoy having guests."

The Cedars Inn

David and Jane
278 Beach Avenue
Kelowna, BC V1Y 5R8
(250) 763-1208 Fax: (250) 763-1109
Cel: (250) 470-3849
E-mail: Cedars@bc.sympatico.ca

• Five minutes from downtown.
• Three rooms. Two people $125–175. Queen-sized bed. Private bathrooms.
On holiday weekends, minimum stay two nights. Weekly and off-season rates.
Golf and ski packages.
• A house with a garden, built between 1906 and 1908, on a landscaped quarter acre surrounded by a cedar hedge. Two guest sitting areas with original stone fireplaces and a reading room. Cobblestone patio with swimming pool and hot tub. Guest rooms have sitting areas. Local wine and appetizers are served between 5:00 and 6:00 p.m. Hosts can arrange golf and ski packages, beach picnics, and esthetician services. Bicycles available. One minute from a public beach. Five minutes from downtown, a city park, and a jogging path. Near award-winning wineries. Full breakfast is served in the dining room, in guests' rooms, or on the patio. Diets accommodated with advance notice. Cancellation notice seven days. Check-in 3:00 to 6:00 p.m.; check-out until 11:00 a.m. or by arrangement. Cash, traveller's cheques, Visa, MasterCard. No children. No pets; cat in residence. Smoking outdoors. **In the hosts' own words:** "We welcome you to experience our beautiful heritage house, private gardens, and exceptional service. Rest and rejuvenate during your stay at our B&B."

The Historic Manor House B&B

Cheryl and Ted Turton
2796 K.L.O. Road
Mail: Box 28202, RPO East Kelowna,
Kelowna, BC V1W 4A6
(250) 861-3932 Fax: (250) 861-4446

• Detailed directions given at the time of booking.
• Two rooms. One person $65; two people $85. King-sized bed; queen-sized bed. Ensuite bathrooms.
• A B&B with antiques and gardens, on a working orchard and vineyard, with a view of the Okanagan Valley. Two minutes' walk down a country lane from golf courses, a pub, and fine dining restaurants. Ten minutes' drive from shopping in Kelowna. Hosts share their knowledge about the history of the valley. Gardens and orchards to walk in. Full breakfast is served in the dining room or on a screened porch surrounded by a garden. Diets are accommodated. Check-in 4:00 p.m.; check-out until 11:00 a.m. Cash, Visa. Adult oriented. No pets. Smoking outdoors. **In the hosts' own words:** "Our elegant, antique-filled heritage house has been home to our family for three generations. We invite you to escape and enjoy an orchard experience."

Comfort and Croissants B&B

Gill and Nonie Davies
3439 Apple Way Boulevard
Westbank, BC V4T 1Y6
(250) 768-0449
E-mail: gill@cnx.net

● From Kelowna, take Highway 97. Cross the floating bridge and exit left at the second set of lights, at Boucherie (Esso gas station and Friends' neighbourhood pub on the corner). Pass Quails' Gate Winery on the left. Turn right onto Mission Hill Road and left onto Apple Way Boulevard.

● Rooms. One person $65–90; two people $70–95. Queen-sized bed; double bed; twin beds. Ensuite and private bathrooms.

● A new, quiet, air-conditioned B&B amid orchards and vineyards, three minutes' drive from Mission Hill, Quails' Gate, and Slamka wineries. Some of the guest rooms have views of Okanagan Lake. Three of the guest rooms are on the lower floor and have separate entrances. One of the rooms has a queen-sized bed and a five-piece ensuite bathroom with Jacuzzi tub. Twelve-metre-long guest sitting room with a TV, a stereo, books, games, and an adjoining patio with loveseat, tables, chaises lounges, and view of garden and lake. Available for retreats and workshops for up to twenty-seven people; this B&B accommodates eight people and is within five minutes' drive of five other B&Bs, two of which are within one block of this B&B. Ten minutes' drive from a beach, golf, horseback riding, parasailing, waterskiing, waterslides, windsurfing, hiking, cycling, skiing, and shopping. Full breakfast is served in the dining room, which has a view of the lake, or on the balcony. Cash, traveller's cheques. Adult oriented. No pets. Smoke-free house; smoking on the patio. **In the hosts' own words:** "Come to our B&B and be pampered in winery and orchard paradise."

Sunnybank B&B

Elvy and Ron Marsh
2479 Reece Road
Westbank, BC V4T 1N1
(250) 768-5110

• Six minutes from the Coquihalla Connector. From Kelowna, take Highway 97 south for 16 kilometres to Westbank. Reece Road is west of Highway 97, between the old Okanagan Highway and Elliah Road.

• Two rooms. One person $45–55; two people $65 85. Queen-sized bed, ensuite bathroom; twin beds, private bathroom. Hide-a-bed available. Weekly and monthly rates.

• A quiet modern house designed as a B&B by one of the hosts, on an acre of flower and herb gardens, with a view of Okanagan Lake, mountains, an orchard, and vineyards. Antiques and art throughout. Guest sitting room with TV, VCR, books, microwave, fridge, and access to a deck and a garden. Guest room with twin beds has French doors that lead to a deck. Three minutes from a shopping centre, golf courses, a waterslide park, and beaches. Fifteen minutes from skiing at Crystal Mountain. An hour from skiing at Apex or Silverstar. Coffee and tea available all day. Full breakfast, including local fresh fruit, homemade bread, muffins, homemade preserves, and an entrée, is served on the deck or in the dining room. Off-street parking for cars and RVs. Cash, traveller's cheques. Adult oriented. No pets. No smoking. **In the hosts' own words:** "We are happy to give information and directions to the four-season playground that surrounds us. We specialize in a dust-free environment at our B&B, and we welcome you to sunshine and relaxation."

The Schroth Farm B&B

Fred and Helen Schroth
3282 East Vernon Road
Vernon, BC V1B 3H5
(250) 545-0010 Fax (250) 260-3757

● One kilometre east of Vernon.
● Room and suite. One person $30; two people $55. Double bed; queen-sized
bed, double bed, and three twin beds. Private bathrooms. Additional person $15.
Child $10.
● A farmhouse with a patio and views of cattle grazing on nearby pastures, miniature goats,
and mountains in the distance. Near sandy beaches for swimming, golf courses, trail riding,
a water slide, wineries, and skiing at Silver Star. Guest room is on the upper floor and has a
TV and a fridge. Three-room suite is on the lower floor, sleeps eight, and has a private
entrance and a living room with TV, VCR, and kitchen facilities. Shaded lawn with barbecue, picnic table, and swing. German spoken. Children welcome. Smoking outdoors. **In the
hosts' own words:** "We have travelled to many parts of the world, and we enjoy guests from
all parts of the world."

The Tuck Inn

Bill and Irene Tullett
3101 Pleasant Valley Road
Vernon, BC V1T 4L2
(250) 545-3252 Fax: (250) 549-3254

• In Vernon, turn east from Highway 97 onto Thirtieth Avenue and continue
for 1 kilometre to Pleasant Valley Road.

• Four rooms. One person $40–45; two people $65–75. Double bed; queen-
sized bed; queen-sized bed and one twin bed. Additional person $15–20. Crib
available.

Ski, golf, honeymoon, and anniversary packages.

• A house built in 1906 that has its original interior doors, casings, and mouldings and is furnished with antiques. Sitting room with books and TV. Twenty-two kilometres from downhill and cross-country skiing at Silver Star. Ten minutes' drive from beaches at Kalamalka
Lake and Okanagan Lake. Five minutes' walk from downtown Vernon's art galleries, museum, theatres, and playhouse. Fifteen minutes' drive from the historical O'Keefe Ranch. Ten
minutes' drive from golf courses. Breakfast is served from 7:30 to 9:00 a.m. in a Victorian-
style tea room with nine-foot ceilings and a circular fireplace. Deposit of 50 percent of total
payment required to hold reservation. Cancellation notice seven days. Check-in 3:00 to 7:00
p.m.; check-out until noon. Visa, MasterCard. Children welcome. No pets; cat in residence.
No smoking indoors. **In the hosts' own words:** "Our large heritage house lets you step back
in time to the Victorian era. Our specialty breakfast is a sumptuous delight."

Castle on the Mountain B&B

Eskil and Sharon Larson
8227 Silver Star Road
Vernon, BC V1B 3M8
(250) 542-4593 Fax: (250) 542-2206
Toll-free from within Canada and the U.S.: 1-800-667-2229
Web site: http://www.monday.com/castle

• Ten kilometres east of Highway 97, on Forty-eighth Avenue, which becomes Silver Star Road.
• Five rooms. One person $65–135; two people $75–165. King-sized bed; queen-sized bed; twin beds. Ensuite and private bathrooms. Additional person $35. Child $15–30.
Honeymoon suite.
Two-storey apartment.
Special occasion packages.
• A Tudor-style house on the way to Silver Star Mountain, with views of the city of Vernon and Okanagan and Kalamalka lakes. In the area are swimming, horseback riding, snowmobiling, and winery tours. Ten minutes from beaches, skating, and downhill and cross-country skiing. Hiking from the B&B. Toboggan slide on the property. Guest sitting room with fireplace and TV, kitchen for light snacks, and outdoor hot tub. Playground and picnic area with fire pit. Six-hundred-square-foot honeymoon suite has a covered balcony with a view, an open balcony, a gas fireplace, a stereo, a TV, and a Jacuzzi. Two-storey apartment has a covered balcony with a view, a gas fireplace, a Jacuzzi, a TV, and a stereo. The house was designed and built by the hosts, who are artists and specialize in custom design picture framing; guests can visit their gallery and studio. Covered parking. Full breakfast with fresh fruit is served between 7:30 and 9:00 a.m. For guests staying in the honeymoon suite, breakfast is served in the suite. Credit cards. Suitable for families. No pets. Smoking outdoors. **In the hosts' own words:** "Our home is your castle. The view, the privacy, the space, the outdoors, and the artwork create a special feeling that you must experience."

Father's Country Inn

David Conover and Brenda Doppert
Tod Mountain Road
Mail: Box 152
Heffley Creek, BC V0E 1Z0
(250) 578-7308 Fax: (250) 578-7334
Web site: http://www.mwsolutions.com/fathersbb

• From Kamloops, take Highway 5 (Yellowhead) north for 45 minutes. Take the exit for Sun Peaks ski area and follow the B&B's signs.

• Rooms. One person $45–65; two people $65–85. Queen-sized bed. Private bathrooms. During ski season (November to April), rates subject to change.

• A B&B in the mountains near the Sun Peaks ski area, with a view of valleys and mountains. Indoor swimming pool in a room with a fireplace, a hot tub, a woodstove, and tropical plants. Nature walks from the B&B through meadows and by streams and cows. Sitting rooms, one with a fireplace. Heated ski room with lockers, drying racks, and benches. A few minutes' drive from downhill and cross-country skiing, golf, mountain biking, hiking, lakes, fishing, and trail rides. Guest rooms have four-post queen-sized beds. Some of the guest rooms have fireplaces and Jacuzzi tubs. Full breakfast includes homemade bread and preserves. Evening meal available on request. Reservations recommended. Deposit required to hold reservation. Cancellation notice fourteen days. In winter, $25 is nonrefundable. Check-in after 3:00 p.m.; check-out until 10:30 a.m. Visa, MasterCard. Adult oriented. No pets. Smoking outdoors.

Macqueen's Manor B&B

Jack and Pat Macqueen
1049 Laurel Place
Kamloops, BC V1S 1R1
(250) 372-9383
Toll-free from within North America:
  1-800-677-5338

• Take exit 367 and turn south onto Pacific
Way. Turn left onto Hugh Allen, left onto
Gloaming Drive, and left onto Laurel Place.
• Two rooms. One person $50; two people $55.
Double bed and hide-a-bed, private bathroom; queen-sized bed, ensuite bathroom.
Additional person $15.
• A five-year-old house in the Aberdeen Hills area of Kamloops, with a view of the city,
within walking distance of shopping, restaurants, and a golf course. Across the highway
from several hundred acres of hiking and mountain biking trails in Mount Dufferin Park,
the largest municipal park in North America. Two decks with views. Guest rooms have
TVs, magazines, coffee supplies and facilities, and fruit baskets. One of the guest rooms
has a double bed and a sitting room with a hide-a-bed. Breakfast includes homemade jam
and baked goods. Laundry facilities available. Two dogs in residence. Smoking outdoors.
In the hosts' own words: "Guests enjoy the beautiful views from our decks and our
wholesome breakfasts. We pride ourselves on providing the little extras that make guests'
stays pleasant and that make our B&B a home away from home."

Park Place B&B

Lynn and Trevor Bentz
720 Yates Road
Kamloops, BC V2B 6C9
(250) 554-2179 Fax: (250) 554-2179
E-mail: bentz@wkpowerlink.com
Web site: http://www.bbcanada.com/
  231.html

• From Highway 5, follow signs for the North
Shore and the airport. After crossing the bridge,
turn right onto Westsyde Road and then take the
fifth right onto Yates Road.
• Three rooms. One person $40–50; two people $55–75. Queen-sized bed; double bed.
Ensuite and shared guest bathrooms.
Cottage. $95.
• A Santa Fe–style house with antiques, on the North Thompson River, with landscaped
grounds, a pool, and a patio. Guest rooms are on the ground floor. Two of the guest rooms
have antique double beds. One of the guest rooms has a TV and a view of the river and
mountains. Resident birds and beavers can be seen. Near golf, tennis, fishing, hiking, boating, shopping, and restaurants. Thirty minutes from skiing at Sun Peaks. Full or light breakfast with homemade preserves is served in a solarium with a view of Mount Paul and the
river. Check-in after 4:00 p.m. Not suitable for children under twelve. Smoking outdoors. **In
the hosts' own words:** "Enjoy our delightful riverfront country house. Stroll around the
landscaped acreage, swim in the pool, or lounge on the patio and watch the river flow by."

Reimer's B&B

Ray and Cookie Reimer
1630 Slater Avenue
Kamloops, BC V2B 4K4
(250) 376-0111 Fax: (250) 554-2717

• Take the Overlander Bridge to the North Shore and follow Fortune Drive, which becomes Tranquille Road. Turn left onto Singh Road, continue for one block, and turn right onto Slater. The B&B is the fourth house on the right.

• Three rooms. One person $30–35; two people $50–60. Queen-sized bed or double bed. Shared bathroom and private bathroom with shower. Open May 15 to December 15. Tent space available.

• A B&B with an outdoor pool on a landscaped, fenced lot, in a quiet area. One of the guest rooms is downstairs and has a private entrance. The other guest rooms are upstairs. One of the guest rooms has a queen-sized water bed. Patio and deck. Ten minutes from golf, tennis courts, and a bike path at McArthur Park. Ten minutes from the airport and downtown. Near a shopping mall, a theatre, and restaurants. An hour from Sun Peaks and Harper Mountain ski areas. Varied breakfast menu includes homemade jam and preserved fruit. Tea or coffee served any time. Check-in any time; check-out until 11:00 a.m. Cash, traveller's cheques. Adult oriented. Guests with alternative lifestyles welcome. Well-behaved pets welcome; dog in residence. Smoking outdoors. **In the hosts' own words:** "We'll make your breakfast any way you like. Our guests say our hospitality is second to none."

The Silvercreek Guesthouse

Gisela Bodnar
6820 Thirtieth Avenue SW
Salmon Arm, BC V1E 4M1
(250) 832-8870

• From Highway 1 west of Salmon Arm, turn onto Salmon River Road (at flashing light) and continue for 2.5 kilometres. Turn right onto Thirtieth Avenue SW and continue for 1.5 kilometres. The B&B sign is on the left.

• One person $25–30; two people $40–45. Additional person $15. Child $5–10. Weekly rates.

• A log house with a deck and a garden, on forty acres, with a view of mountains and a valley. Five minutes' drive from shops, restaurants, a water slide, golf courses, and a community centre with pool and whirlpool. Near beaches and picnic grounds at Shuswap Lake. In the area are trail riding, hiking, biking, and fishing. Twenty-five minutes' drive from cross-country ski trails in the Larch Hills and Skimiken areas. Full breakfast includes eggs from the B&B's chickens and homemade jam and buns. Light breakfast available. Lunch and dinner available with advance notice. **In the hosts' own words:** "Enjoy your stay at our charming, comfortable, and spacious log house."

The Inn at the Ninth Hole

Mike and Karla Van De Kraats
5091 Twentieth Avenue SE
Salmon Arm, BC V1E 1X6
(250) 833-0185 Fax: (250) 833-0113
Toll-free from within Canada and the U.S.: 1-800-221-5955

• From Highway 1, take Highway 97B south for 3 kilometres. Turn right on-to Twentieth Avenue SE. The B&B is the last house on the right.
• Three rooms. Two people $89.95–125. King-sized bed; queen-sized bed. Ensuite bathrooms.
• A colonial-style house with a view of the greens of the Salmon Arm Golf and Country Club, ten minutes from Salmon Arm. Guest rooms have sitting areas, fireplaces, TVs, VCRs, and ensuite bathrooms with jetted tubs. Air conditioning. In the area are hiking, riding stables, cross-country skiing, boating, shopping, and eighteen-hole and nine-hole golf courses. Full breakfast. Reservations recommended. Cancellation notice seven days. Visa, MasterCard, American Express. No pets. No smoking. **In the hosts' own words:** "Our B&B is a place for all seasons. Come and enjoy a relaxing time in peaceful surroundings."

Apple Blossom B&B

Paul and Lillian Scherba
3531 Tenth Avenue SE
Salmon Arm, BC V1E 1W8
(250) 832-0100 Fax: (250) 832-0101
Web sites: http://www.achilles.net/~bb646.html
http://www.bbcanada.com/646.html

• A few minutes from Highway 97B and Highway 1. Call for directions.
• Suite. $75–80 for first night, $60–65 each subsequent night. Queen-sized bed. Private bathroom. Additional person $15. Additional beds available. Extended stay rates.
• A B&B on a small acreage close to golf, tennis, horseback riding, fishing, mountain biking, hiking and cross-country skiing trails, and historical sites. Five minutes from downtown shopping malls and fine dining restaurants. Suite is on the ground floor and has a private entrance, a patio, a flower garden, and a sitting room with chesterfield and TV. Kitchen area with fridge, sink, table, chairs, cooking utensils, dishes, cutlery, and supplies for making tea and coffee. For guests with reservations, a light snack is served on arrival. Full or Continental breakfast, including homemade baked goods, preserves, and fresh fruit, is served between 8:30 and 9:30 a.m. or earlier by arrangement. Parking. German and Ukrainian spoken. No pets. No smoking. **In the hosts' own words:** "Our B&B is designed with our guests' comfort and privacy in mind. Our priority is that our guests are comfortable and enjoy a relaxed stay."

Stone Castle B&B

Lawrence and Sherrin Davis
3325 Allen Frontage Road
Mail: Box 2113
Revelstoke, BC V0E 2S0
(250) 837-5266 Fax: (250) 837-5266

• Off Highway 1, 5 kilometres west of Revelstoke (6 hours from either Vancouver or Calgary).
• Room. One person $45; two people $60.
Queen-sized bed. Private bathroom.
Suite (sleeps five). One person $65; two people $80. Queen-sized bed, one twin bed, and one twin day bed. Ensuite bathroom. Additional person $15.
Golf discounts.
• A stone house near Boulder Mountain, five minutes' walk from two fine dining restaurants. Ten minutes from Revelstoke, a tour of Revelstoke Dam, golf, hiking, summer evening entertainment at the Grizzly Plaza, and a train museum. Hot tub. In the area are downhill and heli-skiing, cross-country ski trails, snowmobiling, and Revelstoke National Park's alpine meadows. Drying room for snow gear. Guest living room with TV, VCR, books, and videos. Suite has a sun room. Full breakfast. Reservations recommended. Cash, traveller's cheques. No pets; cat in residence. Smoking outdoors. **In the hosts' own words:** "We offer a warm welcome and a relaxed atmosphere."

MacPherson Lodge

Lisa Longinotto
2135 Clough Road
Mail: Box 2615
Revelstoke, BC V0E 2S0
(250) 837-7041 Fax: (250) 837-7077
Toll-free from within North America:
  1-888-875-4924
E-mail: bookrev@junction.net
Web site: http://www.bbcanada.com/bc/
  revelstoke

• From Highway 1, go south on Highway 23 for 7 kilometres.
• Two rooms. Two people $60–75. King-sized bed and one twin bed; twin beds side by side with king-sized bedding (or twin beds). Two shared guest bathrooms. Additional person $15. Children under 3 free. Use of kitchen facilities $15 per day. Pets by arrangement $15 per day.
• A log house with two guest rooms. One of the guest rooms has a private balcony and a view of the Columbia River. Guest dining room with stone fireplace. Guest loft with books, TV, and VCR. One of the shared guest bathrooms has a Victorian-style tub and shower. Visa, MasterCard. Children welcome. Pets welcome by arrangement for a fee.

Nehalliston Canyon Retreat B&B

Agnes and Paul Andrews
McNab Road, Nehalliston Canyon
Mail: Box 140
Little Fort, BC V0E 2C0
(250) 677-4272 Fax: (250) 677-4272
E-mail: pandrews@mail.netshop.net
Web site: http://www.bbcanada.com/2052.html

• Six kilometres west of Little Fort, off Highway 24. Turn north onto McNab Road and continue for 3 kilometres.

• Two rooms. One person $44; two people $53–62. Queen-sized bed and one twin bed; double bed. Shared bathroom. Child 6 to 12 $10.
Two-bedroom cottage (sleeps six). Two people $71. Queen-sized bed, twin beds, and hide-a-bed. Private bathroom with shower. Additional person $20. Child 6 to 12 $10. Breakfast not included.
Canoe rentals.

• A hand-hewn log house in Nehalliston Canyon, with a view of Mount Loveway. Near hiking, walking, a six-kilometre toboggan run, alpine skiing at Sun Peaks, and lakes with rainbow trout. Wildlife in the area. One of the hosts conducts scheduled herb walks and gives reiki sessions (an ancient healing art that relieves stress). Living room. Outdoor hot tub. Gardens with herbs and wildflowers. Healing oils and tinctures are made and sold on the premises. Organic, macrobiotic food store on the premises. Two-bedroom cottage accommodates six and has cooking facilities and a wood stove. Full breakfast includes farm-fresh eggs, homemade baked goods, local wild fruit in season, herbal teas, and coffees including espresso and Turkish. Breakfast for guests staying in the cottage is available on request. Macrobiotic breakfast available. Dinner available. Not suitable for small children. **In the hosts' own words:** "Enjoy the seclusion and peacefulness at our B&B."

Wooly Acres B&B

Chris and Jim
1030 Bo Hill Place
Mail: RR 1 Box 1739
Clearwater, BC V0E 1N0
(250) 674-3508 Fax: (250) 674-2316

• Five kilometres from Highway 5. Turn onto Clearwater Valley Road (tourist information centre on corner) and continue for 3.5 kilometres. Turn right onto Greer Road and continue for 1 kilometre. Turn right onto Bo Hill Place and continue for 500 metres to the gate. The B&B has signs on Greer Road and Bo Hill Place.
• Three rooms. One person $40–55; two people $50–65. Queen-sized bed and twin beds; queen-sized bed and one twin bed; double bed and one twin bed. Ensuite and shared guest bathrooms. Additional person $15.
• A house in the country, on ten acres with grazing sheep. Ten minutes' drive from restaurants, shopping, and a nine-hole golf course. Thirty minutes from an eighteen-hole golf course and hiking and sightseeing at Wells Gray Provincial Park. Near snowshoeing and cross-country skiing. Two guest sitting rooms; one has a gas fireplace and a view. Large yard, gardens, and fire pit. Full breakfast, including fresh muesli, farm eggs, berries in season, homemade baked goods, jam, and jelly, is served in the dining room. Children by arrangement. Highchair and playpen available. No pets; sheep on the property and dogs and cats in residence (although not in guests' quarters). No smoking indoors. **In the hosts' own words:** "When visiting Clearwater, enjoy country comfort and sleep like a lamb. Ask for an introduction to Basil, Becky, Queenie, or one of the other sheep."

Trophy Mountain Buffalo Ranch B&B

Joe and Monika Fischer
Clearwater Valley Road
Mail: Box 1768
Clearwater, BC V0E 1N0
(250) 674-3095 Fax: (250) 674-3131

• Between Jasper and Kamloops, on Highway 5. In Clearwater, turn onto Wells Gray Park Road (tourist information centre on corner) and continue for 20 kilometres.
• Six rooms. One person $35–55; two people $50–60. Queen-sized bed and one twin bed; queen-sized bed; double bed; bunk beds. Ensuite and private bathrooms. Additional person $15–25. Children under 6 free.
• A restored 1926 log house in a quiet, rural setting. Horseback riding, hiking, biking, and cross-country skiing trails on the property. Guest entrance. An hour from Wells Gray Provincial Park, Trophy Mountain hiking area, Helmcken Falls, canoeing, river rafting, hiking, cross-country and downhill skiing, and a shopping centre. Hosts keep bison and horses as a hobby. Hosts are outdoor adventure guides and provide information about the area and its outdoor activities. Horse, canoe, and bike rentals. Off-street parking. Visa, MasterCard. Pets welcome outdoors. Smoking outdoors.

Abigail's Garden and Guest House

Abigail and Richard Rutley
Mail: Box 576
Clearwater, BC V0E 1N0
(250) 674-2514

• On Clearwater Valley Road, 19.5 kilometres from Highway 5 (Yellowhead).
• Room. One person $60; two people $80. Double bed. Private bathroom.
Suite. $300 per weekend; $120 per extra day. Queen-sized bed. Ensuite bathroom. Dinner provided.
Teepee. $30 per person.
Cabin. $30 per person. Child 6 to 12 $20.
• A B&B near well-marked hiking trails and twenty minutes from Clearwater, Helmcken Falls, golf, and lake fishing. Forty-five minutes from Clearwater Lake and boat tours. Suite has a balcony, an ensuite bathroom with massage table, and the use of a library with fireplace. Breakfast includes farm-fresh eggs, homemade baked goods, seasonal fruit and jam, garden produce, fresh-ground coffee, mountain water, and garden herb tea. For guests staying in the room or suite, breakfast is served before 9:30 a.m. by a wood stove or on a covered veranda. For guests staying in the teepee or cabin, an early breakfast is served outdoors around a fire circle. Guest room has wheelchair access. For the suite, reservations are required. No pets; dog in residence. No smoking. **In the hosts' own words:** "Enjoy beautiful sunsets, great wilderness, and an abundance of wildlife at our back door."

McKirdy Creek B&B

Jim and Doris McKirdy
3130 McKirdy Road
Mail: Box 158
Valemount, BC V0E 2Z0
(250) 566-4542 Fax: (250) 566-4556

• Five minutes from the village of Valemount.
• Three or four rooms. $45–70. Twin beds; double bed; bunk beds; one twin bed. Shared guest bathrooms.
Self-contained cottage.
Family and group rates.
• A farmhouse with views of a valley and mountains, on a farm with a park and a creek. Bears, deer, and coyotes can be seen. Trails, wildflowers, birdwatching, and ungroomed cross-country ski trails on the property. Near golf, canoeing, rafting, horseback riding, snowmobiling, and groomed cross-country ski trails. Thirty minutes from Mount Robson, the highest peak in the Canadian Rockies. Eighty minutes from Jasper National Park. Full breakfast with wild or garden berries. Picnic area beside a creek has picnic tables, a rain shelter, and a wood range for guests to prepare other meals. Cottage is wheelchair accessible. Smoking on covered porches. **In the hosts' own words:** "We welcome you to our B&B and offer hospitality, friendship, and beautiful scenery."

Mount Robson Mountain River Lodge

Curtis and Claudia Pajunen
13990 Swift Current Creek Road at Highway 16
Mount Robson, BC
Mail: Box 1088
Valemount, BC V0E 2Z0
(250) 566-9899 Fax: (250) 566-9899
Toll-free from within North America:
   1-888-566-9899
Web site: http://www.mtrobson.com

• From Highway 16 (Yellowhead), 2 kilometres
west of Mount Robson Provincial Park and 32 kilometres east of Valemount, turn north onto Swift Current Creek Road. The B&B has signs on the highway.
• Four rooms. One person $60–80; two people $70–90. Ensuite and shared bathrooms. Additional person $15. Off-season rates.
Self-contained cabin (sleeps seven). Two people $90. Breakfast not provided in cabin.
• A log house on a river, on five acres of woodland, with views of Mount Robson and a glacier-fed river. An hour from Jasper National Park. Five minutes from the Berg Lake Trail, river rafting, fishing, hiking, and climbing. Near horseback riding, golf, canoeing, heli-hiking, and heli-skiing. Two of the guest rooms on the upper floor share a balcony with a view. Cabin has a kitchen and a loft. Wrap-around deck on the main floor. Afternoon tea is served on the deck. Guest living room with fireplace and a view of a mountain and a river. Outdoor fire pit, horseshoes, and mountain bikes. Two-course breakfast includes homemade bread, croissants, and muffins. Visa, MasterCard. German spoken. Children in the cabin only. No pets. No smoking. **In the hosts' own words:** "Enjoy warm hospitality in our B&B's beautiful house and setting. We speak German and English, smile in every language, and take pleasure in hosting guests from around the world. We look forward to making your stay with us a highlight of your trip."

Summit River B&B

Bill and Connie Achterberg
19345 Highway 5
Albreda, BC
Mail: Box 517
Valemount, BC V0E 2Z0
(250) 566-9936 Fax: (250) 566-9934
E-mail: sumriver@vis.bc.ca
Web site: http://www.bbcanada.com/
   163.html

• In Albreda (23 kilometres south of Valemount),
on Highway 5 (Yellowhead).
• Five rooms. One person $50–60; two people $60–75. Two double beds and twin beds;
two double beds and one twin bed; two double beds; double bed and one twin bed; twin
beds. Ensuite and private bathrooms. Additional person $12–15. Roll-away cot available.
Twenty-three campsites. $15.
Seniors' rates.
Adventure packages.
• A log house with a glacier-fed river running through the property. Fishing and gold panning in the river. Hiking, snowmobiling, and cross-country skiing on the property. Fifteen
minutes' drive from Valemount, a nature reserve, a golf course, helicopter tours, and a
salmon run in August. Forty-five minutes from Robson Park. One hundred and fifty kilometres west of Jasper. Hosts arrange adventure packages, including nature tours, guided
canoe trips, rafting, guided horseback riding, helicopter sightseeing tours, and golf at an
eighteen-hole golf course. One of the hosts teaches guests tole painting on request. Twenty-
three campsites, ten of which have RV hook-ups, for tents and campers in a wooded area and
a grass field. Pickup from train and bus. Three of the guest rooms are wheelchair accessible.
Deposit of one night's rate required to hold reservation. Visa, MasterCard. **In the hosts' own
words:** "Our area is a paradise for artists and camera enthusiasts."

Brady's B&B

Alan and Mavis Brady
9060 Buffalo Road
Mail: Box 519
Valemount, BC V0E 2Z0
(250) 566-9906

• From Valemount, go north on Highway 5 for 7
kilometres. Turn left onto Blackman Road and
continue for 5 kilometres. Turn left onto Buffalo
Road. Turn right at the B&B's sign.
• Two rooms and one semi-private loft. Two peo-
ple $60. Queen-sized bed; two double beds. Shared guest bathroom and shared guest half
bathroom.
• A log house built by its owners, on wooded acreage with a view of the McLennan River,
Mica Mountain, and the Premier Range. Wildlife on the property. Guest rooms have down
comforters. Upstairs on a mezzanine, a semi-private loft with no door or wall on one side
has two double beds. Living room with fireplace. Deck and backyard swimming pool. In the
area are hiking, climbing, fishing, boating, river rafting, trail riding, cross-country skiing,
heli-skiing, and snowmobiling. Full breakfast is served in the kitchen, which has a view of
a field and mountains. No smoking indoors. **In the hosts' own words:** "Our home is quiet
and comfortable, with spectacular views. Bring your camera; wildlife is just outside the
door."

Rainbow Retreat B&B

Keith and Helen Burchnall
11944 Essen Road, Highway 16W
Mail: Box 138
Valemount, BC V0E 2Z0
(250) 566-9747
Web site: http://www.bbcanada.com

• Twenty kilometres north of Valemount. Half a kilometre west of the junction of Highways 5 and 16 (the Yellowhead highways). The B&B has signs on the highway and a large sign at the driveway.

• Two rooms. One person $60–65; two people $65–70. Queen-sized bed. Shared guest bathroom. Crib and highchair available. Infants free.

• A post-and-beam log house in old-growth forest on the western slope of the Rockies, with a view of the Cariboo Mountains. Ten minutes' walk from the Fraser River. Thirty minutes' walk from Lost Lake. Fifteen minutes' drive from Mount Robson, a world heritage site. An hour from Jasper. A stopover point between Vancouver and Edmonton. Stained glass, original art, sitting/dining room, and stone fireplace. From a deck and a covered porch, hawks, hummingbirds, woodpeckers, and swallows can be seen among the forest trees and wildflowers. Deer, elk, and bears often visit. One of the hosts is an experienced outdoorsperson and shares his knowledge about the history of the area. He is also a pianist and composer and plays for guests on a concert grand piano. Breakfast and dinner are served on fine china and with silver cutlery, in a licensed dining room. Diets are accommodated. Cash, traveller's cheques. Smoking outdoors. **In the hosts' own words:** "Your visit to our B&B will be memorable. Be prepared to stay a while to enjoy scenic wonders, exciting activities, artists, and artisans in this easily accessible and undiscovered destination."

Sunflower Inn B&B

Kathleen Smythe
159 Alpine Road
Christina Lake, BC V0H 1E1
(250) 447-6201 Fax: (250) 447-6592
E-mail: suninnbb@sunshinecable.com
Web site: http://www.Monday.com/tourism

• From Christina Lake village (28 kilometres east of Grand Forks; 70 kilometres west of Castlegar and Rossland), take Highway 3 east for 8 kilometres. Take the Alpine-Texas turnoff to East Lake Drive. At the Y junction, take the left fork on-to Alpine Road. The B&B is on the left, at the corner.

• Three rooms. One person $65–125; two people $70–150. Queen-sized bed and double sofa bed; queen-sized bed. Shared guest bathroom. Additional person $12–15.

Golf packages available. Health retreats.

• A log house on a lake, with a covered deck, a guest entrance, a private beach, and a dock. Near swimming, canoeing, kayaking, hiking, nature trails, birdwatching, mountain biking, golf, cross-country skiing, snowshoeing, and skating. Canoe available. Forty-five minutes from Red Mountain ski area. Guest fridge. One of the hosts is a registered nurse and heal-ing touch practitioner and offers craniosacral and somatoemotional release therapy. Full or Continental breakfast is served on the deck, weather permitting. Diets are accommodated. Visa, MasterCard. Children by arrangement. No pets; dog, who mostly stays outside, in res-idence. Smoke-free environment. **In the hosts' own words:** "Enjoy our beautiful lakeside log house, nutritious breakfasts, and all-season recreation."

Robson Homestead B&B

Linda and Rick Miller
3671 Broadwater Road
Robson, BC
Mail: RR 3 Site 4 C–23
Castlegar, BC V1N 4H9
(250) 365-2374 Fax: (250) 365-2374
E-mail: rimiller@awinc.com

• Eight kilometres off Highway 3A, which runs between Nelson and Castlegar. From Nelson, take the Robson turnoff and follow the signs for Syringa Provincial Park.
From Castlegar, take Robson Bridge and take the first left turn (towards Syringa Provincial Park), which becomes Broadwater Road.
• Two rooms. One person $45; two people $55. Double bed; double bed and one twin bed. Shared guest bathroom. Child 6 to 12 $10. Weekly rates.
• A restored 1909 house with guest rooms furnished with antiques, on three acres across from the Columbia River. Ten minutes' drive from the Hugh Keenleyside Dam, Castlegar, the Doukhobor Museum, Pass Creek, Syringa Provincial Park, Arrow Lake, Selkirk College, a golf course, an airport, and marinas. In the area are mountain biking, hiking, cycling, fishing, and wildlife viewing. Trail rides at a nearby stable. Forty-five minutes from cross-country skiing and three downhill ski areas. Pickup from airport. Babysitting by arrangement. Full breakfast includes seasonal fruit and homemade baked goods. Vegetarian, low-fat, and low-salt diets accommodated. Reservations and deposits recommended. Cash, cheques, traveller's cheques. Children welcome. No pets; goats, horses, and dogs on the property. Smoke-free environment. **In the hosts' own words:** "At our B&B, a warm Kootenay welcome awaits you."

Emory House B&B

Janeen Mather and Mark Giffin
811 Vernon Street
Nelson, BC V1L 4G3
(250) 352-7007 Fax: (250) 352-7007
Web site: http://www.bbcanada.com/
189.html

• In downtown Nelson, one block north of Baker Street, between Hall and Cedar streets.
• Four rooms. One person $60–80; two people $70–90. Queen-sized bed; twin beds. Ensuite and shared guest bathrooms. Additional person $15.Off-season and corporate rates. Golf and ski packages.
• A restored arts and crafts–style house with fireplaces, antiques, and original woodwork and floors, near one of Nelson's guided and self-guided walking tours. Two minutes' walk from shops, cafés, a theatre, and an aquatic centre. Guest living room on the main floor has a tiled fireplace, games, reading material, and information on the area. Guest TV room has lake and mountain views. Backyard with lawn chairs. Air conditioning and fans. Refreshments served when guests arrive. Full breakfast includes homemade baked goods, homemade preserves, and a choice between two hot entrées such as eggs Florentine with herbed hashed brown potatoes and buttermilk huckleberry pancakes. Off-street parking. Ski and bike storage. Check-in 4:00 to 7:00 p.m. Visa, MasterCard. Children over nine welcome. No pets; two cats in residence. No smoking indoors. **In the hosts' own words:** "Our B&B is a home away from home with lots of extras. Come and enjoy our spacious heritage house and all that Nelson has to offer. Discover why our guests return again and again."

Kootenay Lake Homestays

June and Dennis Ray
7459 Mauriello Road
Procter, BC
Mail: RR 3 Site 26 C–10
Nelson, BC V1L 5P6
(250) 229-5688 Fax: (250) 229-5688
Toll-free from within British Columbia,
Alberta, Washington, Idaho, and Montana:
  1-800-256-8711
Web site: http://www.bbcanada.com/
  1904.html

•Thirty-five minutes north of Nelson. Twenty-five minutes south of Ainsworth Hot Springs.
•Self-contained suite. Two people $85. Double bed and double hide-a-bed.
Room. Two people $65. Queen-sized bed. Private bathroom.
Open February to June and September to November. Weekly rates.
• A log house on Kootenay Lake, between Nelson and Ainsworth Hot Springs. Guest room is a six-hundred-square-foot loft with a view of the lake and mountains, a Jacuzzi tub, and fitness facilities. Suite, which is seven hundred square feet and is on the side of the house facing the lake, has a kitchen, a living room, laundry facilities, a gas fireplace, a TV, a CD player, a barbecue, and double French doors that lead to a private covered patio and a garden. Small powerboat, canoe, and bicycles available. Hosts provide information on nearby attractions. Visa. **In the hosts' own words:** "We are well travelled and enjoy exchanging plans for fun destinations near and far. You'll love our peaceful surroundings on the edge of Kootenay Lake—come prepared to stay a while."

Willow Point Lodge

Anni Mühlegg and Florent Barillé
2211 Taylor Drive
Mail: RR 1 Site 21 C–31
Nelson, BC V1L 5P4
(250) 825-9411 Fax: (250) 825-3432
Toll-free: 1-800-949-2211
E-mail: willowpl@insidenet.com

• From Nelson, take Highway 3A north for 6.5 kilometres.
• Six rooms. One person $60–135; two people
$75–150. Queen-sized bed; double bed; twin beds. Private bathrooms. Additional person $15. Two honeymoon suites. Ski packages at Whitewater ski area.
• A lodge built in 1920, on acreage with extensive landscaped grounds, with a view of the west arm of Kootenay Lake and mountains. Garden hot tub. Hiking trails from the lodge, including a trail to a forty-foot waterfall. Birds and wildlife on the property. Five minutes from sandy beaches. Thirty minutes from Ainsworth Hot Springs and Whitewater ski area. One of the hosts is a tour guide. Drawing room with large fireplaces. Two honeymoon suites. Period furnishings. Outdoor shoes are not worn in the house; guests bring slippers or indoor shoes. Full breakfast. Visa, MasterCard. French spoken. Adult oriented. Golden retriever in residence. Nonsmoking house. **In the hosts' own words:** "At our lodge, enjoy the pristine lake and mountain views. A stroll in the forest to the spectacular waterfall is a must all year round. Our home is in a quiet setting where many birds and animals dwell. Come and enjoy the rejuvenating experience and our gourmet French breakfasts."

Inn the Garden B&B

Lynda Stevens and Jerry Van Veen
408 Victoria Street
Nelson, BC V1L 4K5
(250) 352-3226 Fax: (250) 352-3284

• In downtown Nelson, one block south of Baker Street, between Stanley and Ward streets.
• Five rooms. One person $65–80; two people $70–90. Queen-sized bed; double bed. Ensuite, private, and shared guest bathrooms. Additional person $15.
Suite. One person $105; two people $120. Additional person $25.
Self-contained cottage. One person or two people $150; four people $180; six people $210.
Ski and golf packages.
• A restored Victorian house with plants, wicker, and antiques, two minutes' walk from shopping, restaurants, and theatre. Lake and mountain views, terraced front garden, and guest living room. Suite is on the third floor and has a private entrance. Suite and self-contained cottage are suitable for groups. In the area are historical walking tours, hiking, golf, fishing, canoeing, and downhill and cross-country skiing. Full, varied breakfast is served in an old-fashioned dining room. Off-street parking and ski/golf/bike storage facilities. Check-in 4:00 to 8:00 p.m. Visa, MasterCard, American Express. Adult oriented. No pets. No smoking. **In the hosts' own words:** "We offer bright, comfortable rooms, modern amenities, and a friendly atmosphere, in our elegant turn-of-the-century heritage house. The charming 1920s cottage is perfect for romantic getaways and groups."

Three B's Balfour B&B

Austen and Dianne Megyesi
7722 Highway 3A
Mail: Box 73
Balfour, BC V0G 1C0
(250) 229-5223 Fax: (250) 229-5223
Web site: http://www.bbcanada.com/248.html

• Half an hour east of Nelson.
• Three rooms. One person $35; two people $55–60. Queen-sized bed, ensuite bathroom; double bed, shared guest bathroom; twin beds, shared guest bathroom. Off-season rates.
• A country-style B&B overlooking Kootenay Lake, with lake access. Five minutes from golf, fishing, and boating. Twenty minutes from hot springs. A few blocks from Kootenay Lake ferry. Near hiking. Hot tub. Guest rooms open onto a guest sitting area, which has books and a view of the lake. Full breakfast is served in the dining room. Cancellation notice two days. Cash. No pets. No smoking. **In the hosts' own words:** "Come and explore the beautiful Kootenay country. Our visits over breakfast are fantastic."

Mistaya Country Inn

Sue and George Iverson
Mail: Box 28
Silverton, BC V0G 2B0
(250) 358-7787 Fax: (250) 358-7787

• On Highway 6, 10 kilometres south of Silverton. Ninety kilometres north of Nelson.

• Five rooms. One person $45–50; two people $60–65. Double bed; queen-sized bed; twin beds. Shared guest bathrooms. Additional person $15.
Riding lessons, trail rides, and three-day pack trips.

• A lodge with walking trails on ninety acres in the Slocan Valley, between Valhalla and Kokanee Glacier parks. Guest sitting room with fireplace. Near ghost towns and old mining trails in the Selkirk Mountains. A few minutes' drive from Slocan Lake, hiking, golf, and cross-country skiing. Fire pit. Full breakfast. Visa, MasterCard. No pets. Smoking on the porch.

La Chance Swiss Guest Lodge

Caroline and Werner Faessler
16818 Highway 3A
Mail: Box 34
Kootenay Bay, BC V0B 1X0
Toll-free from within British Columbia,
   Alberta, Saskatchewan, Washington, and
   Idaho: 1-888-366-3388
Fax: (250) 227-9477
E-mail: faessler@neticlea.com

• Seventy-five minutes north of Creston. Three
hundred metres from the Kootenay Lake ferry terminal.
• Six rooms. One person $49; two people $65. Queen-sized bed and double sofa bed;
queen-sized bed; two double beds. Private bathrooms. Additional person $10. Child under
12 $7. Four self-contained cottages. Two people $80. Additional person $10. Breakfast not
provided; available at on-site restaurant. Extended stay rates.
• A B&B in several buildings that resemble a small Swiss village, on two and a half landscaped acres. Within walking distance of a beach and fishing and boating on Kooteney Lake.
Seven minutes' drive from a golf resort. Ainsworth Hot Springs Resort and a golf course at
Balfour are accessible by the Kootenay Lake ferry, a free ferry. Guest rooms have fridges
and TVs with movie channels. Two of the guest rooms have jetted tubs, and two have fireplaces. Dining room, sitting areas, ping pong table, and canoe. Cottages have kitchens, covered porches, and fire pits. European breakfast buffet. Visa, MasterCard. **In the hosts' own
words:** "Find tranquillity around our large goldfish pond, and take pleasure in the beautiful
flowers visible in all directions. Enjoy an exquisite dinner in our dining room or on the deck."

Wedgwood Manor Country Inn

Joan Huiberts and John Edwards
16002 Crawford Creek Road
Mail: Box 135
Crawford Bay, BC V0B 1E0
(250) 227-9233 Fax: (250) 227-9233
Toll free from within northwest North
   America: 1-800-862-0022
Web site: http://www.bbcanada.com

• In Crawford Bay, 80 kilometres north of Creston, on Highway 3A.
• Six rooms. One person $79; two people $79–110. Queen-sized bed; queen-sized bed and
one twin bed; double bed. Ensuite bathrooms. Additional adult or child $20. Open April
15 to October 15. Golf packages and Ainsworth Hot Springs packages.
• A country inn built at the turn of the century by the Wedgwood China family, on fifty acres
at the foot of the Purcell Mountains. Across the road from Kokanee Springs golf course. A
few minutes from beaches, fishing, and boating on Kootenay Lake. Hiking, walking, and
biking from the B&B. Landscaped grounds and gardens. Library and sitting room. Guest
rooms have Victorian furnishings. Some of the guest rooms have Jacuzzis and some have
fireplaces. One of the rooms is a honeymoon suite. One is wheelchair accessible. Tea and
snacks served any time. Visa, MasterCard. Smoking on the veranda. **In the hosts' own
words:** "Snuggle up in the library, sip tea by the parlour fireplace, stroll the garden paths.
Our goal is to make you welcome in the most restful and beautiful surroundings."

Anita's Old Fashioned B&B

Anita Johnston
110 Twelfth Avenue South
Cranbrook, BC V1C 2S1
(250) 426-7993 Fax: (250) 426-7965
Toll-free: 1-888-452-2221
E-mail: anitaj@cyberlink.bc.ca

• Three rooms. One person $60–70; two people $70–80. Queen-sized bed and one twin day bed; double bed. Ensuite bathrooms. Additional person $10. Three-quarter-sized roll-out cot available. Honeymoon packages.

• A B&B with a west-facing front porch, an east-facing deck, and guest rooms that have views of mountains, one block from downtown and within walking distance of shopping, theatres, and business services. Near the heritage town of Fort Steele, the Canadian Museum of Rail Travel, hiking, biking, horseback riding, swimming, boating, windsurfing, waterskiing, fishing, skiing, waterslides, and golf. Sitting room with fireplace and books. Sun room with TV and VCR. Dining room and refreshment service available for small meetings. Secretarial and laundry service. Guest rooms have percale linen, telephones, microwaves, fridges, kettles, coffee makers, teapots, and refreshments. Choice of full or Continental breakfast, including homemade baked goods, homemade butter and preserves, fresh-squeezed juice, farm-fresh free-range eggs, and local organic produce, is served in the dining room or on the deck. Vegetarian and vegan diets accommodated. Room service and picnic lunches available on request. Check-in after 3:00 p.m.; check-out until 11:00 a.m. Deposit of one night's rate required to hold reservation. Cancellation notice seven days. Cash, traveller's cheques, Visa, MasterCard. School-aged children welcome; babysitting service available. Dog and cats in residence. **In the hosts' own words:** "You'll be treated to first-class service in our heritage-style house."

Cranberry House B&B

Gloria Murray
321 Cranbrook Street North
Cranbrook, BC V1C 3R4
(250) 489-6216 Fax: (250) 489-6216

• Four rooms. One person $60; two people $65–70. Queen-sized bed, ensuite bathroom; twin beds, shared guest bathroom.

• A B&B three blocks from downtown and thirty minutes from golf courses, ski hills, the heritage town of Fort Steele, and hiking and climbing areas. Hot tub. Guest rooms have duvets, percale linen, robes, soap, shampoo, telephones, and TVs. Fax, fridge, microwave, and coffee and tea supplies available. Central air conditioning. Breakfast includes fresh-ground coffee, purified water, homemade jam, and homemade baked goods. Parking. Deposit of one night's rate required to hold reservation. Cancellation notice seven days. Traveller's cheques, Visa, MasterCard, American Express. Adult oriented. No pets. Smoking on the patio. **In the hosts' own words:** "If you want to be spoiled, a warm welcome awaits you at our heritage B&B."

Singing Pines B&B

Sandra and Robert Dirom
5180 Kennedy Road
Mail: Box A SS 3 Site 15 C–9
Cranbrook, BC V1C 6H3
(250) 426-5959 Fax: (250) 426-5959
Toll-free from within North America:
   1-800-863-4969

• From Highway 3/95, take the airport/Kimberley exit to Highway 95A north. Four kilometres north, turn right onto Kennedy Road. Continue for 700 metres. The B&B is the second driveway on the right.

• Three rooms. One person $65–70; two people $75–90. Queen-sized bed and extra-long twin beds; two queen-sized beds. Ensuite bathrooms. Additional person $20. Open April to October and in winter by arrangement.

• A modern ranch-style house on eleven acres in the Rocky Mountain Trench, with views of the Rocky and Purcell mountains. Country furnishings and antiques. Guest rooms are on the main floor and have pine sleigh-style beds. Two of the guest rooms have patio doors that lead to a deck. Guest living room with TV and VCR. Guest phone line. Guest outdoor hot tub. Robes and hair dryers. Three to twenty-five kilometres from three championship golf courses and two par-three golf courses. Fifteen minutes from the heritage town of Fort Steele. Twenty-five minutes from downhill and cross-country skiing at Kimberley. Ten minutes from cross-country skiing at Cranbrook. Sixty minutes from skiing at Fernie. Five minutes from the Canadian Museum of Rail Travel. Breakfast has a varied menu. Deposit of one night's rate required to hold reservation. Cancellation notice seven days. Cash, traveller's cheques, Visa, MasterCard, American Express. Children over eleven welcome. No pets; dog in residence and wildlife in area. Smoking on the deck. **In the hosts' own words:** "We look forward to welcoming our guests and take pleasure in sharing our home and the beauty of our natural setting."

Mountain Magic Ventures

Gordon Burns and Sue Boyd
Wardner Road
Mail: Box 94
Wardner, BC V0B 2J0
(250) 429-3958 Fax: (250) 429-3958
E-mail: mtnmagvent@cyberlink.bc.ca

• In the East Kootenays. From Cranbrook, go east on Highway 3/93 for 35 kilometres. Turn right onto Wardner Road and continue south for 1 kilometre. Follow the B&B's signs.

• Two cabins. One person $65; two people $75. Private bathrooms. Additional person $15.

Vacation and guided adventure travel packages.

• Two log cabins on a working cattle and horse ranch, with views of the Rockies and Lake Koocanusa. Each cabin accommodates up to six people and has a kitchen, a wood stove, and a deck. Walking and hiking trails on the property. Hosts offer guided trail riding, sleigh rides, extended backcountry packhorse trips, and guided and unguided canoeing, fishing, mountain biking, hiking, and cross-country skiing. Cat-skiing and whitewater rafting packages arranged. Ranch has a farm animal petting zoo, a fire pit, a volleyball court, a basketball hoop, a horseshoe pit, bicycles, and cross-country ski trails. Five minutes' walk from swimming. Ten minutes' drive from golf and restaurants. Forty minutes from Fernie and Kimberley ski areas. Choice of Continental breakfast served in the cabins or full breakfast, including farm-fresh eggs and homemade baked goods, served in the ranch house or on the deck. **In the hosts' own words:** "We offer friendly western hospitality."

McMillan Chalet B&B

Ken and Bonnie McMillan
5021 Fairmont Close
Mail: Box 989
Fairmont Hot Springs, BC V0B 1L0
(250) 345-9553 Fax: (250) 345-9553
E-mail: kenmcm@rockies.net

• At Fairmont Hot Springs, turn east off
Highway 93. Behind the Fairmont Grocery, turn
left and then take two immediate right turns. The
B&B is at the southeast corner of Fairmont
Close.
• Two rooms. One person $49–54; two people $54–59. Queen-sized bed. Shared guest
bathroom.
Suite. One person $64; two people $69. Queen-sized bed. Ensuite bathroom.
Additional person $20. Child under 11 $10. Rates for children over 10.
• A B&B near Windermere and Columbia lakes, at the foot of the hill leading to Fairmont
Hot Springs and near five golf courses—Mountainside, Riverside, Radium's two courses,
and Windermere Valley. Thirty minutes from skiing at Fairmont's ski hill and at Panorama.
An hour from skiing at Kimberley. Two hours from Fernie and Lake Louise. Fine dining at
Fairmont Hot Springs Resort. Some of the guest rooms have TVs and sofa beds.
Refreshments served when guests arrive. Breakfast is served in the dining area. Deposit of
one night's rate required to hold reservation. Cancellation notice three days. Cash, Visa,
MasterCard. Children welcome. No pets. Smoking on the deck. **In the hosts' own words:**
"We offer a warm welcome—come, relax, and enjoy the scenic Windermere Valley."

Nipika Lodge

Lyle and Dianne Wilson
9200 Settler's Road
Mail: Box 802 RR 1 Timber Ridge
Invermere, BC V0A 1K0
(250) 342-6516 Fax: (250) 342-0510
E-mail: realestate@nipika.com
Web site: http://www.nipika.com

• From Banff, take Highway 1 west, for 29 kilometres to Highway 93. Take Highway 93 south
for 84 kilometres. Turn left onto Settler's Road
and continue for 13 kilometres to the B&B. There is truck traffic on Settler's Road; use ex-
treme caution.
• Four lodge rooms. One person $40–50; two people $55–65. Shared bathrooms. Breakfast
not provided; guests bring their own food. Extended stay rates.
Entire lodge (sleeps fourteen). $225–275. Breakfast not provided; guests bring their own
food. Minimum stay two nights. Extended stay rates.
Cabin. One person or two people $30–40. Double bed and loft. Outhouse. Breakfast not
provided; guests bring their own food. Additional person $10. Children under 6 free. Ex-
tended stay rates.
• A traditional timber-frame lodge and a restored log trapper's cabin on the Kootenay River,
bordering on Kootenay National Park. Cross-country skiing, hiking, canoeing, kayaking,
rafting, river fishing, and mountain biking. Twenty minutes from Radium Hot Springs.
Lodge has a kitchen and a sitting room with a fireplace and a view of the mountains. No
telephone or TV. Cabin is heated by wood and has a kitchen but no plumbing. No restaurant
on the property; guests bring their own food. **In the hosts' own words:** "Come to our lodge
in the wilderness in the heart of the majestic Rockies and feel the magic."

Delphine Lodge

Anne and David Joy
Main Avenue
Wilmer, BC
Mail: Box 2797
Invermere, BC V0A 1K0
(250) 342-6851 Fax: (250) 342-6845

• In Wilmer (5 kilometres north of Invermere), on the corner of Main and Wells streets.

• Six rooms in a lodge separate from the hosts' house. One person $50–80; two people $60–80. Queen-sized bed; double bed; twin bed; double bed and one twin bed. Ensuite, private, and shared guest bathrooms. Additional person $20. Child under 11 $10.

• A restored lodge, separate from the hosts' house, on an acre of gardens, in a small village in the Windermere Valley. Lodge has quilts, lace curtains, early Canadian antiques, and a double-sided stone fireplace. Hiking, mountain biking, and cross-country skiing from the B&B. Five kilometres from Lake Windermere. Twelve kilometres from Panorama ski resort. Birdwatching in the area. Breakfast includes homemade baked goods, eggs, and fruit. Visa. Dog and cat in residence. No smoking. **In the hosts' own words:** "Our lodge has an outstanding garden. Guests relax, surrounded by majestic mountains."

Emerald Grove Estate B&B Inn

Lorraine Klassen and Glenda Lindsay
1265 Sunridge Road
Mail: Box 627
Windermere, BC V0B 2L0
(250) 342-4431 Fax: (250) 342-7220
Toll-free from within North America: 1-888-835-3959
E-mail: emerald@adventurevalley.com
Web site: http://www.discoveryweb.com/emeraldgroveestate

• Off Highway 93/95, fifteen minutes south of Radium Hot Springs and fifteen minutes north of Fairmont Hot Springs.

• Three rooms. One person $65–80; two people $80–105. Queen-sized bed, twin day bed, and double sofa bed. Ensuite bathrooms.
Honeymoon suite. Queen-sized bed. Ensuite bathroom.
Additional person $20. Children under 6 free. Child 7 to 16, $1 per year of age.
Honeymoon and ski packages.

• A house on three acres, a few minutes from golf courses, miniature golf, swimming, fishing, parasailing, boating, hiking, and horseback riding. Ten minutes from shops, a museum, a theatre, and restaurants. Honeymoon suite has a canopied bed, a sofa, a window seat, robes, a double Jacuzzi tub, and a down duvet. Guest rooms have TVs, VCRs, and movies. Upper balcony and lower decks. Guest living room with fireplace on the main floor. On the property are a gazebo, a barbecue, picnic tables, a waterfall, a fish pond, benches, and a large backyard with flower beds, bocci balls, croquet, and a lawn area that accommodates weddings, staff parties, and reunions. Hot tub. Tray with tea and coffee is delivered to the guest rooms and the suite before breakfast. Full three-course breakfast, including homemade baked goods, is served in the dining room. One of the guest rooms is on the main floor and is wheelchair accessible. Cancellation notice twenty-one days. Check-in after 3:00 p.m.; check-out until 11:00 a.m. Deposit of one night's rate required to hold reservation. Cash, traveller's cheques, Visa, MasterCard, Diners Club/enRoute, American Express. Smoking on the deck. **In the hosts' own words:** "Our B&B offers comfort, luxury, warmth, and hospitality in a location of great natural beauty."

Windermere Creek B&B

Scott and Astrid MacDonald
1658 Windermere Loop Road
Mail: Box 409
Windermere, BC V0B 2L0
(250) 342-0356 Fax: (250) 342-0356
Web site: http://www.bbcanada.com/849.html

• From Windermere, take Highway 95/93 south for 1 kilometre to the south end of Windermere Loop Road. Turn left and follow the loop road past Windermere Valley golf course. The B&B is the third house on the right, 1.5 kilometres past the golf course entrance.

• Three rooms. $60–75. Queen-sized bed. Private and shared guest bathrooms. Three log cabins. $90. Queen-sized bed. Private bathroom. Romance and ski packages.

• A B&B on one hundred and seven forested acres with lawns, gardens, five hours of walking trails, a heated pool, creekside hammocks, an orchard, lookout benches, picnic areas, and beaver ponds. One of the log cabins is an 1887 homestead and the two other cabins are new and have kitchens. Cabins have bathrooms with Jacuzzi tubs. Guests staying in the rooms share a guest living room with fireplace, a dining room, a sun room, a deck, and a breakfast nook with wood stove. Near swimming and golf at Radium Hot Springs and Fairmont Hot Springs. Five minutes' drive from Windermere's public beach and art shops. Ninety minutes from Lake Louise and Banff. Full buffet breakfast. Not suitable for children. Smoking restricted. **In the hosts' own words:** "We offer dream cabins in the Rockies with a private forest at your doorstep."

Wells Landing B&B

Ron and Jan van Vugt
4040 Sanborn Road
Mail: Box 89
Parson, BC V0A 1L0
(250) 348-2273 Fax: (250) 348-2278
E-mail: wellsldg@rockies.net
Web site: http://www.rockies.net/~wellslan/

• From Golden, take Highway 95 south for 35
kilometres. At Parson, cross the Columbia
River to the west side of the valley. Go south
on Sanborn Road for 3 kilometres. The road ends at the B&B.
• Three rooms. One person $60; two people $90. Additional person $25.
• A log house on thirty acres, with rock and flower gardens, at a historical riverboat landing on the Columbia River. The acreage is bordered by the river, forests, wetlands, and the Rocky Mountains. An abandoned logging road parallel to the river is suitable for walking and mountain biking. Over two hundred species of birds travel through the valley; a great blue heron rookery can be seen from the living room. Guest rooms have views. One of the guest rooms has a private entrance. Hot tub and music area on the main floor. Gazebo with a view of the river. Canoeing, fishing, hiking, birdwatching, mountain biking, and photography on the property. An hour's drive from whitewater rafting, mountaineering, natural hot springs, and hang-gliding. Near Banff, Yoho, Kootenay, and Glacier national parks. Breakfast includes homemade baked goods, a fruit plate, a hot entrée, fruit smoothies, and edible flower and herb garnishes. Cancellation notice twenty-four hours. Visa, MasterCard. Cats and a dog in residence. Nonsmoking house. **In the hosts' own words:** "Enjoy our beautiful house, spectacular view, and terrific breakfasts."

McLaren Lodge

George and Lou McLaren
1509 Lafontaine Road
Mail: Box 2586
Golden, BC V0A 1H0
(250) 344-6133 Fax: (250) 344-7650

• Off Highway 1, on the eastern limits of Golden
(45 minutes west of Lake Louise).
• Ten rooms. One person $60; two people $65.
Queen-sized bed; twin beds. Ensuite bathrooms.
Guided flatwater kayaking trips. Guided white-
water rafting trips. Guided all-terrain vehicle mountain trail tours. Guided heli-fishing in mountain lakes.
• A log house between the Purcell and Rocky Mountain ranges, with views of the Columbia Valley and the Kicking Horse River Valley. Sitting room with books, wood stove, and TV. Decks and garden gazebo. Near hiking, horseback riding, golf, scenic water tours, hang-gliding, and parasailing. Guided whitewater rafting trips leave daily from the lodge. Full breakfast. Adult oriented. No pets. No smoking. **In the hosts' own words:** "We invite you to stay a while and enjoy the mountain beauty."

H. G. Parson House B&B

André and Ruth Kowalski
815 Twelfth Street South
Mail: Box 1196
Golden, BC V0A 1H0
(250) 344-5001 Fax: (250) 344-2900

• One block off Highway 95.
• Three rooms. One person $55–70; two people $70–85. Extra-long twin beds (or extra-long twin beds side by side with king-sized bedding); queen-sized bed; queen-sized bed and one extra-long twin bed. Ensuite bathrooms and private bathroom with shower. Additional person $15.
• A 1893 house, in a quiet residential area, that was originally the family home of H. G. Parson, a merchant and MLA for the Golden area. Furnished with antiques. Guest rooms are decorated in themes. Two of the guest rooms have ensuite bathrooms with Jacuzzi tubs; the other guest room has a private bathroom with shower. Within walking distance of shopping and restaurants. Near golf, whitewater rafting, horseback riding, wetlands slowfloating, skiing, and snowmobiling. Hosts arrange outdoor activities for guests. A base for day trips to Banff, Yoho, and Kootenay national parks. Full breakfast. Cancellation notice five days; 30 percent is nonrefundable. Cash, traveller's cheques, Visa, MasterCard. French and Polish spoken.

Kapristo Lodge

Roswitha Ferstl
1297 Campbell Road
Mail: Box 90
Golden, BC V0A 1H0
(250) 344-6048 Fax: (250) 344-6755
E-mail: KapristoLodge@redshift.bc.ca
Web site: http://www.redshift.bc.ca/
business/kapristo/

• Fourteen kilometres south of Golden and 1.5 kilometres off Highway 95.

• Six rooms and a suite. King-sized bed; queen-sized bed; twin beds (or twin beds side by side with king-sized bedding). Ensuite, private, and shared guest bathrooms.

• A lodge on ninety acres on the side of Kapristo Mountain, close to snowmobiling, dog sledding, horseback riding, hiking, ice walks, mountain biking, downhill and backcountry skiing, birdwatching, fishing, and golf. A base for day trips to Yoho, Banff, Jasper, Kootenay, Glacier, and Mount Revelstoke national parks. Lodge has views of mountains and the Columbia River Valley. Living room with fireplace. Dining room and adjoining sun room. Terrace. Sauna and outdoor hot tub. Guest rooms have down quilts. Suite has a kitchen, a fireplace, and a Jacuzzi tub. Host shares knowledge of the area. Other meals by arrangement. Helicopter landing port on the premises. **In the hosts' own words:** "Our lodge is family owned and operated and is well known for its hospitality and world-class accommodation. Whether you are looking for an outdoor adventure, a quiet getaway, a location for a business meeting, or the perfect spot for a wedding, our lodge is the place for you."

Bears Den Guest House

Lorraine Zirke
414 First Street West
Mail: Box 127
Field, BC V0A 1G0
(250) 343-6439

• In Field (27 kilometres west of Lake Louise).

• Self-contained two-bedroom suite. Two people $85. Queen-sized bed and two extra-long twin beds. Bathroom in suite. Additional person $15. Open May to mid-October.

• A B&B in Yoho National Park, near hiking and mountain biking trails, canoeing on Emerald Lake, and rafting on the Kicking Horse River. Suite has handmade log beds, a private entrance, a TV, books on the area, and a kitchen with fridge, stove, and cooking utensils. In the park are spiral tunnels, a natural bridge, Takkakaw Falls, and Lake O'Hara. Cash, traveller's cheques, MasterCard. German spoken. No pets. No smoking. **In the hosts' own words:** "Yoho is one of the best-kept secrets in the Rockies. We invite you to make it a highlight of your holiday."

Kelly Lake Ranch B&B

Karin H. Lange
Kelly Lake Road
Mail: Box 547
Clinton, BC V0K 1K0
(250) 459-2313 Fax: (250) 459-2313
E-mail: klrbnb@wkpowerlink.com
Web site: http://www.beacom.com/kellylakeranch

• Seventeen kilometres west of Clinton, on a paved road. The B.C. Rail train stops at Kelly Lake.
• Four rooms in a ranch house. One person $45; two people $50. Queen-sized bed; twin beds. Shared bathroom.
Three log cabins. Two people $60–75. Shared guest showers in separate cabin. Additional person $10. Group rates. Minimum stay two nights.
Four RV hook-ups $12. Tent sites $8.
Group rates.
Horseback riding arranged. Canoe, paddle boat, and mountain bike rentals.
Pottery and watercolour and silk painting workshops $25–65.
• A B&B with a ranch house and three log cabins, surrounded by lakes, mountains, and wildlife, on a 240-acre ranch on the Cariboo Gold Rush Trail. During the gold rush, the trail passed between the barn and the present-day ranch house. B.C. Rail runs through the ranch; trains stop to pick up and drop off guests. Horseback trail riding, hiking, biking, swimming, canoeing, trout fishing, cross-country skiing, and a trampoline. Each cabin has kitchen facilities, an electric stove, a wood stove, a horse paddock, a flower garden, a fire pit, and lawn chairs. Breakfast is served in the ranch house in a glassed-in sun room with a view of gardens and corrals. Other meals by request. MasterCard, traveller's cheques. German spoken.
In the hosts' own words: "Guests ride the train to the Kelly Lake station and spend a few days at our ranch riding and hiking. Two rustic creekside cabins and one historical log cabin house hikers, nature lovers, artists, and horse enthusiasts. Our B&B is ideal for family reunions and retreats."

Ruth Lake Lodge

Klaus and Susanna Kaiser
Ruth Lake Road
Mail: Box 315
Forest Grove, BC V0K 1M0
(250) 397-2070 Fax: (250) 397-2284
E-mail: ruthlake@netshop.net

• Thirty-two kilometres northeast of 100 Mile House. From Highway 97, turn right onto Canim Lake Road. At Forest Grove, go straight ahead onto Eagle Creek Road and continue for 6.5 kilometres. Turn left onto Ruth Lake Road and continue for 3.5 kilometres.

• Five rooms. One person $59; two people $89. Queen-sized bed; queen-sized bed and sofa bed; bunk beds.

Three self-contained cabins (each sleeps up to six). $130. Queen-sized bed and four mattresses in loft. Breakfast not included.

Early booking discounts.

Boat, mountain bike, and skidoo rentals.

• A lodge and three cabins separate from the hosts' house, on the shores of Ruth Lake. Fishing, swimming, and hiking from the lodge. Hosts arrange golf, horseback riding, dog sled rides, and fly-ins by float plane. Guest sauna by the lake. Lodge has a guest TV and video room and a guest living room with a fireplace. Each cabin has a bedroom with queen-sized bed, a loft with four beds, a bathroom with shower, kitchen facilities, a dining and living area, a wood stove, and electric heaters. A restaurant in the lodge serves European cuisine. Full breakfast is served in the restaurant for lodge guests. For guests staying in the cabins, breakfast is available in the restaurant for an additional charge. Reservations required. Visa, MasterCard, American Express. **In the hosts' own words:** "The sumptuous breakfast we serve in our restaurant will make your day."

The Log House B&B

Dale and Joan Bummer
4785—U81 Kitwanga Drive
Mail: Box 347
108 Mile Ranch, BC V0K 2Z0
(250) 791-5353 Fax (250) 791-5631
Toll-free from within North America: 1-800-610-1002
Web site: http://www.achilles.net/~bb/623.html

• Thirteen kilometres north of 100 Mile House. Thirteen kilometres south of
Lac La Hache. From Highway 97, turn off at the heritage site rest stop. Turn
right onto Kitwanga Drive and follow it around the lake for 2 kilometres. The
B&B is on the lake side.

• Two rooms. One person $60–70. Queen-sized bed. Ensuite bathrooms.
Additional person $10. Children under 8 free. Cots and small crib available.
Off-season rates.

• A log house on 108 Mile Lake in the Cariboo, near swimming, canoeing, hiking, and
downhill and cross-country skiing. Three kilometres from a golf course and restaurants. Half
a block from riding stables. Sixteen kilometres from downhill skiing at Mount Timothy and
Lac La Hache. Hosts arrange covered wagon rides, hay rides, sleigh rides, helicopter rides,
and dog sled rides. Large landscaped yard. One of the guest rooms, the living room, and a
deck are wheelchair accessible. Tea, coffee, and cold drinks provided. Full breakfast is
served in the dining room or on the deck. Parking. Reservations recommended. Deposit of
one night's rate required to hold reservation. Cancellation notice two days. Visa, MasterCard.
Children welcome. No pets; cat in residence. No smoking. **In the hosts' own words:**
"Experience the Cariboo."

The Chilcotin Lodge

Pamela and Joe Bishop
Mail: Box 2
Riske Creek, BC V0L 1T0
(250) 659-5646 Fax: (250) 659-5646

• From Williams Lake, go 64 kilometres west on Highway 20. The B&B is
at the intersection of Highway 20 and Stack Valley Road.

• Ten rooms. One person $55; two people $75. Two shared guest bathrooms.
Washbasins in the guest rooms.

• A log building built in 1938 as a hunting lodge, on the edge of the Chilcoltin grasslands,
with a view of Riske Creek Valley that extends for over forty kilometres. Art, memorabilia, and antique furniture. In the area are wildlife, birdwatching, hiking, fishing, cycling,
and river rafting. Continental breakfast. Licensed restaurant with a limited menu. Visa,
MasterCard. No pets. No smoking. **In the hosts' own words:** "After a full day's exploring
you'll enjoy having dinner and spending a relaxing evening by the stone fireplace in our
old western hotel."

Eagle Bluff B&B

Mary Allen and Bryan Cox
201 Cow Bay Road
Prince Rupert, BC V8J 1A2
(250) 627-4955 Fax: (250) 627-7945
E-mail: eaglebed@citytel.net

• From Highway 16, take the Cow Bay turnoff (Third Avenue East) onto Cow Bay Road. Turn left one block past Smile's Seafood Café. The B&B is next to Cow Bay Wharf.

• Rooms. One person $45–55; two people $55–70. Queen-sized bed and hide-a-bed; queen-sized bed and one twin bed; queen-sized bed and single futon. Ensuite and shared guest bathrooms. Cot available.

Suite. Two people $70. Queen-sized bed, twin beds, and double hide-a-bed.

Additional person $10. Child 7 to 12 $5. Children under 6 free. Weekly and winter rates.

• A B&B with a view of a yacht club, on a harbour where cruise ships, sailboats, freighters, and commercial fishing boats come and go. Five minutes' walk from downtown Prince Rupert, the Northern Museum, and Mariner's Park. Ten minutes' walk from a library, tennis courts, an indoor swimming pool, and a performing arts centre. Near a public boat launch and mooring, boat rentals and charters, a hiking trail by the ocean, an eighteen-hole golf course, and a racquet centre. Two of the guest rooms are downstairs, and the other two guest rooms and the suite are upstairs. Suite has a bedroom with twin beds and a sitting room with a queen-sized bed and a hide-a-bed. Laundry facilities available. Within a block of two seaside cafés and a neighbourhood pub. Full breakfast includes muffins and fruit salad. Deposit of one night's rate required to hold reservation. Cancellation notice seven days. Visa, MasterCard. Families welcome. No pets. No smoking. **In the hosts' own words:** "Experience Prince Rupert's waterfront and enjoy the view from our B&B of the sunset over the harbour."

Raindrop B&B

Bob and Judy Warren
2121 Graham Avenue
Prince Rupert, BC V8J 1C9
(250) 624-5564 Fax: (250) 624-5564

• One person or two people $70. Double bed.
Private bathroom.
• A B&B with bay windows that have a view of
the harbour, ten minutes' drive from downtown, a
golf course, a swimming pool, hiking trails, and
parks. Guest sitting room. Gardens and decks.
Pickup and drop-off from and to transportation terminals. Hosts arrange tours of the city and
the North Pacific Cannery Museum. A choice of breakfasts is served with linen, china, and
silver and with a view of the harbour. Visa. No pets. No smoking. **In the hosts' own words:**
"Enjoy peace and tranquillity. Feed the wild deer who are almost daily in the yard, and watch
the ships go by."

Parry Place B&B

John and Danielle Wood
133 Parry Place
Prince Rupert, BC V8J 4B1
(250) 624-5887 Fax: (250) 624-8176
Toll-free from within Canada and the U.S.:
  1-800-565-3500
E-mail: norwood@citytel.net
Web site: http://www.bbcanada.com/
  1720.html

• Two rooms. One person $55; two people $65.
Queen-sized bed. Shared guest bathroom.
Suite. One person $65; two people $75. Queen-sized bed, couch, and cot. Additional person $15.
• A B&B five minutes' walk from ferries to points in B.C. and Alaska. Guest living room
on the main floor with fireplace, TV, stereo, books, games, and refreshments. Suite has a
view of a garden. Backyard with sitting area next to a mountain stream. Covered front
porch. Harbour walks and trails from the B&B. Hosts provide information on fishing charters, tours, and local points of interest. Buffet breakfast, including coffee, homemade
baked goods, and seasonal fruit, is served in the dining room. Pickup and drop-off from
and to transportation terminals. Visa, MasterCard. French spoken. Children welcome by
arrangement. Dog in residence. Smoking on the porch and in the garden. **In the hosts'
own words:** "Il nous ferait plaisir de vous servir en français."

A&A Terrace B&B

Joanne and Jerry Peltier
3802 DeJong Crescent
Terrace, BC V8G 4W6
(250) 635-0079 Fax: (250) 635-0180
Toll-free from within North America,
for reservations: 1-888-635-0079
E-mail: jpeltier@kermode.net
Web site: http://www.bbcanada.com/
**   1043.html**

• Room. One person $45; two people $50.
Queen-sized bed. Private bathroom.
One-bedroom suite (sleeps five). One person $50; two people $55. Queen-sized bed, double sofa bed, and one twin day bed. Bathroom in suite. Additional person $10.
Children under 6 free. Weekly rates. Seniors' rates.

• A modern house within walking distance of shopping, downtown, and a children's park. Suite sleeps up to five and has a bedroom and a sitting room with TV, VCR, phone, and fridge. Guest room has a TV and a VCR. Forty-five minutes from skiing and hiking at Shames Mountain. An hour from Nisga'a Memorial Lava Bed Park. Twenty minutes from Lakelse Lake and Mount Layton Hot Springs. Thirty minutes from fishing. Backyard with lawn chairs, barbecue, and picnic table. Laundry facilities. Pickup and drop-off for guests travelling by train, plane, or bus. Fax machine and computer available. Choice of full or Continental breakfast. Cash, traveller's cheques, Visa. Family oriented. Smoke-free environment. **In the hosts' own words:** "Our B&B is centrally located. Come and spend time in northern B.C. and let us show you northern hospitality."

Merkodei Meadows

Inke Kase
4507 North Sparks Street
Terrace, BC V8G 2W4
(250) 635-7808 Fax: (250) 635-9727
E-mail: merkodei@kermode.net
Web site: http://www.kermode.net/merkodei

• Five minutes from downtown Terrace.
• Self-contained one-bedroom suite. One person $45; two people $50. Queen-sized bed and day bed. Ensuite bathroom. Additional person $10. Winter rates.
Ski packages.

• A B&B on two and a half acres of gardens and woods, five minutes' walk from a heritage park, tennis courts, the Terrace Mountain trail, a playground, and a transit route. Suite has a kitchen, a private telephone line, a TV, and a VCR. Pickup from plane, train, and bus for a fee. Ski packages at Shames Mountain can be arranged. In the area are Skeena River fishing, Lakelse Lake, and Mount Layton hotsprings. An hour south of the Tseax lava beds. Computer equipment rental and Internet access can be arranged. Continental breakfast is served at guests' convenience. Visa. Children welcome. No dogs; cats in residence. **In the hosts' own words:** "We would like to welcome you to the hub of B.C.'s northwest."

The Forks B&B

Heather and Bill Beamish
1005 Lieuwen West Road
Mail: Box 361
Houston, BC V0J 1Z0
(250) 845-2464 Fax: (250) 845-2464
E-mail: forks@mail.netshop.net

• Seven kilometres west of Houston and one block south of Highway 16, on Silverthorne Hill.
• Suite. One person $50; two people $56.
Double bed and hide-a-bed. Ensuite bathroom.
Additional person $10. Children's rates at $1 per year of age.
• A log house with views of the Telkwa Mountains and the Bulkley River. Birds, black bears, moose, deer, coyotes, and foxes can be seen in the area. Near hiking, fishing, trail rides, cross-country skiing, snowmobiling, mill tours, and wildlife viewing. Suite has a TV, a VCR, a selection of children's and family videos, and a living room with hide-a-bed and double-sided fireplace. Reservations recommended. Deposit required to hold reservation. Cash, traveller's cheques. Children welcome. Smoking outdoors. **In the hosts' own words:** "Relax and enjoy the comfort of our log house after a busy day of work or travelling."

La Mia Casa, E'Sempre Aperta B&B

Luciano and Georgina Dotto
2555 Dominion Avenue
Mail: Box 43
Houston, BC V0J 1Z0
(250) 845-7775

• From Highway 16, turn onto Butler Avenue (forestry building on the corner). Turn left onto Eleventh Street. Turn left onto Avalon Avenue. Turn right onto Star Street, which leads to Dominion Avenue. The B&B is on the left and has a tree-lined driveway.
• Three rooms. One person $40; two people $50. Double bed; twin beds. Shared guest bathrooms. Children under 6 free. Child 7 to 12 half rate. Queen-sized hide-a-bed available in family room. Highchair and playpen available. Monthly rates.
Fishing packages.
• A quiet house at the end of a tree-lined driveway, with a yard, a garden, a greenhouse, a patio, a woodworking shop, and a family room with fireplace. Near shopping. Ten minutes from a nature walk along a creek, two nine-hole golf courses, tennis courts, basketball, bowling, fishing, and cross-country skiing. Forty-five minutes from downhill skiing at Hudson Bay Mountain. In the area are sawmill and forestry tours. Coffee, tea, and other beverages provided when guests arrive. Choice of full breakfast, which includes waffles, fresh strawberries and raspberries with whipped cream, pork sausages, and bacon, or Continental breakfast, which includes toast made with homemade bread, homemade preserves, cereal, and fresh fruit. Other meals by arrangement. Ground floor is wheelchair accessible. Cash, traveller's cheques. Italian spoken. Children welcome. No pets; small dog in residence. Smoking outdoors. **In the hosts' own words:** "Your comfort is our main concern, so come and enjoy your stay in our quiet, peaceful, and friendly house."

Little Madness on Francois Lake B&B

Meg and Ron Opas
Colleymount Road West
Mail: Box 606
Francois Lake, BC V0J 1R0
(250) 695-6673

• Thirty kilometres (20 minutes) south of Burns
Lake. From Burns Lake, take Highway 35 south
to the Francois Lake ferry landing. Take the
lakeshore road west for 4 kilometres.
• Three rooms. One person $50; two people $60.
Shared guest bathroom.
• A traditional European-style B&B in a log house on five acres, with views of Francois
Lake, rolling ranch lands, forests, and distant snowcapped mountains. Within twelve hours'
drive of Prince Rupert, Jasper, Banff, Vancouver, Yukon, and Alaska. In the area are boating,
sailing, horseback riding, birdwatching, cycling, hiking, and cross-country skiing. Garden.
Living areas with art, books, music, and TV. Full breakfast. Outdoor shelter for pets and
smokers. **In the hosts' own words:** "Our peaceful and picturesque place is far away from
the big madnesses of other parts of the world. An ideal spot to take a break from road touring."

Mead Manor B&B

Laura and Bob Mead
4127 Baker Road
Prince George, BC V2N 5K2
(250) 964-8436 Fax: (250) 964-8449
E-mail: meadmanor@bc.sympatico.ca
Web site: http://www.bbcanada.com/356.html

• From downtown Prince George, take Highway
16 west for five minutes. Turn right onto Tyner
Road. At the first right, turn onto Baker Road.
Continue past the stop sign at Davis Road.
• Two rooms. One person $50; two people $60. Queen-sized bed. Private bathrooms.
Seniors' rates.
• A four-level house in a quiet neighbourhood, five minutes from downtown Prince George.
Near the University of Northern British Columbia, the Fort George Museum, a railway
museum, golf, shopping, and casual and fine dining restaurants. Ten minutes from bus and
train stations. Twenty minutes from the airport. Eight hours from Prince Rupert. One of the
guest rooms has a TV and a VCR. Another guest room has a private entrance, a Jacuzzi,
access to a guest sitting room with TV and VCR, and a selection of movies. Guest outdoor
hot tub. Laundry facilities. Full breakfast is served in a sun room that has a view of a garden or in the breakfast room. Cash, Visa. Smoking in a designated area. **In the host's own
words:** "A quiet, convenient location with privacy at a reasonable price is what you can
expect at our B&B."

Tangled Garden B&B

Cynthia and Dave
2957 Sullivan Crescent
Prince George, BC V2N 5H6
(250) 964-3265 Fax: (250) 964-3248
E-mail: dpcc@mag-net.com
Web site: http://www.mag-net.com/tangledgardenb+b

• From Highway 16, at the University of Northern British Columbia sign, turn west onto Tyner Boulevard. At the first right, turn onto Baker Road. Immediately turn left onto Sullivan Crescent. The B&B is near the top of the curve, on the left.

• Room. One person $50; two people $60. Double bed. Private bathroom. Twin futon bed available.

Self-contained suite. One person $50; two people $60. Queen-sized bed. Ensuite bathroom. Additional person $15.

• A modern house with a terraced garden, next to a greenbelt and five minutes from shopping, the University of Northern British Columbia, golf, and nature trails. Suite has a kitchen, a loveseat, a TV, a VCR, and a private entrance. Guest room is upstairs and has a view of mountains. Adjoining private living room with TV, VCR, CD player, and twin futon bed for an additional person. Beds have duvets. Outdoor hot tub; robes provided. Deck with flowers. Sitting room with books and fireplace. Fax service and laundry. Full breakfast is served in the dining room or on the deck. Off-street parking. Adult oriented. No pets; cat in residence. Smoking outdoors. **In the hosts' own words:** "In summer, relax among flowers on our deck, which overlooks the terraced garden—a hummingbird paradise. In winter, our secluded hot tub is a serene place for viewing stars and snowflakes."

Bedford Place B&B

Walt and Ruth Thielmann
135 Patricia Boulevard
Prince George, BC V2L 3T6
(250) 562-3269
Toll-free from within North America:
  1-888-311-9292
E-mail: c/o bedandbreakfastassc@
  pgonline.com

• From First Avenue, take Queensway Street.
Turn left onto Patricia Boulevard and continue
for eight blocks to Taylor Drive.

• Two rooms. One person $65; two people $75. Queen-sized bed. Ensuite and private bathrooms.

• A B&B with a view of the Fraser River and the Yellowhead Bridge. One of the guest rooms has a queen-sized Murphy bed, maple wainscoting, and an ensuite bathroom. The other guest room has a queen-sized sleigh-style bed and a private bathroom with clawfoot tub. Ten minutes' walk from three parks, regional and railway museums, and the Heritage River Trail. Full breakfast is served in a formal dining room or on the patio. German spoken. **In the hosts' own words:** "Relax and enjoy our beautiful garden and backyard patio."

Huntley Place B&B

Bette and Cy Mackay
218 Huntley Place
Prince George, BC V2M 6W1
(250) 562-4597 Fax: (250) 564-2588
E-mail: wally_mackay@bc.sympatico.ca

• Twelve minutes from the city centre.

• Rooms. One person $40–50; two people
$50–60. Queen-sized bed; twin beds (or twin
beds side by side with king-sized bedding).
Ensuite bathrooms.

Self-contained suite. Two or three people $60–75. Queen-sized bed and hide-a-bed.
Private bathroom.

• A B&B surrounded by trees, on a quiet cul-de-sac next to a greenbelt. Patchwork quilts, duvets, and maple furniture. Self-contained suite is in the basement and has a kitchen, a gas fireplace, duvets, a telephone, a TV, a VCR, and a private entrance as well as an entrance through the house. Breakfast is served in the dining room or on the deck. Off-street parking. Adult oriented. No pets. **In the hosts' own words:** "Our patchwork quilts and maple furniture will take you back in time, while you enjoy such modern conveniences as a private phone and a fax machine. The suite is cool in the summer, and the gas fireplace and the duvets will keep you warm on winter nights. We specialize in turning strangers into friends."

Eleanor's House

Eleanor House and Rick Kunelius
125 Kootenay Avenue
Mail: Box 1553
Banff, AB T0L 0C0
(403) 760-2457 Fax: (403) 762-3852
E-mail: house@banff.net
Web site: http://www.banff.net/house

• On the south side of the river, one block above the road to the Banff Springs Hotel.

• Rooms. In spring (February to April), two people $100. In summer (May to October), two people $125. Queen-sized bed; extra-long twin beds. Ensuite bathrooms. Open February to October.

• A B&B in a quiet residential area, ten minutes' walk from the Banff Springs Hotel and the town centre. In the area are golf, hiking, mountain climbing, rafting, fishing, downhill skiing, cross-country skiing, heli-skiing, heli-hiking, wildlife viewing, the Banff Centre for the Performing Arts, museums, a theatre, art galleries, and restaurants. Hosts help guests plan activities. Each guest room is 350 square feet and has a mountain view. Ensuite bathrooms with soaker tubs. Guest library/sitting room has a private entrance, a fireplace, a wet bar, and books. Continental breakfast. Elk and deer can often be seen grazing on the front lawn. Visa, MasterCard. Adults only. **In the hosts' own words:** "Our guest house reflects mid-century elegance for the discerning traveller."

Mountain Home B&B

Lynne and Ecki Treutler
129 Muskrat Street
Mail: Box 272
Banff, AB T0L 0C0
(403) 762-3889 Fax: (403) 762-3254
E-mail: mountainhome@banff.net
Web site: http://www.banff.net/mountainhome/

• One and a half blocks from Banff town centre.

• Four rooms. In winter, two people $85–100. In summer (May to October), two people $110–125. King-sized bed; queen-sized bed and one twin bed. En-suite bathrooms.

• A house half a block from a riverside walk along the Bow River and one and a half blocks from Banff's shops, gourmet restaurants, and boutiques. Each guest room has a sitting area, down duvets, and an ensuite bathroom with soaker tub, shower, and Victorian-style pedestal sink. Guest entrance. Living room with a rundlestone fireplace on the main floor. In the area are golf, hiking, horseback riding, kayaking, river rafting, fishing, mountain climbing, biking, downhill and cross-country skiing, snowshoeing, ice fishing, dog sledding, heli-hiking, heli-skiing, sleigh rides, art galleries, museums, and the Banff Centre for the Performing Arts. Hosts provide information on the area. Breakfast includes homemade bread, muffins, scones, blueberry pancakes, homemade preserves, fresh fruit, and juice. Visa, MasterCard. Not suitable for young children. No pets. Nonsmoking environment. **In the hosts' own words:** "Our B&B offers affordable charm, a relaxed, friendly atmosphere, and Rocky Mountain hospitality."

Cedar Springs B&B

Deborah J. Robillard
426 First Street
Canmore, AB T1W 2K9
(403) 678-3865 Fax: (403) 678-1938
E-mail: cedarspr@telusplanet.net
Web site: http://www.canadianrockies.net/cedarsprings

• On the south side of Canmore (15 minutes from Banff; an hour west of Calgary).

• Rooms. In winter, two people from $85. In summer (May to October), two peoplefrom $95. King-sized bed; queen-sized bed; twin beds. Ensuite bathrooms.

Suite and honeymoon suite. Call for information.

Extended stay and group rates.

Special occasion packages.

• A quiet cedar chalet in a forest, with country décor and a view of the Three Sisters Mountains. Guest sitting room has a fireplace, books, decks, and a fridge with beverages. Guest entrance. Guest rooms have skylights and fireplaces. Wildlife can be seen in the garden area. A few minutes' drive from the Bow River and Banff National Park. River walkways lead to Canmore's shops, galleries, and restaurants. Host helps plan recreational activities. Marriage commissioner available to perform wedding ceremonies. Full breakfast is served in the guest sitting room or in the suite. Deposit of one night's rate required to hold reservation. Visa, MasterCard. French spoken. Adults only. No pets. Smoke-free environment. **In the hosts' own words:** "Come for the mountains and experience our friendly hospitality, affordable luxury, relaxing atmosphere, secluded setting, and spectacular mountain views."

McNeill Heritage Inn

Alan and Sharon Cole
500 Three Sisters Drive
Canmore, AB T1W 2P3
(403) 678-4884 Fax: (403) 678-4884
E-mail: info@mcneillinn.ab.ca
Web site: http://www.mcneillinn.ab.ca

• From Highway 1, at Canmore (15 minutes east of Banff; an hour west of Calgary), follow the signs to the Canmore Nordic Centre. After crossing the Bow River, Rundle Drive ends. Turn right onto Three Sisters Drive and continue for 1 kilometre up the hill. The road becomes the B&B's private driveway, marked with a stone entrance.

• Five rooms. June to October, one person $110–130, two people $125–145. November to May, one person $85–105, two people $100–120. Queen-sized bed; twin beds. Ensuite bathroom. Additional person $25.

• A 1907 house on a wooded acreage adjacent to trails on the Bow River and the Canmore Olympic Nordic Centre. Hardwood floors, antique pine and oak furniture, and a wraparound veranda with mountain views. Guest living room/library with games table and stone fireplace. Guest rooms are 250 to 400 square feet and have pine Canadiana antiques, writing desks, chairs, and down duvets. Hosts are experienced outdoor enthusiasts. Full breakfast is served in an old-fashioned dining room. Ski and bike storage available. Deposit of one night's rate required to hold reservation. Cancellation notice forty-eight hours; for long weekends and stays of four or more nights, cancellation notice seven days. Visa, MasterCard. Adult oriented; older children by arrangement. No pets. Nonsmoking house. **In the hosts' own words:** "We are pleased to welcome visitors from around the world to relax at our B&B while experiencing the beautiful Rockies."

Mountain Ash B&B

Henk and Mimi Waterreus
218 Lady MacDonald Drive
Canmore, AB T1W 1H3
(403) 678-0066 Fax: (403) 678-0066
Web site: http://www.bbcanada.com/
   1903.html

• In Canmore, on the north side of Highway 1.
From Banff, take the Canmore city centre exit.
Turn left onto Benchland Trail. Where the road
divides, keep right and follow Elk Run
Boulevard. Turn right at the second street, which is Lady MacDonald.
• Three rooms. One person from $55; two people from $65. Queen-sized bed; double bed;
twin beds. Private and shared guest bathrooms.
• A modern house with mountain views, near hiking and cross-country skiing trails. Guest
entrance. Guest deck on the upper floor. Guest sitting room with TV, VCR, games, and
books. Ski wax room with storage space. Fifteen minutes from cross-country skiing trails
and the Canmore Olympic Nordic Centre. An hour from Calgary and Lake Louise. Twenty
minutes from Banff. Forty minutes from Kananaskis Country. Evening snacks and beverages served in guest sitting room. Full breakfast includes yogurt, fruit salad, and homemade baked goods. Visa, MasterCard. Dutch and German spoken. Smoke-free. **In the
hosts' own words:** "Our warm hospitality and comfortable house will help make your stay
a memorable one."

By the Brook B&B

John and Joan Middleton
4 Birchwood Place
Canmore, AB T1W 1P9
(403) 678-4566 Fax: (403) 678-4199
E-mail: jmiddle@riscan.com
Web site: http://users.uniserve.com/~cadeau/
   bythebrook

• Ten minutes east of Banff. One hour west of
Calgary.
• Rooms. Queen-sized bed. Ensuite bathrooms.
• A modern house on a quiet cul-de-sac by a mountain stream and trails for hiking and cross-
country skiing. Guest rooms have TVs, down duvets, and sitting areas with bay windows and
mountain views. Sauna and hot tub. Five minutes' walk from downtown Canmore. Fifteen
minutes' drive from Banff. Twenty to fifty-five minutes' drive from five downhill ski areas.
Forty minutes' drive from four golf courses. Full breakfast. Cancellation notice seven days.
Visa, MasterCard. No pets. No smoking. **In the hosts' own words:** "After enjoying the
activities and sights the mountains have to offer, relax in our hot tub or sauna."

Enjoy Living B&B

Garry and Nancy Thoen
149 Cougar Point Road
Canmore, AB T1W 1A1
(403) 678-3026 Fax: (403) 678-3042
Toll-free from within North America: 1-800-922-8274
E-mail: enjoy@telusplanet.net
Web site: http://www.canadianrockies.net/enjoyliving

● From Calgary, take the second exit to Canmore. At the stop sign, turn right. At the traffic lights, turn left. Take the next right onto Cougar Creek Drive and the next right onto Cougar Point.
From Banff, take the third exit to Canmore. At the traffic lights, turn left. Take the next right onto Cougar Creek Drive and the next right onto Cougar Point.
● Two rooms. $70–100. Queen-sized bed; queen-sized bed and fold-out double futon bed. Ensuite bathrooms. Additional person $20. Children's rates negotiable.
● A quiet B&B with mountain views in all directions, ten minutes' walk from downtown Canmore's cafés, specialty shops, art galleries, antiques, and fine dining restaurants. Five minutes' drive from Banff National Park and fifteen minutes' drive from the town of Banff. Near golf courses, ski hills, hiking trails, fishing, climbing, rafting, and sightseeing. Guest rooms have mountain décor. One of the bathrooms has a whirlpool tub. Refreshments area with coffee, tea, and cookies. Guest living room with fireplace, stereo, TV, and VCR. Deck with hot tub. Guest rooms, refreshments area, living room, and deck are on the main floor of the house, which is for guest use only. Phone and fax available. Fire pit for campfires. Ski and bike storage. Full breakfast is served indoors or on the deck. Early breakfast available by request. Cancellation notice seven days. Check-in times flexible. Cash, traveller's cheques, MasterCard. Smoking outdoors. **In the hosts' own words:** "The name of our B&B is more than a name; enjoying living is an attitude that we try to make a way of life. It is our goal to make you feel welcome and at home during your visit to the Rocky Mountains."

Reservations Jasper Ltd.

Debbie Taylor
Mail: Box 1840
Jasper, AB T0E 1E0
(403) 852-5488 Fax: (403) 852-5489
E-mail: resjas@incentre.net
Web site: http://www.inshuttle.net/resjas/
default.htm

• A reservation service covering Jasper, Banff, Lake Louise, Canmore, Edmonton, Calgary, and Mount Robson. B&Bs, in-house accommodation without breakfast, hotels, motels, cabins, and bungalows. Booking fee of $20 for one destination; $5 for each additional destination. Additional $5 fee for overseas clients. Visa. Non-commissionable. **In the agents' own words:** "We offer a fast, reliable, and informative service for our clients. You need only make one call for your Canadian Rockies vacation accommodations."